The Nighttime Butterfly

The
Nighttime Butterfly

A Catholic Woman and Her Jewish Family in
Warsaw at the Turn of the Twentieth Century

KAREN AUERBACH

Yale UNIVERSITY PRESS
New Haven and London

Published with assistance from the foundation established in memory of Philip Hamilton McMillan of the Class of 1894, Yale College.

Copyright © 2025 by Karen Auerbach.
All rights reserved.
This book may not be reproduced, in whole or in part, including illustrations, in any form (beyond that copying permitted by Sections 107 and 108 of the U.S. Copyright Law and except by reviewers for the public press), without written permission from the publishers.

Yale University Press books may be purchased in quantity for educational, business, or promotional use. For information, please e-mail sales.press@yale.edu (U.S. office) or sales@yaleup.co.uk (U.K. office).

Printed in the United States of America.

Library of Congress Control Number: 2024951297
ISBN 978-0-300-27083-9 (hardcover)

A catalogue record for this book is available from the British Library.

Authorized Representative in the EU: Easy Access System Europe, Mustamäe tee 50, 10621 Tallinn, Estonia, gpsr.requests@easproject.com

10 9 8 7 6 5 4 3 2 1

For my father, Robert Auerbach,
and my grandmother,
Hilda Yellin Auerbach
In loving memory

Contents

Introduction 1

ONE. A Coming-of-Age Chronicle 15

TWO. A Jewish Circle in a Polish City 40

THREE. The Disillusionment of a Polish Jew 74

FOUR. "The Nighttime Butterfly" 104

FIVE. "The Sword of Damocles" 130

SIX. From a Manor House in the Countryside to
Interwar Poland 160

SEVEN. The "Road to Total Assimilation" 177

Epilogue 194

Notes *205*
Acknowledgments *249*
Index *253*

Introduction

Kneeling in a church pew in Warsaw in the first year of the twentieth century, twenty-year-old Alicja Lewental, the eldest daughter of a prominent Polish publisher and granddaughter of a Jewish communal leader in Warsaw, ruminated on the meaning of the transformation she was about to undergo.

She thought about the man she was preparing to marry, a deeply believing Catholic for whom she was being baptized that day, and she contemplated the break from her family's past that her conversion signified for her as a daughter and granddaughter of Jewish leaders in Warsaw. Her father, Salomon Lewental, a publisher and bookseller of Polish literature, was a member of Warsaw's Jewish leadership council, and her maternal grandfather, Mathias Bersohn, was among the most esteemed Jews in Warsaw—head of a Jewish children's hospital founded by his father, former member of the Jewish communal board, and collector of Judaica. Alicja's mother, Hortensja, was an eminent salon hostess who helped to oversee the charities established by her family.

Alicja's conversion was not entirely a break from the religious faith of her home. Her mother attended church regularly, and despite Hortensja's upbringing in a Jewish home, she was raising her five children in the Catholic faith before any members of the Lewental family were baptized. Until several years earlier, Alicja had prayed frequently under an image of Jesus in her bedroom. Nevertheless, she viewed her conversion as a formal separation from her family. "On the first of June, I will already belong to another faith than my parents do, than my family, than my entire past," she wrote less than two months before the baptism. Days before the ceremony, she continued, "And the day after tomorrow I will throw off my entire past forever, I will never again return to it[,] and perhaps this would be to no avail."[1]

It was Alicja's mother who had insisted that her daughters marry Catholic men, preferably of aristocratic background—a path to her family's acceptance into Polish society at a time when the role of Catholicism in Polish national identity was strengthening. In the end, however, Alicja never married her fiancé. Her parents called off the wedding just days before the marriage for reasons that are not entirely clear from Alicja's anguished diary entries. Her initial recounting indicated that her parents had been furious when her fiancé asked them about money days before the ceremony was to be held. But in an entry a month later, she recalled comments he had reportedly made to another woman at one of the social gatherings that were regularly held in Warsaw's salons, and an acquaintance had repeated these comments to Alicja: "A long time ago in Warsaw I had already been told something I did not want to believe: that his dear old friend Karłowicz had tried to convince him how much good comes out of the assimilation of the races; apparently he was saying that to one girl at a ball, and he added, 'And he convinced me so that I got engaged to a woman from a different race than mine.'"[2]

Introduction 3

For Alicja Lewental, who had no knowledge about the religious content of her Jewish background beyond a vague sense of heritage, the experience led to a devastating realization that she could not decode the rules of belonging, and that the terrain of identity—Polish, Jewish, Catholic—was changing beneath her.

For nearly seven years, beginning in the last days of 1895, when she was sixteen years old, until shortly after her father's death in 1902, Alicja Lewental chronicled the search for belonging that transcends time and place for many a diarist her age. In three volumes bound in red covers with her initials embossed in gold lettering, she documented the despair that accompanied her passage from childhood to young womanhood. Yet she was also grappling with the challenges of being a woman with her background in fin-de-siècle Warsaw: a Polish woman from a prominent Jewish family who was being raised in the Catholic faith. Alicja's life and her family's path unfolded at the center of Polish society, surrounded by luminaries of Polish culture in exclusive salons. Yet her journal was permeated with feelings of alienation because of what she viewed as the stigma of her Jewish background.

This book tells the story of a young woman's coming of age, her disenchantment in her search for acceptance, and her family's path from Judaism to Catholicism at the turn of the twentieth century. It is a generational history of the Lewentals, their social circles, and their aspirations for belonging in Polish society, playing out in Warsaw's homes, salons, and bookstores in a modernizing city. Their history sheds light on the everyday lives of those who straddled the borders of Polish and Jewish belonging at a time when those borders were shifting. Alicja's chronicle provides access to a life history that is an example of the "exceptional normal": a marginal individual whose experiences cast in sharp relief historical developments that shape society more broadly.[3]

Diary of Alicja Lewental. Front cover, 1895–1897. Muzeum Warszawy, MD247/AR.

The narrative lens of this book is the unpublished diary of Alicja Lewental. In the Warsaw of twenty-first-century Poland, there are still glimpses of the fin-de-siècle world in which she lived as a young woman more than a century earlier. Traces of an old world rise to the surface in contemporary Warsaw: the elegant nineteenth-century handwriting of Polish writers whose countless letters have survived in library archives; the archivist who kissed the hand of a visitor by way of formal greeting, an aristocratic tradition with faint traces in today's

Introduction

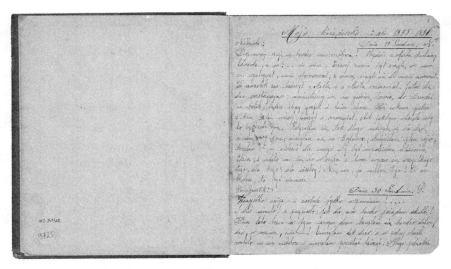

Diary of Alicja Lewental, first entry on December 29, 1895.
Muzeum Warszawy, MD247/AR.

Poland. Alicja's journal has been preserved in the archive of the Museum of Printing, which I first visited in 2012. It was located at that time a few blocks away from Warsaw's pastel-colored old town, which was reconstructed after its destruction during World War II. The museum, which has since moved to the right-bank Praga district of Warsaw, consisted at the time of just a few cramped rooms. It acquired the Lewental family's furniture, together with the family's personal papers, in 1991. Among the letters, old receipts for furniture and jewelry, and photographs of elegantly dressed family members is Alicja's diary.

During my first visit to the museum, the well-intentioned archivist dismissed Alicja's diary as merely a chronicle of a young girl's crushes, nothing of worth for a historian. The melodramas of her romantic life dominated her journals for years, and the first few months of entries were mainly lamentations about her heartbreak over a man who was soon to be engaged to another woman. But other details she recounted about her life were immediately intriguing: books she was reading, concerts and plays she attended, balls and dances in the homes of the most prominent Jewish families of nineteenth-century Warsaw. She wrote of salons where sought-after invitations allowed her and her family to mingle with journalists, poets, children of the city's financial elites, and descendants of the Polish aristocracy. Her diary is a coming-of-age tale of a young woman, her family, and their social circles. As I pored over the diary entries, the social lives of Jews who were integrated into Polish culture began to come into focus.

Then, after reading several months of journal entries, I came across these lines from an entry in March 1896: "No, no, let Edward remain who he is; I do not want him to be baptized!" she wrote of her second cousin. And later that year, in August, she wrote: "Today I was in church for a lamentation prayer for the soul of Anielka Strassburger. . . . Also there were the Fuchs, the Rossmans. . . . Mrs. Rossman and Stefcia constantly looked over at me, wondering that I had come to church, that I was kneeling and crossed myself like the others; but only in prayer do I truly find peace, comfort, and forgetting that even despite this, I would not be baptized for anything!"[4]

Confused, I read further. I had begun research about Jewish publishers of Polish books in the nineteenth century— Jewish families were among the most important Polish publishers at that time—and I was searching for materials about their private lives. An early question of my research was how their publishing work, which drew them into Polish cultural circles, shaped their families' sense of belonging and social integration, both in their own lifetimes and among their children and grandchildren. Central to this question was the degree to which

Introduction

it was possible for Jews who identified as Polish to be accepted as part of the Polish national community across generations.

My research up to that point had led me to believe that for many of these publishing families, leaving Judaism behind was what I viewed at the time as the ultimate price of acceptance. Usually that price was paid not by the first generation of family members who aspired to integration while maintaining a dual identity as both Polish and Jewish, but rather in the generations of their children or grandchildren. The most prominent Jewish publishers of Polish books were leaders in Jewish communal life, but most of their children or grandchildren converted to Christianity. I knew that Salomon Lewental had been baptized as Catholic along with his wife, Hortensja, at the end of his life. It did not entirely surprise me, therefore, that their daughter wrote in her diary about attending church and praying beneath an image of Jesus on her bedroom wall even before their baptism. But why would she be disappointed by her cousin's plans to convert, and why was she averse—at times—to being baptized herself?

What nearly seven years of Alicja's diary entries revealed was that confusion about her religious identity, and about what her family's Jewish background meant for her own life, was inseparable from the alienation that was at the heart of her internal struggles as she came of age. The experiences she recounted are a denouement to the gradual and complicated process by which her family left behind a dual sense of belonging as both Polish and Jewish by the beginning of the twentieth century. This book is the story of that arc and its aftermath.

The evolution in the Lewental family's religious and cultural identifications across three generations is rooted in tensions in the last decades of the nineteenth century between Jewish integration into Polish culture and society, on one hand, and changing ideas about the relationship among nation, state, religion, and culture in the Polish lands, on the other. Alicja's parents and their contemporaries in the circle of Warsaw's "Jewish plutocracy"—those who were immersed in Polish culture and integrated into the upper reaches of the Polish economy—came of age in the middle of the nineteenth century, when they believed they did not have to choose between two communities, one Polish and the other Jewish. They expected that Jews could be accepted as Polish as long as they spoke the language, considered themselves true "patriots" of the Polish nation, and pored over the classics of Polish literature.[5] But the 1890s, when Alicja, the Lewentals' eldest daughter, was coming of age, were a time of increasing ambivalence among some circles of Poles and Jews about the possibility for Jewish belonging to the Polish national community as an exclusionary definition of Polish national identity was gaining ground. Alicja's father was at the center of these debates as a leading publisher of Polish books and co-owner of Warsaw's largest daily newspaper. When Alicja was a young girl, Salomon became the "whipping boy" of polemics against Jewish involvement in Polish culture.[6]

In Central Europe, meanwhile, in Germany and Austria, a racial definition of the Jew developed in the 1870s and 1880s that challenged theological conceptions of anti-Jewish thought. These ideologues—journalists, politicians, and others— rejected even converts to Christianity, arguing that being Jewish was rooted in blood and was contaminating European cultures. Racial ideology was still on the margins of Polish politics as Alicja began chronicling her life at the end of the nineteenth century. But whereas studies of Polish nationalism and its impact on Polish-Jewish relations have focused on developments in politics, journalism, and other areas of public life, Alicja's chronicle of her family life and the family's social circles shifts the focus to the private realm: How did individu-

Introduction

als in their everyday lives, beyond polemics in newspapers and politics, understand and experience evolving definitions of "Pole" and "Jew"? How did the ideology of exclusionary nationalism and changing ideas about the nation in the political realm affect everyday relations between Jewish and Catholic societies in social circles, romantic relationships, and other areas of private life? To what extent did racial ideology influence these relations? And how did these notions impact the lives of Jewish families that had adopted a Polish political and cultural identification in earlier generations with the expectation that this would lead to their acceptance as part of the Polish nation?

Exclusionary boundaries around the nation developed gradually. Historians who have traced attitudes toward Jews among Polish political figures, journalists, secular Polish intellectuals, and Catholic writers have emphasized the last decades of the nineteenth century and the early twentieth century as the key time frame for the consolidation of an understanding of the Polish nation rooted in ethnicity, even as Catholicism became more central to national belonging by the end of the nineteenth century. Nationalism emphasized not only culture and language, but also a shared past and historical connection to land at the center of the national community. The perception of ethnicity as an immutable element of national belonging conflicted with the emphasis on Catholicism as integral to Polishness, a religious identity that an individual could choose to embrace.[7]

Historians' findings have differed, however, over the extent to which racial ideas influenced political rhetoric and conceptions of exclusionary ethnic nationalism in those years. I argue that even before racial notions of what it meant to be Polish gained traction in politics, Alicja Lewental and her peers encountered these ideas in their private lives. The challenge to her identity as a Pole, at times using the language of race, suggests that racial ideology was having an influence at the grass roots even at a time when these ideas were still marginalized in the political realm. From the perspective of individuals beyond ideologues who sought to make sense of these exclusionary conceptions of national belonging, the difference between "ethnicity" and "race" could be ambiguous. The Lewental family's generational history and Alicja's life path provide a case study from below of how European societies understood political conceptions of nation, ethnicity, and race; the blurred boundaries between these ideas; and contradictions in the role of religion, culture, and ethnicity in notions of national belonging. These tensions and ambiguities were at the root of Alicja's confusion in her search for acceptance.[8]

Alicja experienced political ideologies about the national community as uncertainty about where she belonged in her social world. The public and private, the political and the social, were not separate realms for her. Her narrative of everyday life casts in sharp relief how conceptions of national belonging in the public realms of political ideology and cultural life were experienced in the private realms of social life, the home, and an individual's emotional world. Alicja longed to be accepted as Polish, which she feared excluded her. "They are Catholics, playing with a Jew, even liking or loving you, of course . . . but then, what are the consequences?" she wrote in her diary at eighteen, overcome with melancholy over her latest romantic disappointment even as she continued to pray under a cross in her bedroom. "He makes jokes, jeering, makes fun of you and will go away in a cold stoicism, saying 'But this is a Jew after all.' . . . Do you again want to fly into the light, you poor nighttime butterfly? . . . So close yourself up in yourself, coat your heart with armor, and always remember that this world is not yours, that you are an intruder, that you alone are a Jew, among all of these Catholics!"[9]

Introduction 11

Alicja's perception of her Jewish background as an inescapable stigma left her adrift, caught between the Polish Jewish world that her mother sought to leave behind and the Polish Catholic world in which Alicja felt like an outsider. Her life as a young woman was limited by the social conventions of the time, despite her youthful literary ambitions, and it was only through marriage, her mother came to believe, that Alicja could be accepted as a Pole. She bore the burden of her mother's aspirations to leave behind the family's Jewish past as the price for belonging to the Polish nation. The Lewentals' path was one in which the public lives of parents intersected with the private lives of children in a process of integration that unfolded over generations. Her family's history underscores the need to examine shifts in belonging and identifications among Jews as a multigenerational process. Only by understanding the lives of the Lewentals, their friends and colleagues, and the broader circle of Jews who integrated into Polish culture in the nineteenth century does her path come into sharper light.

Alicja's diary chronicles not only her own experiences, but also the lives of her extended family and social circles. The Lewentals crossed paths with nearly every one of Warsaw's most prominent Jewish families among the Polish-speaking economic elites, as well as lesser-known families who followed similar paths as the Lewentals. Her parents encountered them at meetings of Warsaw's Jewish communal and philanthropic institutions in which they were active, socialized with them in their homes, and traveled with them during vacations. Alicja and her siblings mingled with the younger generation at the salons they visited and the dances and concerts they attended. In her diary, Alicja chronicles the broader circle's social world and family life, from marriages and funerals to baptisms. Many were connected by marriage to Hortensja Lewental's family. They were, as Alicja described them in her diary, "the

Jewish circle of our world"—however much some of them sought to leave behind that circle. At the same time, her father's fate as a Jewish publisher of Polish books and periodicals, and his path from a Jewish leader in Warsaw to the baptismal altar shortly before his death in 1902, played out in the political realm.[10]

The Lewentals and their social circles were not typical of Polish Jewry. They were exceptional in their wealth, their immersion in Polish culture, and their distance from Jewish religious traditions at a time when most Polish Jews spoke Yiddish and observed the laws and rituals of rabbinic Judaism. But unlike most Polish Jews at that time, who had limited contact with Polish cultural life and social circles, they encountered increasingly exclusionary conceptions of the Polish nation as a challenge to their own sense of belonging as Polish or as both Polish and Jewish at the same time. Their embrace of Catholicism as a radical response to this challenge shaped the lives of their children. The experiences of the Lewentals and their circle reflect broader shifts in both Polish and Jewish history because of their view from the margins.

While Alicja's diary is the narrative lens of the story, this book is also rooted in more widespread research in Poland. The history of the Lewentals, their extended family, friends, colleagues in the publishing business, and relationships with writers is preserved in extensive correspondence and other documents scattered across more than a dozen archives in Poland. The reconstruction of Salomon Lewental's experiences and the history of Jewish publishers who were his predecessors in the Polish book trade are based on letters to and from the writers whose works they published, newspapers from the time, and materials from publishing houses. Letters among Alicja, her family, and friends helped to trace her life before and after she ended her diary in 1902. Woven into the broader historical

Introduction

context are memoirs, newspaper articles, and other sources documenting Polish and Polish Jewish life.

The challenges that Alicja Lewental recounted at the turn of the twentieth century are as relevant today, more than two decades into the twenty-first century, as they were in her lifetime, and not only for Polish, and Polish Jewish, history. This history echoes with the experiences of those who are growing up at a time when what it means to be "American" is in dispute and when politics is increasingly infused with discrimination against minority groups, whether they be Muslim, African American, Asian American, Latino, or Jewish. It is a time when these groups are at the center of political debates about the relationship among national belonging, culture, religion, and citizenship, just as Jews were in a similar role in the Polish lands and elsewhere in Europe since the eighteenth century. "I graduated from high school last year. But the Muslim girl at prom did not—does not—exist in a vacuum. She becomes the Muslim woman on a college campus, at the office party," a college student, Romaissaa Benzizoune, wrote in an essay titled "The Muslim Prom Queen and Me" in the *New York Times* in 2017. "The Muslim woman in America, breathing American air, occupying American public space and generally making the mind-blowing political statement of being an American. It is no surprise that under so many eyes, she cannot fit in. . . . What is lost in the conversations about Islam and terrorism and media representation is that a teenage girl is a teenage girl. When her high school heartthrob asks someone else to prom, she will be—without fail and without exception—devastated."[11]

Alicja Lewental's story is both a tale of a Polish Jewish family and a universal tale, a narrative of coming of age as a young person whose place in society and in the national community is contested in political life. The Lewentals' story is one of continuities and ruptures between past and present and across generations. Alicja's diary provides a window onto a life path that separated her from her ancestors, a chronicle of her anguish over where she and her family belonged.

A guide to pronouncing the names of key individuals in this book might be helpful for the reader. The name "Alicja" is pronounced "a-LEE-tsee-a" ("tsee" is short); "Hortensja" is pronounced "hor-TEN-see-a" ("see" is short); and "Zosia" is pronounced "ZO-sha." When, because of border changes, cities have different contemporary names than the names by which they were previously known, I have used the contemporary names (L'viv instead of Lwów, Vilnius instead of Wilno). Warsaw and Krakow are referred to according to their common English usage. When referring to the newspaper *Kurjer Warszawski* and other newspapers, I have used the spelling employed at that time rather than the contemporary spelling of Kurier.

1

A Coming-of-Age Chronicle

In the last days of 1895, sixteen-year-old Alicja Lewental sat on her bed in her family's apartment in Warsaw and confessed to the blank pages of a notebook the emotional turmoil that she could not share with those closest to her—neither with her mother, a woman of high society who hosted a renowned salon in their home, nor with her younger sister Marta, whom she viewed as a competitor for both friendships and suitors. Hanging over Alicja's bed was a picture of Christ, under which she often knelt to pray. She had spent the past week celebrating Christmas at balls and other gatherings with relatives and acquaintances, among them the man with whom she had fallen in love, and now she lamented her unfulfilled hopes for a future with him. Her uncertainty about the future, and her vacillations between pessimism and romantic hopes for love, had begun even then. "Oh, the night is full of mysticism and superstitions!" she wrote on the first day of 1896, shortly after she began writing her diary. "What do people not do behind your black curtains in order to ask you about the future! And what will it bring me? Happiness or sadness, joy or worries? Oh, new year!"[1]

16   A Coming-of-Age Chronicle

Over the next seven years of entries, Alicja turned to her diary as she sought to make sense of her emotional fluctuations and questions of belonging while marking the passing of time. Her journal is a narrative of emotions at the extremes, moving back and forth between hope and despair, elation and disappointment. From the time of her seventeenth birthday in 1896, when she exchanged her short childhood skirts for the long, elegant dresses of a young woman, she spent countless evenings at balls and salons, dancing with men whom she thought of as marriage prospects. They seemed to court her as well, only to stop short of pursuing her further as suitors—experiences she often attributed to her Jewish background. She hoped, as her mother did, that conversion and marriage to a Catholic man from an aristocratic family could make her an equal to her Polish Catholic peers. But she eventually despaired over her unfulfilled hopes for romantic love, a despair that became intertwined with her yearning for acceptance in Polish society.

Alicja kept a record of her life in Polish, her native tongue and a language that was central to the identity she cultivated as a culturally sophisticated woman in Warsaw's elite social circles. Occasionally she wrote down quotes that moved her from books or poems she was reading in French, German, and English, but nowhere in her journal does Yiddish appear. Growing up in a home that was fully immersed in Polish culture, with a mother who was raised in a modernizing Jewish home by parents who themselves were integrated into Polish culture, she was unlikely to have known the language.

Alicja wrote in plain, light-brown notebooks, most of which she later had bound into three red volumes. She planned to have at least one of those volumes bound while abroad in Germany; she and her suitors were the subjects of gossip in Warsaw, and in Germany, she noted, the bookbinder would not be able to read the deeply personal thoughts and experiences

A Coming-of-Age Chronicle

she recorded in Polish. For the first five years of her diary, Alicja wrote almost daily and noted her failure to write when she missed more than a day or two. But each time the fulfillment of her hopes for marriage seemed imminent—just before a courtship that stopped short of engagement; on the eve of her engagement to another man, whom she did not marry in the end; and finally before the commitment of marriage to the man who became her husband—she lamented that she would have to end her diary, as was expected of her, and confess her deepest feelings to her husband instead. "It is a pity, my dear diary, that in several months, in a year at most, I will have to burn you because I will not be able to show you in any way, and Mamusia [Mommy] says that it is forbidden to me to be secretive toward a husband!" she wrote just before a courtship with one suitor seemed to be heading toward marriage. "It is a pity to burn so many notebooks, my entire maiden life." Young women who kept diaries throughout Europe in the nineteenth century often stopped writing when they were married, as Hortensja Lewental had expected of her eldest daughter. Just before Alicja's marriage in 1901, she seemed to have stopped writing entirely. But defying convention, she returned to the journal the following year, when she lamented the absence of conversation and fulfillment in her marriage and sought solace in writing.[2]

Alicja often wrote at her desk in the bedroom she shared with her younger sister Marta, who was keeping her own diary, which Alicja sometimes read without her sister's knowledge. In the summers, when her family vacationed in the Polish mountain resort of Zakopane or other respites from the big city, she wrote in pensions and apartments with views of the mountains. Other times she took pen in hand as she traveled with her family by train to the cities and resort towns of Central and Western Europe and the Ottoman Empire. During vacations, Alicja wrote about the beauty of the Polish landscape, the charms of Constantinople,

Alicja Lewental, 1898–1899. Muzeum Warszawy, MD170/Fot.

Marta and Alicja Lewental, circa 1900. Muzeum Warszawy, MD168/Fot.

Drawing of Alicja Mińska by Zygmunt Miński, 1901–1902. Muzeum Warszawy, MD396/AR.

and the crowded marketplaces of Italy. On a trip to Switzerland, where she traveled with her family to escape from gossip in Warsaw after her broken engagement, she wrote on a hotel balcony overlooking the mountains, on a boat traveling to Lucerne, and on a train winding through the Alps.

Alicja ruminated on her diary writing, reflecting on when and where she wrote and why she felt compelled to do so. Sometimes she wrote late at night after returning from a long evening of dancing. Other times she wrote early in the morning, before her family awoke. "How good it is to write so peacefully, in the morning in bed, while everyone is still sleeping and no one disturbs me [or] interrupts my thoughts," she wrote one morn-

A Coming-of-Age Chronicle   21

ing while her family was vacationing in the Polish mountains. "I also like to write in the evening, when everyone is sleeping and there is nothing to hear in the nighttime darkness, only the barking of the dog and the scraping of my pen." Occasionally she wrote of reading earlier entries in her diary, lamenting the passing of childhood and reliving her romances and trips abroad.[3]

Alicja's diary became a confidante and witness to her young life. She expressed gratitude that she could confide in her diary about feelings she was able to reveal to no one else: "It is good to have a place where it is possible to tell [and] think everything, where it is possible to write about everything. To have such a witness of paper that it is possible to trust completely." A year later, at a time of disillusionment after her hopes for marriage had been stymied by her mother's decision that she must marry a Catholic man, she wrote, "Sometimes when I sit alone, I think I am missing a good friend terribly, such a dear friend for whom I would give everything and who would also give everything for me! And I am missing her so much that I wonder how I have been able to live without her until now and to have only my diary as a confidante and to never desire anything more!" When she came to the end of the first notebook of her diary, she bid farewell as if to a dear friend. "So farewell, notebook; it is already the end!" she wrote. "Still a few [more] words, and I will close you in order to no longer write in you! Farewell, my faithful notebook," she added before ending with a prayer to Christ.[4]

Alicja's angst over her first romance seems to have prompted her to begin the journal, but if she had an audience for her diary in mind aside from herself, it was perhaps her mother, Hortensja. When she first confided to her mother that she was keeping a diary, Hortensja told her that she would read it the day before her wedding, when Alicja planned to give her the volumes for safekeeping. Even before then, Alicja gave her the first notebook of her diary to read, but she agonized over whether to do so and viewed the act as a substitute for confiding in her more directly. "On New Year's, I would like to make a gift of my diary to Mamusia!" she wrote in 1896, a year after her first entry. "I know that Mamusia would be in heaven! But I do not know whether to give it or whether to keep it for a year? I reread it in its entirety myself in the dawn hours and then courage, Mon Coeur. . . . Yes, in the new year I will give Mamusia these notebooks, in which I poured out my entire soul and my entire heart!"[5] Hortensja returned the diary to her daughter with only a passing comment that it was well written, according to Alicja's recounting. She never again mentioned sharing her notebooks with her mother, and the diaries seem to have remained in Alicja's possession even after her marriage.

Diary writing was in some ways an extension of Alicja's perpetual internal conversation with God about her struggles over religious faith. Often she wrote down entreaties as if the pages of her journal stood in for the ears of God. At times, the diary seemed to be a literary undertaking as well, a way to channel literary ambitions and cultural interests that had no place in the expectations that her parents and social world had for her. When she told one man at a salon that she was keeping a diary, she refused his repeated requests to read it, but her very mention to him that she kept a journal was perhaps an expression of literary ambitions within the confines of what was permitted to her by the social norms of that time.

The self-portrait that Alicja created through the words of her diary was of a romantic girl and then an anguished, often pessimistic young woman who eventually resigned herself to a life without romantic love even as she longed for it; a cultured woman who was moved to tears by poetry, who valued education and refinement in men and female acquaintances alike, and who criticized the materialism of her social world. She luxuriated in the elegant clothes that a local tailor sewed for her

A Coming-of-Age Chronicle

and that her father brought home from his travels abroad, appreciating the fashionable dresses that drew attention at social gatherings. But she eventually lamented the focus on wealth and status that permeated her social life and aspirations for marriage. The life of the spirit was her consolation, but that, too, was the cause of anguish. Alicja's disappointments in romance and courtship soon became inseparable from her increasing alienation over her ambivalent desire to leave behind what she viewed as the burden of a Jewish heritage.

The formal photographs of Alicja that have survived with her diary show a woman with dark, wavy hair and almond-shaped eyes. In images taken in a photography studio on Plac Zielony (Green Square) in the city center, near Saski Garden with its grand palace, Alicja sits on a plush armchair as a toddler, first on her own holding a doll, and then with her infant sister Marta. It was a ritual of childhood for Varsovians with the means for such luxuries: childhood photographs taken by the renowned Warsaw photographer Konrad Brandel, whose work appeared in the illustrated journal *Kłosy*, the jewel in the crown of Salomon Lewental's publishing business when Alicja was a young girl. A decade later, in a photography studio on Miodowa Street, Warsaw's traditional "book row," a photograph shows the sisters as young girls, Alicja at eleven years old, leaning against one another, heads touching, with long hair and wearing white dresses with high collars. As young women sitting for a portrait in the same studio years later at a time when Alicja was writing her diary, their long hair has been pinned up, Alicja wearing a bow tying her hair back at the nape of her neck. Later, as a married woman with the last name Mińska and with her mustachioed husband observing her from a distance, Alicja is wearing a wide-brimmed hat and a long fur coat, her head bowed and looking down, no longer with the expectant gaze of the earlier photographs.

In many ways, Alicja Lewental's record of her life followed conventions that had developed over the nineteenth century and earlier as private diary writing became increasingly popular across Europe, especially among adolescent girls and young women. It was at once a personal endeavor, a window onto an individual life, and a cultural practice—marking entries by date, writing to the diary as a friend, and often addressing the entries to the paper itself ("dear diary"). The nineteenth century was the "golden age of the diary," as the historian Peter Gay termed it. Until recent decades, it has often been men's diaries that have found their way to contemporary audiences—prominent women writers and other cultural figures such as Anaïs Nin and Virginia Woolf are among the exceptions—and women's diaries are preserved less frequently than men's. When a woman's diary is preserved, it is often part of an archival collection under her husband's name or, as in Alicja's case, under her father's name, making it less visible to a historian searching for records. But young women were the ones making diary writing a popular pursuit in the nineteenth century.[6]

The diary as a record of private life evolved from a much longer history. The chronicling of everyday life has its root in ancient times, when some individuals kept account books and recorded mundane details of household events, but these were not records of personal life and were often taken down by a secretary. For centuries in Japan, young women wrote down musings about daily life in what were called "pillow books," the most famous of which was written by a woman of the Japanese imperial court, Sei Shonagon, who completed her writing in 1002. By the seventeenth and eighteenth centuries, the greater availability of paper and the standardization of the calendar turned journals into what some historians have asserted is the defining feature of the modern diary: the keeping of dated records of daily life. Those characteristics allow a reader of diaries

A Coming-of-Age Chronicle

to trace the mundane, day-to-day experiences that influence an individual's emotional life; the construction of a sense of self; and the decisions that shape a life path. The diary of Samuel Pepys, a British naval administrator and parliamentarian who began writing in 1680, became a prototype for the personal diary. But even then the practice was limited mainly to prominent individuals who recorded historical events affecting their country or their personal finances and mundane details such as the weather, more so than their private thoughts and inner life.[7]

It was only in the mid-nineteenth century that more diaries began to be published and drew the attention of a broader readership. Pepys's diary manuscript had circulated in private hands among a small group of individuals but was first published only in 1825 as the practice of diary writing became a more public phenomenon. By then, it had begun to be viewed by many as a "female" pursuit, especially among middle-class women whose lives were increasingly relegated to the private sphere. Often they were "spiritual diaries," an accounting of good deeds and sins or an exploration of faith, while other diarists confided romantic longings, creating a "secret space" between the covers of their journals, a sentiment that weaves throughout Alicja's diary. Many diaries, like Alicja's, combined threads of private life and inner world.[8]

In France, where girls had begun keeping diaries in increasing numbers in the late eighteenth century, the practice became more common around the 1830s, and even before then in England. Adolescent girls and young women throughout Europe, in the United States, and beyond took pen in hand to record their lives. Diary writing required a degree of education and the leisure of time, thus silencing the voices of women without those luxuries, and diaries that have found their way to a public readership are skewed toward those that shed light on elite cultural circles. A decade before Alicja began her journal, the diaries of Marie Bashkirtseff, a Russian painter who died in 1884 at the age of twenty-five, became a "cult of a kind" throughout Europe and later in the United States after they were published in France in 1887 and in English translation in 1889. Just over two years before Alicja wrote her first entry, Julie Manet, the daughter of prominent Impressionist painters who was a niece of the artist Edouard Manet, began to keep a diary, documenting the everyday lives and social world of the artists in Paris who raised her after she was orphaned. And two years after Alicja began her diary, the writer Virginia Woolf took pen in hand to write the first entry in a journal she kept until shortly before her death in 1941. Closer to home for Alicja, Zinaida Poliakova, the daughter of a Russian Jewish railroad magnate and a generation older than Alicja, kept a journal for more than seventy-five years beginning in the 1870s, recording her everyday life among the acculturated bourgeoisie in Moscow and St. Petersburg and later as an émigrée in France. A century and a half would pass before Poliakova's diary found its way to a public audience.[9]

In the United States, too, young women documented their lives, from the large cities of the Northeast to small towns throughout the country. The "spiritual diary" and the travel journal were central to American literary traditions, paving the way for secular chronicles with a "focus on the inner reality of the diarist." A steep increase in literacy in the nineteenth century expanded the practice of diary writing. While keeping a diary was more common among men than among women into the second half of the nineteenth century in the United States, journal writing became a predominantly female pursuit by the end of the century, particularly among middle-class women. The popularity of Bashkirtseff's journal in the United States led young women "from Massachusetts to Montana" to write diaries

A Coming-of-Age Chronicle

not only with themselves as an audience, but "with the explicit expectation that their journals would make them famous too."[10]

Historical developments, from westward expansion to the Civil War, further shaped the content and function of diary writing in the United States. Several African American women who kept diaries in the nineteenth century and whose journals have found their way to a public audience recorded the impact of racism in public and private life on their personal travails and identities. Alicja Lewental's record of her life, while reflecting the very different contexts of European Jewish history, contains echoes of the nineteenth-century diary of an African American woman born in Philadelphia, Charlotte Forten Grimké, who kept her journal for thirty-eight years, from 1858 to 1892. The daughter of an anti-slavery activist, Grimké grew up in a bourgeois home where she learned to play the piano, studied foreign languages, and wrote poetry. Her diary writing and her immersion in books, from African American literature to the essays of Ralph Waldo Emerson and the poetry of William Wordsworth and Elizabeth Barrett Browning, gave her solace and an escape from her despair over the enslavement of African Americans in the southern states, as well as from the racism she experienced herself, according to Geneva Cobb-Moore. During the Civil War, Grimké documented her experiences providing medical assistance to Union soldiers and teaching African Americans who had escaped behind Union lines. Unlike Alicja's more ambiguous response to the ideology of racial antisemitism, Grimké sought to challenge racism, but she lived on the margins, as Alicja did. She "felt the paradox of her unique place in a society where her color gave offense and connected her irremediably to the unprivileged and illiterate slaves, but where her background was greatly different from that of the slaves," Brenda Stevenson wrote of Grimké.[11]

28 A Coming-of-Age Chronicle

Diary writing was in some ways a shared endeavor, even in its solitude. Three of the four Lewental sisters were writing diaries, and Alicja's sister Marta sometimes read pages of her journal to her sisters, as Alicja recounted in her own diary. Often educated at home and secluded from the broader world of work and public life, women from Alicja's social class who kept diaries often focused on events and details that were considered trivial: daily life and romance, or, as the scholar Valerie Raoul put it, "any event or non-event [that] can be considered worthy of comment." Yet sometimes diaries also provide a window onto a moment in time, a picture of a "particular time and place in the exterior world." The "paradox of the private diary," wrote Raoul, "is that, in order to remain private, it should not survive. Yet a written record remains, until destroyed—like a message in a bottle which may evoke, years later, a barely elicited response unknown to the sender."[12]

Alicja's writing was usually introspective, chronicling a sense of despair that, she lamented, she must mask behind the refinement and proper conversation that were expected of her. "I am tired of everything, of this life, constant lies and hypocrisy, tired of this mask that I constantly must wear!" she wrote in early January 1898 as she contemplated how her life would unfold in the new year. While nineteenth-century diaries of adolescent girls often lacked a literary narrative and a consistent cast of characters, as some literary scholars have described the genre, Alicja's diary reads at times like a travelogue or one of the romance novels in which she frequently sought solace. "Only an hour before leaving Pest, we returned by steamship from Constantinople," she wrote in 1896 during a trip with her family and members of the Natanson, Brühl, and Perlmutter families, from their social circles in Warsaw, as she thought about her romantic feelings for a man back home. "The ship went slowly enough, the moon shone wonderfully, [it was] so

A Coming-of-Age Chronicle 29

warm that we were only in cotton dresses, and this quick departure so affected me that I sat in the corner of the ship, and, completely drenched in the rays of the moon, I started thinking, and I did not even notice as tears began to flow down my face at first slowly, then faster and faster! . . . And the exhilaration lasted such a short time!"[13]

Yet Alicja's journal also transcended the quotidian and the introspective. Alicja ventured outside of the private realm, which was the expected domain of a woman of her time and social class, even as a movement for women's emancipation developed in the Polish lands. She provided a window into the literary life around her. Her diary rarely mentioned her father's publishing work, but she and her sisters sometimes worked in his bookstore, and she lived in a home where writers socialized and where their books stood on the shelves of the family's private library. While she referred at times only matter-of-factly to a book she was reading or expressed her reaction by relating the storyline to her personal troubles, she sometimes commented on a book's literary value. After attending a concert or play, she evaluated the skill of the actors and the talent of the musicians, even if her ruminations were only tentative. "Yesterday I was at [Ignacy Jan] Paderewski's [concert]," she wrote after attending a performance by the renowned Polish pianist and future prime minister. "He played like God! It was not so much his technique that amazed me, because he is great, he is dazzling, yet [it was] the soul, this animated playing of his emotion! He does not play, he actually, truly, is crying and yearning and musing through the sounds. Yesterday, listening to his mazurka by Chopin or his etudes or nocturnes, [his] preludes, it made me want to throw myself on the floor and cry, cry, the soul weeps, he played like that! . . . He is deep like the depths of the sea, he plays with his heart and thought and not with his fingers!"[14]

As the daughter of a publisher whose cultural role drew him into politics and who brought home the latest issues of the journals he published, Alicja would have been privy to news about political developments. She wrote with awareness that cultural life had political significance. Her chronicle helps to reconstruct both her own life path as a young woman and a social history of cultural life in which politics played a central role. The publishing role of Alicja's father, together with the wealth and prestige of her mother Hortensja's family, the Bersohns, opened doors for Alicja not only to the material luxuries that her family's financial success brought, but also to literary events and social gatherings where the Polish writers in attendance lent prestige to all those present. Salomon and Hortensja Lewental turned their own home into a venue of Polish cultural and social life, hosting a salon in their apartment, where their children encountered writers and journalists whose works Salomon published.

Alicja's diary reflected her education as well as the central role of culture in her sense of belonging. Like many other young women of her economic class and social status, she took private lessons in foreign languages and read books in French, English, and German. More than the foreign works she read, however, of greatest interest to her were the novels of the Polish writer Józef Ignacy Kraszewski, with whom her father had frequent contact as one of his publishers until Kraszewski's death in 1887. She was especially interested in Kraszewski's descriptions of the Volhynian region—"his beautiful fatherland," she wrote, referring to the region where a suitor had grown up—which was in the eastern part of the Polish-Lithuanian Commonwealth before the late eighteenth-century partitions by the surrounding empires. Those eastern lands were central to some ideologues' multinational vision of a hoped-for Polish state that could incorporate regions whose populations were not predominantly

A Coming-of-Age Chronicle 31

ethnic Poles. "And now I am in the process of reading Krasze-wski's Volhynian story, *Two Worlds*. I am more interested in it because this is his fatherland!" she wrote about the suitor. "I am throwing myself now into the Ukrainian-Volhynian stories of Kraszewski and Sienkiewicz, and I want to know his homeland from books [literally, description]. . . . Because I have to behold it someday, this is his Volhynia, his beautiful fatherland!" Lewental's emotional connection to Polish culture and language and to the historic lands of the former Polish-Lithuanian Commonwealth reflected the very elements of heritage that some ideologues professed to be at the core of Polish nationality.[15]

Alicja often wrote of savoring the classics of Polish litera-ture. She was enraptured by the works of Adam Mickiewicz and Juliusz Słowacki, the bards of nineteenth-century Polish Ro-manticism, with their themes of ardent Polish patriotism. She read Mickiewicz's works "a thousand times," she noted in one entry. After reading *Quo Vadis*, Henryk Sienkiewicz's novel about a romance between the Roman consul and a Christian woman in the first-century Roman Empire, just three years after the book was published, Alicja wrote in her diary that the novel had renewed in her the spark of religious faith.[16]

She sometimes read literature by Polish writers whose works her father published. Among these authors were Polish intellectuals who had begun to rethink the romantic traditions of Polish patriotism after the failure of the Polish insurrection against Russian rule in 1863–64. The collapse of the rebellion was a crucial turning point in the views of some Polish writers about the relationship between Russian authorities and the Congress Kingdom of Poland, a semi-autonomous region of the Russian Empire that included Warsaw. The tsarist rulers had largely stripped the region of its limited autonomy follow-ing the failed revolt. Grouped around several newspapers in Warsaw, these writers believed that a fractured Polish society had doomed the uprising to failure and that the way to throw off the Russian yoke was not by launching armed insurrections but by fostering economic and social unity in Polish society at the grass roots: aristocrats and peasants, Christians and Jews. These writers became known as Polish Positivists; they wanted to adapt to Polish conditions the French philosopher Auguste Comte's conception of science as the basis for human development. The Positivists viewed the Hasidic masses as a backward population that followed an outdated way of life and held irrational beliefs in mysticism. They believed that Jews could become part of Polish society only by shedding external markers of difference, from the Yiddish language to distinctive traditional clothes. Only then could they be accepted on an equal footing with their neighbors in Polish society. The Positivists were at first optimistic that Jews could become an organic part of Polish society.

The novels of the eminent writer Eliza Orzeszkowa, whose works Alicja's father published, were particularly influential in developing the Positivists' views on Jewish integration, and her works appeared in Alicja's accounts of her reading life. She disliked Orzeszkowa's *Marta,* a feminist novel that lamented the fate of a widowed woman who searches in vain for a job in Warsaw to support her daughter. It was a criticism of the harsh realities of the industrialized city, and Alicja's reaction underscored the class divide that separated her wealthy world from most residents of Warsaw. "It made a depressing, unpleasant impression on me. Poor Marta," she wrote of the novel, which her mother had recommended to her—perhaps an attempt by Hortensja to elicit Alicja's interest in the charity work in which her mother remained active. Alicja expressed sympathy but also discomfort with poverty. She ruminated more extensively on Orzeszkowa's best-known books on Jewish themes, *Meir Ezofowicz* and *Eli Makower,* which Alicja read at a time when she

A Coming-of-Age Chronicle

was struggling with the meaning of her Jewish background in her own life. In 1896 she read *Meir Ezofowicz*, which contrasted the "enlightened" Ezofowiczes with a family of traditional Jews who were spiritual leaders in a small town's Jewish community. The work, which was first published in 1878 and was reissued by Alicja's father, together with Orzeszkowa's entire corpus of writing, was strongly critical of traditional Jewish life.[17]

Alicja related the books she read to her own experiences, sometimes comparing them with her romantic life but also, in a handful of entries, with the influence of Jewishness on her social world. After reading *Eli Makower*, a novel by Orzeszkowa about Jewish relations with the Polish nobility that focuses on the moral awakening of Eli Makower, an employee of a dishonest Polish agent, Porycki, Alicja reflected on the character of Lila, the sister of a nobleman who would have been ruined financially by Makower in order to pay his debt for Lila's dowry. The Positivist message of cooperation between Poles and Jews—that they "must work together for their mutual benefit," according to the literary scholar Ursula Phillips—is at the heart of the novel. "I have read these days the wonderful book by Orzeszkowa, *Eli Makower*, a Jewish history," Alicja wrote. "Poor Lila, entwined so terribly in a web by Porycki that she fell so low, that she can no longer raise herself up. How wonderful is the section where she thinks about what she believes in and comes to the conviction that she believes in nothing—that there is darkness and coldness in her heart, that she always strove only for her personal happiness, that she was an egoist and became a nihilist. . . . The scene of Eli with his father is very beautiful, especially in the third volume, when Judel [Eli's father] speaks about the equality of Jews." As Alicja ruminated on the novel, her anguish over rejection by a Catholic man of aristocratic heritage was at its height. Her comment about the

34 A Coming-of-Age Chronicle

novel was one of few references she made regarding the legal equality of Jews.[18]

Alicja did not view her identity as a Polish patriot as contradictory to a cosmopolitan immersion in the literature of other cultures, travel to other countries, and the study of foreign languages. Interspersed in her entries are phrases in French, the foreign language favored by the Polish aristocracy, and she wrote of nineteenth-century Polish classic literature in the same entry in which she makes a reference to Victor Hugo, whose works she was also reading. In 1896 she read a work by the philosopher Baruch Spinoza, a favorite in later years of some secularizing Jews who left behind Jewish observances but did not embrace Christianity. She did not comment in her diary about her reactions to Spinoza's philosophy or life path. For a historian of modern Jewish life, her very interest in his writing evokes the dilemma of the "non-Jewish Jew," who "looked for ideals and fulfillment" beyond Jewish identity when it was devoid of religious significance, in the words of Isaac Deutscher. Yet the phrase "non-Jewish Jew" could not describe Alicja, who was raised as Catholic since childhood.[19]

Reading was both a way to make sense of romantic disappointments and an escape from them. Alicja seemed to read constantly. Early on in her diary, she commented that Goethe's *The Sorrows of Young Werther* was her favorite book; she had read it repeatedly, she wrote, and each time it evoked in her "a new thought and new feeling." Plots of unrequited love, as in Goethe's book, seemed to resonate with her most, but in the novel, the noblemen's platonic rejection of Werther, an artist with no aristocratic background, also mirrored Alicja's perceptions of her own experiences. On vacations, Alicja spent much of her time reading the books she brought with her, sitting alone in a hotel library or on the balcony of a hotel room. "Often we go to the forest with books, and we sit on one of the most

A Coming-of-Age Chronicle

frequented roads in a beautiful pavilion with a view of the Jungfrau [mountain] and Lake Brienz," she wrote during her travels in Switzerland. In Zakopane, reading contributed to the tranquil atmosphere that she savored in the Polish mountains. "I do not know anyone here," she wrote. "I do not go anywhere! Life is very calm. I read a lot, play [croquet], study, and write many letters."[20]

Alicja was particularly drawn to music and poetry. At home she studied piano and learned to sing, and she described her deep emotions when listening to Chopin, the Polish-born composer who was a symbol of Polish national culture. She frequently wrote down her favorite verses and occasionally recited poems at the requests of men at the dances or balls she attended. After her broken engagement following her baptism, when her parents sent her to a spa town abroad to escape from the gossip and disappointment, she filled pages of her diary with poems and passages from novels about tormented love in four languages—mainly in Polish, but also in French, German, and English, which she was learning with tutors at home. Alicja sometimes wrote eloquently, with a hint of literary ambition, about the landscapes during her travels, her inner life, and her existential anguish. When she first began keeping a record of her life, she mentioned writing her own short stories, and several years later she tried her hand at literary writing once more, penning several pages of a novel before setting it aside, as she noted in her diary. Binding the notebooks of her diary into hard-covered volumes resembling books reflects, perhaps, a vision of herself as a writer, shaped by the world of books that surrounded her in her social world, education, leisure time, and family life.

Alicja's chronicle also depicts the stifling world of a woman whose young life was expected to be above all about the search for a husband with a social status that would be suitable to her family's economic position. Her education was intended to cultivate her cultural interests and tastes with an eye toward social life and marriage to a man of culture and aristocratic bearing. Her cousin Zuzanna Rabska later flouted those conventions by becoming a part of Polish journalistic and cultural circles, and in a handful of entries, Alicja recounted conversations with men about feminism and women's emancipation at social gatherings. But Alicja's immersion in literature, her education in foreign languages, and the seeds of literary talent were not a prelude for her to become part of public life beyond friendships with writers and financial support for them after her marriage. A young man of her economic and cultural background would likely have been educated in a school where he could become part of a circle of peers who developed intellectual ideas about culture and politics together. Alicja's uncle, the lawyer and historian Aleksander Kraushar, had followed that path when he attended the Warsaw Real-Gymnasium, a Polish school (similar to a high school) where students and teachers alike were involved in patriotic circles. But the education of Alicja and her sisters—unlike that of their younger brother Stefan, who attended a gymnasium despite his disappointing grades—was limited to lessons with private tutors within the home: Polish history and literature; instruction in foreign languages; and classes in music, dancing, and painting.[21]

Despite her initial explorations of literary ambitions, Alicja soon abandoned the path to a life of the intellect, if she had ever seriously contemplated it. Her intellectual interests became an element of her desire for social acceptance and marriage. Salons and other social gatherings were the main settings where she and her sisters displayed their affinity for Polish culture, and her entries were soon dominated by accounts of dancing and conversations with men she met at balls and salons and by her hopes and disappointments in romance. She re-

A Coming-of-Age Chronicle

corded detailed descriptions of the silk blouses, elegant gloves, and stylish dresses that were essential in her social world. Often, when she sat down at her desk with her diary in the wee hours of the morning after a long evening of dancing, she noted which young women were the most elegantly dressed, who looked particularly attractive, and which ones had drawn the most attention from potential suitors. And always she recounted in detail her conversations with men, the wittiness or dullness of their comments, the refinement or boorishness of their manners, and their dancing finesse or lack thereof. Her appreciation for literature, music, and theater became a thread within the narrative of romance as she recounted ideas about culture mainly through her interactions with the latest suitors. Her journal became an outlet to give vent to frustrations over romantic life and her search for a husband.

Woven throughout Alicja Lewental's narrative of social and cultural life, her romantic hopes and disappointments, and her longing for friendship—through nearly all of her everyday life—was her confusion over religious identity and about the meaning of her family's Jewish background for her own life. She felt increasingly alienated from her social world. Her interactions were characterized by emotional distance, according to her ruminations. Feelings of loneliness and isolation prevailed. If only she could find a confidante as close as her mother's closest friend, Alicja lamented, she would no longer need a diary. "From time to time I reread to myself what was long ago! It would be so good to be able to recount this conversation to someone. . . . I do not have anyone!" She wrote of friendship as of romantic love, eagerly awaiting letters from a young woman who she hoped would finally fill her need for close female companionship, a feeling she did not express when writing about her sisters.[22]

Alicja's identity—on the margins of the Catholic and Jewish worlds, at the intersection of "Polish" and "Jewish"—exaggerated the struggle with a developing sense of self that often motivated young diarists of that time to record the details of their private lives. She wrote as a way to make sense of that struggle. The desire to chronicle one's daily life often stems from a "malaise based on a questioning of selfhood" and an attempt to bring meaning to the disorder of "fractured lives," as literary scholars have interpreted the motivations of diary writers. In her diary, a youthful search for belonging reinforced the inner turmoil caused by the challenge that exclusionary conceptions of the Polish nation posed to her self-identification.[23]

Alicja's narrative of everyday life allows for an examination of often elusive issues of evolving identifications. The diary conveys a mindset—a set of assumptions and attitudes that shape one's behavior, decisions, and interpretation of experiences—of an individual on the brink of conversion whose understanding of herself and the world is in flux. She explicitly connected that developing worldview to her identity as a Pole from a Jewish family. Her outlook as a woman of Jewish background who did not gain prominence in public life is rare in extant sources from the nineteenth-century Polish lands written contemporaneously with the experiences they recount. Alicja's chronicle is not only a window into daily life among the acculturated, urban bourgeoisie of East European Jewry, but also a conversion narrative, one that points to the heightened dilemmas of Jewish families who felt a sense of belonging to the Polish nation, even as they experienced the pressures of nationalism.

Alicja wrote her chronicle at the very moment when she was grappling with her religious identity. It is therefore more revealing of motivations for baptism than are other types of conversion narratives. These narratives, whether in memoirs or in official documents such as petitions to church and government authorities, did not simply recount "actual events, but self-consciously refashioned them into a seamless story that

A Coming-of-Age Chronicle

ended at the baptismal font," as the historian ChaeRan Freeze wrote. Alicja, on the other hand, wrote without hindsight as her religious beliefs were in formation and unstable. She had not yet woven these beliefs into a coherent set of ideas. To be sure, her diary is a constructed narrative as well, but it is a contemporaneous construction, providing a glimpse into both the details of everyday life that helped to shape the formation of identity and her interpretations of these experiences as she made decisions about her life. Because religious identity is only one element of her broader narrative, the details of her romantic life, social interactions, family life, education, and other aspects of her private world expand our understanding of the "complex of motives, needs and perceptions" that, in addition to belief, shape even "spiritual" conversions.[24]

Alicja's diary, its undercurrents of confusion and alienation, help to reconstruct the "historical sensation," to use the historian Johan Huizinga's term, of an individual from a Jewish family who sought acceptance by the surrounding society at a time of changing ideas about what bound individuals to a community. The city of Warsaw, with its salons, bookstores, and medieval old town, was central to her story.

2

A Jewish Circle in a Polish City

When Ferdynand Hoesick, an up-and-coming young journalist, visited the book-lined home of Alicja Lewental and her family near fashionable New World Street (Nowy Świat) for the first time at the dawn of the twentieth century, he took in his surroundings and felt the rush of having "made it" in Warsaw. On Saturday evenings each week, Hoesick, the son of a bookseller himself, recalled that "the entire Warsaw literary and journalistic world" gathered at the Lewental home, sitting under paintings by famous Polish artists on the walls. The women might have been dressed in gowns like the ones Alicja described in her diary, and the men in waistcoats made in Western Europe or sewn perhaps by the local Jewish tailor known simply as Szabsio, "known to all of literary-journalistic Warsaw," as one memoirist recalled. After dinner and dancing, the guests—writers and poets, journalists and artists—retired to the sitting room or the Lewentals' private library, deep in conversation about the newest literature and poetry or the latest political news. The journalists among them sometimes discussed an article or essay planned for an upcoming issue. Musicians from abroad who were

A Jewish Circle in a Polish City

invited to the salon sometimes found that discussions there led to favorable reviews by the writers they met.[1]

The gatherings were known as "Saturdays at the Lewentals," and receiving an invitation from Hortensja, printed in elegant script on formal stationery, was considered a privilege among Varsovians. On Sunday afternoons, a dozen or more new guests would arrive for tea and conversation. The Lewental home was "exceptionally hospitable, open, and genuinely Polish," Hoesick recalled. The lane where the Lewentals lived was so strongly associated with Hortensja that in 1883 it was named after her. Occasionally Alicja played piano for the guests, a prelude or mazurka by Chopin. Late at night or in the early morning hours, after the last guests had gone, Alicja recorded the details of the evening in her diary: the conversations she had had with writers, the clothes she and other women had worn, and the men with whom she had danced. Some writers who attended the gatherings hoped to be suitors for the daughters of such a prominent publisher. Hoesick was one of them, wooing Alicja's younger sister Zosia whom he later married. Alicja sometimes considered some of the writers as marriage prospects.[2]

Decades later, after World War II had reduced New World Street to rubble, the Polish poet Stanisław Baliński evoked the atmosphere of the Lewental home, a symbol of old-world Warsaw, as he took the reader on a walk through the city. The poet first imagined the books in the window of Gebethner and Wolff's bookstore—one of the largest publishers in Poland and a competitor of the bookstore owned by Alicja's father—and the legendary Blikle café of Warsaw lore before continuing through nearby streets to the Lewental home:

At the Blikle sweet shop, just after Warecka [Street],
Is a home shrouded in a faint, old-world mist,

> Walking there, I always look with a wistful eye
> Into the window half-veiled with curtains.
>
> That is how we walked once, as if through a dream I re-
>   member,
> For Sunday tea to Mrs. Lewental's,
> Where in a plush salon, in the Secessionist style,
> There gathered in the evening so many famous people.
> We children, with cake in our hands, hidden behind the
>   curtain,
> Looked through the slit at the faces of artists.

Baliński recalled the colorful characters who were regular guests at the Lewental salon: Maria Konopnicka, the feminist writer and poet, wearing a "pince-nez with a complexion as if [she were] sick"; the "stooped Tetmajer . . . with sunken eyes, frayed nerves," a poet with whom Alicja Lewental often engaged in conversations at salons and dinners; and, about the presence of one of the giants of nineteenth-century Polish literature, "in the adjacent drawing room through a half-open door, the shadow of [Henryk] Sienkiewicz can be seen as he deals cards."[3]

In the Lewental salon of Baliński's memory, there are also actresses, one dressed "in a black boa, in long gloves," another "in an old frock coat"; the writer and actress Gabriela Zapolska, "with a cigarette in her mouth." The Lewental home was a symbol of the venerable traditions and colorful personalities of old Warsaw—"everyone as if taken today from a book by Proust," in Baliński's memory:

> Behind the window in the courtyard the winter night
>   flows,
> And the yellow gas streetlight burns.
> Snow falls and casts satins on the city,
> Burying this salon, these people, these times.

Turn-of-the-century Warsaw was a city of multiple, evolving worlds beyond Baliński's sentimental recollection. As Hortensja prepared for the Lewentals' evening salon each Saturday, the famed Yiddish writer I. L. Peretz held court in his own apartment on Ceglana Street, across the city from the Lewentals' home. Peretz's modest dwelling, not far from the factories of the Wola district, was a world away from that of the Lewentals: two small bedrooms, a kitchen, and a study, where he wrote some of the plays and novels that would earn him the moniker of a "father of Yiddish literature." Peretz, who was known to help a maid fold clothes, might have viewed Hortensja Lewental's refined world as haughty, and Hortensja would no doubt have looked down her nose at the Yiddish writer. Peretz had moved to Warsaw just four years before Alicja began her diary, but a pilgrimage to his home quickly became a rite of passage for aspiring Yiddish writers throughout the Russian Empire. Arriving in Warsaw from a provincial town, such a writer would climb the stairs to Peretz's apartment, nervous but hopeful, "carrying a bundle of manuscripts in his hand or in his coat pocket," as a memoirist recalled. A sign on the door informed these hopefuls: "I. L. Peretz receives visitors between 3 and 4 on Saturdays."[4]

Modern Yiddish culture was beginning to come into its own in the 1890s, and wherever Peretz lived in the city, his home became its center of gravity. It was a symbol of the changing times that the participants in the salon in his apartment gathered on Saturdays. Many young Jews newly arrived in Warsaw had grown up in small towns, the *shtetlekh* of traditional Jewish life, where religious observance set the rhythm of the week for many of them. Now, as their move to big cities uprooted them from their old communities, they searched for new roots. In the decade before Alicja Lewental began her diary in 1895, the Jewish population in Warsaw had grown exponentially, and of

44 A Jewish Circle in a Polish City

more than half a million residents in the city, over one-third were Jewish by the time she first took pen in hand. Often alone in a new city, living in the tenements of the expanding Muranów neighborhood where the Yiddish-speaking masses lived, many young Jews debated the questions that were beginning to transform Jewish life: what it meant to be Jewish when, for some, religious traditions no longer governed their lives as much as they had in the small towns they had left behind, and what bound them to one another and to the country in which they lived. Language was becoming central to a sense of belonging. As Warsaw became a center of secular Yiddish culture, from high-brow literature to culture for the broader Jewish population, writers such as Peretz were the new *rebbes,* the authorities to whom they looked for guidance.[5]

The Lewentals distanced themselves from that Yiddish-speaking world. Polish culture governed their lives in Warsaw at a time when the Russian authorities that ruled the city sought to impose their own culture and language on it. After the failure of the 1863 uprising, the Russian authorities increasingly restricted Polish culture, a symbol of Polish aspirations for independence. And Alicja's family was at the center of it all. At Salomon's prestigious bookstore and in the salon at the family's apartment nearby, Salomon and Hortensja Lewental became mediators at the intersection of culture, politics, and social life. The reading of banned Polish poems at salon gatherings, the smuggling of censored Polish books across the border—such expressions of Polish culture became a kind of resistance to Russian rule.

The journey of the Lewentals and their social and professional circles played out in the crucible of modern Polish and Polish Jewish history in the last third of the nineteenth century and into the twentieth. Salomon, who was fifteen years older than Hortensja, was at the beginning of his publishing career in 1862, when legal restrictions on Jews were lifted in the Congress Kingdom of Poland and when Poles launched the unsuccessful revolt the following year. The Lewentals were new parents in 1881 during a Christmas Day pogrom in Warsaw, part of a wave of anti-Jewish violence in the Russian Empire. In the following decade, as Salomon became an eminent publisher of Polish literature, as Hortensja turned her home into a space of Polish social and cultural life, and as Alicja and her siblings were growing up, the underlying question in the Lewentals' lives and the broader circles of Warsaw's Jewish bourgeoisie was whether identification as both Polish and Jewish was a viable path in an era of evolving nationalism in Central and East Central Europe. Some Jews continued to embrace a dual sense of belonging. But for the descendants of the economic elites among Polonizing Jewish families in Warsaw, their paths seen in retrospect suggest that the answer, for many of them, was no. In their search for new answers to that dilemma, they had often left Judaism behind them entirely by the early twentieth century.

The Lewentals' family history over the course of the nineteenth century is drawn from varied threads: Alicja's esteemed maternal grandfather, Mathias Bersohn, whose philanthropy and leadership in both Jewish institutions and Polish culture epitomized the integrationist ideal, at least as some Jews envisioned it; her father, who was an important publisher of Polish literature as he too became a leader in Warsaw's Jewish community; and her mother, whose Catholic faith and her renown as a salon hostess shaped Alicja's childhood home.

The family of Alicja's mother had risen to prominence in Warsaw generations before Alicja's birth. Hortensja's grandfather, Me'ir Bersohn, amassed a fortune in the first half of the nineteenth century when he established a sugar refinery in Warsaw, and he turned his profits toward the public good when he founded a Jewish children's hospital. Me'ir Bersohn's son, Mathias—Alicja's grandfather—was successful in business like his father. He founded a private bank and became a renowned philanthropist, overseeing the hospital established by his father and opening soup kitchens for Warsaw's impoverished Jews. Mathias's philanthropy extended beyond the Jewish community. He donated to Polish cultural institutions, especially art museums, a symbol of his sense of belonging to the Polish national community. Alicja herself occasionally helped to raise funds for the family's charities for the Jewish population and attended fundraising events organized by her mother. Mathias's brother, Jan, was active in both Jewish and Polish life as well, serving as head of the committee that planned the Great Synagogue in Warsaw and as a member of the city's municipal body.[6]

The Bersohns were part of a circle of Jewish economic elites that began to develop in Warsaw nearly a century before Alicja's birth. Between 1795 and 1806, the growth of the Polish economy gave rise to a Jewish bourgeoisie whose members were economic pioneers. They supplied the military, developed the textile industry, and financed the developing infrastructure of the Polish lands, as well as helped to found Warsaw's Jewish philanthropic institutions. In the first decades of the nineteenth century, this bourgeoisie consisted of about a dozen families at a time when most Polish Jews lived a modest existence as small shopkeepers and traders, tavern keepers, artisans, and peddlers, or eked out a living on the margins. While Jews of the middle class were not admitted in practice into craft guilds and merchants' associations, the "plutocratic circle in Warsaw" became integrated into the upper reaches of the economic sphere over the course of the nineteenth century. In order to do so, some of these Jews separated themselves from the Jewish masses, including by seeking exemptions from restrictions on an individual basis, even as they advocated on behalf of the broader Jewish population.[7]

A Jewish Circle in a Polish City   47

The economic involvement of these elite families brought them into contact with Polish Catholic society: with social activists whose trade schools and social welfare organizations they helped to fund and with writers and artists whose works they supported financially. These Jewish families took pride in their connections with Polish patriotic organizations that plotted to throw off the yoke of Russian rule, providing financial resources, surreptitiously publishing maps for planners of Polish uprisings, and sometimes taking part in the rebellions themselves. First through their economic roles and then through involvement in Polish culture and conspiratorial politics, these Jewish families in the mid-nineteenth century embraced a Polish national identity, often without rejecting their sense of belonging to the Jewish community.

As they aspired to acceptance in the Polish nation, however, these families remained a tight-knit group, often marrying within their own circle for several generations. They gathered for meals in one another's homes in Warsaw and at times vacationed together. It was in this circle that Alicja came of age in the last decades of the nineteenth century. Not far from the Lewentals' apartment lived Hortensja's sister and brother-in-law, Jadwiga and Aleksander Kraushar, who were among the Lewentals' closest relatives, and the two families frequently spent time together in one another's homes. Aleksander was a well-known Polish lawyer, legal advisor to Polish nobles, and historian of Jews "with an assimilationist slant." He wrote articles and poems for the Polish-language Jewish newspaper, *Jutrzenka*, and its successor, *Izraelita*, which represented the worldview of those who believed they could be both Jews and faithful Poles—"Poles of the Mosaic faith." At the same time, Aleksander was active in the Polish political underground and romanticized Polish aristocratic traditions. Jadwiga was a writer as well, penning essays about Polish literature and cultural figures while developing close friendships with prominent Polish intellectuals.[8]

48 A Jewish Circle in a Polish City

Among the Lewentals' social circles were Hortensja's closest friend, Franciszka Perlmutter, a widowed Jewish woman who was a frequent guest with her son in the Lewental home, and Dawid Ludwik Brühl, a doctor whose relatives were involved in Polish musical culture. Hortensja and Salomon often socialized with Kazimierz and Antoni Natanson, who sometimes traveled with them to the Polish mountains and cities abroad. The Natansons, who were half-brothers, were descended from one of nineteenth-century Warsaw's most eminent Jewish families, one that followed a similar path as the Bersohns did. Their grandfather, Volf Zelig Natanson, was an industrialist and banker who established a reform-minded synagogue in his home in 1850 and helped to finance the Great Synagogue nearly three decades later, while their father, Henryk, was a leader in Warsaw's Jewish institutions. Henryk owned a bookstore that was a gathering place where acculturated Jews interacted with Polish cultural figures. Henryk's brother Ludwik, a doctor involved in public health, served for a quarter century as president of Warsaw's Jewish communal board, into the 1890s. It might have been through Ludwik that Antoni and Kazimierz became friends with the Lewentals; before Hortensja's birth, Ludwik was married to Mathias Bersohn's sister before she died at an early age. After Henryk Natanson's death earlier in the year when Alicja began her diary, Salomon and Hortensja would likely have been among the mourners who gathered at his funeral in Warsaw's Jewish cemetery.[9]

The close-knit circles of Alicja's parents and their contemporaries shaped the social lives of their children, many of whom, like Alicja, never knew Jewish traditions but grew up surrounded by other families of Jewish background. Among her peers at balls and concerts were descendants of financier families of Jewish background, even as the young women among

A Jewish Circle in a Polish City

them eyed Polish Catholic writers and men from noble families as marriage prospects. At social gatherings, Alicja encountered the daughter and other relatives of Hipolit Wawelberg, her great-uncle and a member of one of Warsaw's most prominent Jewish banking families, who had taken part in the 1863 uprising and helped to finance the publication of Polish literature and Jewish communal organizations alike. Alicja frequently crossed paths with members of the Rotwand family, connected to the Kraushars through marriage. Alicja's father encountered Jakub Rotwand at meetings of the Jewish communal board, where Jakub was the longtime secretary. Another Rotwand of Salomon's generation, Stanisław, was a lawyer and banker who was sixteen when he was baptized as a Lutheran before going on to study law in Moscow and St. Petersburg and co-founding a school with Hipolit Wawelberg that became Warsaw's Polytechnic Institute. Alicja commented in her diary about the suitors of a female friend, Zosia Rotwand, who was the same generation as the Lewental sisters, and she noted in another entry that a young member of the Rotwand family, Kazimierz, had been baptized several years earlier because "he does not want a Jewish woman for a wife."[10]

At social events, Alicja and her sisters often encountered Mania Kronenberg, a great-granddaughter of a Prussian Jew, Samuel, who founded a bank in Warsaw at the end of the eighteenth century and who served on Warsaw's Jewish community board while becoming friends with Polish aristocrats. The Kronenbergs had traveled the road from prominence in Jewish life to the baptism of family members years before Mania's birth in the 1880s, though often as Protestants rather than as Catholics. By the time Mania Kronenberg was attending dinners and dances with Alicja Lewental and her sisters in the 1890s, most of Samuel Kronenberg's descendants had been baptized. The Kronenbergs and Lewentals visited one another when the

50 A Jewish Circle in a Polish City

families both spent summers in the Polish mountains. Back in Warsaw, when Alicja attended the piano performance by Paderewski, Mania Kronenberg and her family were among the "masses of acquaintances" who sat in the rows around the Lewentals.[11]

They were "the Jewish circle of our world," as Alicja described them, even as her mother perceived the Jewishness of their circle to be the very obstacle she sought to overcome.[12]

The Making of a Polish Jewish Publisher

At the time Alicja was coming of age, Warsaw was a burgeoning city, crowded and industrializing, with new tenement houses being built to accommodate tens of thousands of newly arrived workers from the provinces. Alicja's Warsaw, on the other hand, seemed at times like a small town. She took carriage rides along elegant boulevards and the narrow streets of the medieval old town and through the green oasis of Łazienki Park, sometimes passing an acquaintance or a young man who had disappointed her in love.

At the center of the Lewentals' life in Warsaw was the world of books, which was woven into the fabric of the city. Bookstores selling new Polish books, including the Lewentals', were clustered on streets in the medieval center, while book lovers and students alike searched on Holy Cross (Świętokrzyska) Street through the shelves of used bookshops or piles of books at street stalls for an obscure title or a cheap school textbook. Writers and poets debated literature and politics in bookstores that served as salons. Although Polish-language bookstores sometimes sold Russian books, the book rows on Warsaw's streetscape were largely divided by language: stores selling Yiddish and Hebrew books were on Franciszkanska Street and on Nalewki Street, a center of economic life in the largely

Jewish neighborhood of Muranów. Books were a visible part of urban life.[13]

In the years before Alicja's birth, Salomon had built his Polish publishing business into one of the largest in Warsaw. His bookstore sold the books he published, and he met there with writers whose works he supported or was considering for publication. Salomon's predecessors in the Polish book trade owned bookshops on narrow Miodowa Street, which was the city's book row until the mid-1860s, but by the time Salomon opened a bookstore under his name in 1863, Warsaw's largest bookstores were beginning to move to fashionable Krakowskie Przedmieście nearby. Salomon's bookshop was located at first further west, several blocks from a trade area that developed not far from Warsaw's train station. By the mid-1870s, he had moved his business just down the street from the new center of Warsaw's book trade on Krakowskie Przedmieście, in a building he owned on New World Street.

Salomon's path to success in the Polish book trade beginning in the 1860s is the story of an encounter between the Jewish heritage of his birth and a sense of belonging to the community of Polish culture. He grew up in a Jewish family of modest means that was influenced by the modernizing currents of the *haskalah,* the Jewish Enlightenment, which sought to integrate Jews into the cultures of the countries in which they lived while renewing distinct Jewish culture. Salomon was shaped by aspirations for Jewish emancipation that accompanied these modernizing ideas, rooted in notions of equality and individual rights at the heart of liberalism. As a young adult, he was drawn to the institutions of religious reform. His education at the reform-minded Rabbinic School in Warsaw, a state-run institution where knowledge of Polish was fundamental to its agenda, paved the way for his professional success and social advancement. That path—a childhood in a modernizing family,

52 A Jewish Circle in a Polish City

education at the Rabbinic School, and a professional life immersed in Polish culture, often while maintaining an active involvement in the Jewish community—was a common one among the men in the families of Warsaw Jewry's nineteenth-century Polish-speaking elites. The families that later became part of the Lewentals' social world followed a gradual trajectory across generations from economic integration, to involvement in Polish political and cultural life, and then, by the end of the century, to an ambiguous social integration.

Salomon came of age in the emerging metropolis of mid-nineteenth-century Warsaw, but his modernizing path and rise to prominence had roots in a small-town childhood. He was born in 1841 in Włocławek, a small town in central Poland northeast of Warsaw, where the Jewish population was rapidly increasing. Fifteen years before his birth, the town had restricted nearly all of its Jewish residents to a handful of streets, but in the 1830s and 1840s, a small number of wealthier Jews received permission to move out of the quarter as the Jewish population increased. By the 1850s, nearly one in five of the town's 6,200 residents was Jewish. Most Jews in Włocławek, as elsewhere in the Polish lands, spoke Yiddish and maintained a traditional way of life revolving around religious rituals. Many of the town's Jews worked as petty traders, shopkeepers, and tailors, common professions for small-town Jews. But Włocławek was not the proverbial *shtetl* of Jewish lore. The town was industrializing in the second half of the nineteenth century, and among its Jews were also factory owners and well-to-do traders. Some were descended from German Jews who had moved to the Polish lands earlier in the century and sought to reform traditional Jewish life as many German Jews had, though more modestly in the Polish lands than further west. They wanted children to receive a secular education in addition to instruction in Judaism, encouraged Jews to speak the language of their non-Jewish neighbors instead of Yiddish, and supported other transformations that would allow Jews to become more "modern" and integrated into the broader society.[14]

Salomon's father, Dawid, was a proponent of the movement for reform, and the elder Lewental's fellow modernizers from Włocławek were among the subscribers to one of two Hebrew booklets the father published. Few traces remain of Dawid Lewental's life, but a brief mention of him in a memorial book written about the Jews of Włocławek hints at his path. He might have been a transplant from the German lands, for after the family moved to Warsaw in the 1840s, Dawid taught German and Hebrew as a private tutor in the homes of wealthy Jewish families. Among the families for whom he worked were the children of Mathias Rozen, a member of a prominent Warsaw banking family who was a Jewish communal leader and part of the social circles in which Salomon's future father-in-law, Mathias Bersohn, was immersed.[15]

More than a half century later, when Salomon recounted his family's history in a brief autobiographical sketch he wrote in the last months of his life, he described a family heritage in which Jewish traditions coexisted with the principles of the Jewish Enlightenment. He was descended from rabbis, he wrote, and his father was a Hebrew philosopher who knew other languages so well that he translated sections of the Talmud into French and the Polish stories of Ignacy Krasicki, an eighteenth-century theologian and poet who was the first major Polish writer of the Enlightenment, into Hebrew. It would be an unusual combination of knowledge for a nineteenth-century Talmudic scholar in Eastern Europe. The narrative that Salomon retold about his father's life was just as much a reflection of the dual sense of belonging that came to shape his own path: a Jewish identity that could coexist with Polishness, symbolized by the language of Polish culture and by French, the foreign language traditionally favored by the Polish aristocracy. Salomon's account reflected his own rootedness in the religious background of a Jew and a cultural identity as a Pole.[16]

As the son of a *maskil,* a promoter of the Jewish Enlightenment, it is unlikely that Salomon spoke Yiddish as a child. Memoirists who recalled him in their writings did not mention a Yiddish accent, a characteristic that Polish writers often noted about the Hasidic owners of Warsaw's antiquarian bookshops that sold used Polish books. Had Lewental spoken with even a slight accent, the challenges to his Polish identity during his lifetime would likely have referred to a Yiddish-inflected Polish. But if Salomon's father was a Talmudic scholar, then the son would likely have grown up in a home imbued with Jewish observance and rituals.

Salomon's entry into the Polish publishing world followed his attendance at the Rabbinic School, whose list of graduates was a who's who of Warsaw Jewry's elite families in the nineteenth century. The authorities established the seminary in 1826 to create a cadre of "modern" rabbis as part of their efforts to reform Jewish religious life. The political authorities pursued that goal at times in cooperation with supporters of the Jewish Enlightenment, some of whose aims overlapped to a degree with the government's agenda. Central to the goals of both the government and the maskilim was ridding Jewish life of Yiddish, which they viewed disdainfully as the "Jewish jargon," a corrupted form of German. Instead, the school's students attended Hebrew-language classes on religion and learned about Jewish history and secular subjects in Polish. Many students were the sons of Warsaw's prominent Jewish families that had begun to integrate into Polish culture in earlier generations. Others, like Salomon Lewental, came from families of more modest means but grew up in homes where their parents

A Jewish Circle in a Polish City 55

had adopted some of the reforms promoted by the Jewish Enlightenment.[17]

Scant traces exist of Salomon's coming of age. He and some of his classmates at the Rabbinic School would likely have attended one of the two small synagogues in Warsaw that followed reforming trends, one of which was just a few blocks away on Daniłowiczowska Street. The synagogue was founded by a German Jew a half-century before Salomon studied at the school. Although the synagogue adopted only modest elements of religious reform, one of the main symbols of its modernizing character was the language of the sermons: at reforming synagogues sermons were at first delivered in German. By the second half of the 1850s, however, the sermons began to be given in Polish, a sign of the congregants' evolving cultural identifications.[18]

To be sure, those who prayed at Warsaw's progressive synagogues at the time—the Daniłowiczowska Street synagogue and another one in a private home on Nalewki Street, founded in 1852—were a small fraction of the seventy-three thousand Jews who lived in the city at the time. Language was often (though not always) an indication of cultural identification, and the numbers of Polish-speaking Jews remained only a slim minority of Warsaw's Jewish population into the twentieth century. Even in 1897, only twenty-nine thousand Warsaw Jews—13.7 percent of the city's Jewish population—reported Polish as their native language. The Polish-language Jewish newspaper *Izraelita* counted just 350 subscribers at the end of 1870, its fifth year of publication, with 230 of them in Warsaw, although the number of readers was likely larger as subscribers shared newspapers with other readers. But by the 1870s, circles of acculturated and reforming Jews outgrew the synagogues where they prayed. Their leaders began planning a new synagogue, one whose monumental structure would symbolize their aspirations for acceptance on the urban landscape. The Great Synagogue was built between

56 A Jewish Circle in a Polish City

1876 and 1878 with sitting room for 2,000–3,000 individuals; this seating availability was reportedly insufficient. Hortensja's uncle Jan Bersohn chaired its planning committee, and Salomon was a member of the committee.[19]

The Rabbinic School sought to produce religious leaders who would help to reform Jewish religious life. But it did not fulfill the task set for it. Its goals were too far removed from the reality of Polish Jewish life at the time, when the vast majority of Polish Jews continued to speak Yiddish and observe traditional Jewish rituals and piety. The Jewish masses did not recognize the Rabbinic School graduates as religious leaders. None of them served as rabbis; only two became religious leaders, giving sermons in Polish at the private synagogue on Nalewki Street and later at the Great Synagogue in Warsaw.[20] The school's alumni became influential, nevertheless, as Polish-speaking Jewish intellectuals— among them journalists, publishers, and communal leaders—as they continued the quest to reform Jewish life.[21]

Salomon followed other alumni of the Rabbinic School into the Polish book trade, including at least five other graduates who, like him, became prominent publishers of Polish books. It might have been through the school that he met his early patron, Jan Glucksberg, who was a scion of one of Warsaw's most eminent publishing families, pioneers in the Polish book trade for generations. Glucksberg had helped to establish the Rabbinic School, and before Salomon graduated in 1856, he began working for Glucksberg's firm. Perhaps Lewental's success in the publishing business also benefited from connections with the town of his birth. In the early years of his professional life, the first mechanized paper mill in the Polish lands was established in Włocławek, providing the raw material for the books and newspapers that publishers needed for their trade.[22]

Salomon's personal ties to Jan Glucksberg solidified Lewental's role at the center of the Polish book trade. Upon his

A Jewish Circle in a Polish City 57

employer's death in 1859, Salomon married Glucksberg's daughter Ernestyna and inherited his deceased father-in-law's publishing business. Salomon continued the success of Glucksberg's thriving firm. For several years the business remained under the Glucksberg name, but in 1863, the Lewental bookstore and publishing house were born. It was the most significant step in Salomon's transformation into a mediator of Polish culture.

Salomon was still in his thirties when Ernestyna died. She had remained involved in Jewish communal life until her death, and she was buried in Warsaw's Jewish cemetery. Salomon's rise to prominence was cemented when, one year after his wife's death, he wed Hortensja Bersohn, marrying into the royalty of Warsaw Jewry. They were married in 1878 in the Great Synagogue, which had opened less than two months earlier. In honor of the marriage, Hortensja's parents donated a wedding canopy to the synagogue, and they gave money to support numerous charities—"half for Christians, half for *starozakonnych*," according to the newspaper *Kurjer Warszawski*. (The latter term means "[those] of the Old Law," sometimes used in Polish at that time to refer to Jews.) For his part, Salomon made donations to charities as well: to Warsaw's city hospital; to support the widows and orphans of writers, as well as the families of elderly printers; and to the Warsaw Jewish community's charity fund for girls. His marriage to Hortensja would likely have required sufficient status and a sophisticated demeanor to earn her parents' permission despite his more modest family background. Salomon Lewental had arrived.[23]

Salomon's second marriage brought him further into Warsaw Jewry's most elite strata. He now found himself at the very center of circles that sought to bring Jewish society closer to Polish culture while at the same time serving as leaders in Jewish communal life. He became an overseer of the Bersohn and Bauman hospital for Jewish children founded by Hortensja's

58   A Jewish Circle in a Polish City

grandfather, and he later asserted that the hospital had never turned away patients under his watch, whether Jewish or Christian. Hortensja oversaw Jewish charitable institutions that her father had founded, even after she began raising her children in the Catholic faith.[24]

It was Salomon and Hortensja Lewental and their descendants who continued the work of the Glucksbergs' publishing business into the twentieth century. And, for most of his adult life, Salomon embraced the dual identifications that Jan Glucksberg and the patriarchs of other Jewish publishing families had developed decades earlier.

The Book Rows and Salons of Warsaw

Salomon Lewental and other publishers and booksellers of nineteenth-century Warsaw were at the center of Polish cultural life not only in producing and selling books. In the leading Polish-language bookstores on Warsaw's book rows in the medieval old town, writers, journalists, and poets debated literature and conspiratorial politics, sharing the latest news and journals from abroad. The most prominent publishers also owned bookstores, so writers often met with their publishers to discuss their manuscripts at the front of a bookstore, where the owner sat. A few bookshops that specialized in music had a piano in the store for customers, turning the space into a center of musical life for professors and students. Customers were sometimes not free to take books off the shelves themselves—many bookshops selling new books in Warsaw were not yet "self-service" even by the early twentieth century—so interactions between employees and their customers were extensive since clients had to request books from the shelves. Readers often relied on the knowledge of the bookstore's owner and employees about the latest books.[25]

The central role in Polish cultural life of bookstores owned by Jewish families also transformed economic, cultural, and political interactions between Jews and Catholics into social contacts. Aleksander and Jadwiga Kraushar's daughter Zuzanna Rabska recalled that in the mid-nineteenth century, the "literary world of the time" gathered in the Warsaw bookstore of the Jewish publisher Samuel Henryk Merzbach. He opened his store with his brother Zygmunt in 1830, and it became a locus of Polish conspiratorial politics, attended by Polish cultural figures who were at the center of political intrigue after he began selling banned patriotic literature during the Polish uprising that year. Just as Salomon Lewental was entering the book trade, Merzbach's nephew Henryk Merzbach took over his uncle's firm and continued the salon gatherings. The younger Merzbach then opened his own bookstore, which, like his uncle's establishment, also became a meeting place for Polish political conspirators and cultural figures. The police forced the younger Merzbach to close his business after he was found to have circulated censored poems during the 1863 rebellion, and the following year he fled to Brussels, becoming part of the Polish émigré community there. He continued to publish Polish books, some of which were smuggled into the Polish lands.[26]

Publishers' homes, too, were part of the salon culture that permeated Warsaw's intellectual life in the nineteenth century. While invitations to the gatherings at the Lewental home were sought after, it competed with other salons, of greater or lesser prestige, in the last decades of the century. They were literary gatherings, a space away from the eyes of the censors that "became the cultural center in which literary works were evaluated, in which political ideas were analyzed and in which, above all, readings were held from the works of the Polish romantic poets banned by the Russian authorities," the historian Jacob Shatzky noted. Each salon had its own character. "If the excellent Bechstein pianos attracted musicians to the salon of the Grossmans and the Wertheims," wrote the memoirist Anna Leo, referring to banking families of Jewish background in Warsaw, "writers, journalists, and also . . . actors gladly went to more modest homes." On Marszałkowska Street, mathematicians and other scholars gathered late into the evening on Sundays at the home of the Dicksteins, a Jewish family whose members were prominent in both Polish culture and Jewish communal life.[27]

Generations of the families that owned one of Salomon Lewental's main competitors in the publishing world, Gebethner and Wolff, who were descended from families of ethnic German background, invited writers to their literary salon, with the prominent Polish Positivist writer Bolesław Prus often holding court in the Gebethner home just down the street from the Lewentals. On Sundays, conservative Catholic circles gathered in the home of the editor of a Catholic-oriented newspaper. Nearby lived a doctor from a Hungarian aristocratic family and his wife, and their daughter recited poetry at their social gatherings. Conversations often centered on conspiratorial politics at the salon in the Benni home on Bracka Street, which, as Anna Leo noted, drew "everyone who thought and felt in Warsaw." The Benni salon was "exclusively male," Leo recalled, but in the 1890s, many women were in attendance at other salons. The home of the Wolffs, the Gebethner family's partners in the publishing business, was a literary gathering place for women. On Thursdays the poet Jadwiga Łuszczewska, known as Deotyma, invited dozens of artists, writers, and journalists into her home nearly every week until her death in 1908. After Deotyma died, Hortensja Lewental took over the tradition.[28]

Aleksander and Jadwiga Kraushar, Hortensja's sister and brother-in-law, were often guests in the Lewental home, but the Kraushars hosted their own salon in a home on nearby Senatorska Street. The Kraushars' road to the center of Polish cultural life was a variation on the Lewentals' path. In the midnineteenth century, Aleksander and his younger brother, Ludwik, attended the Warsaw Real-Gymnasium, a Polish institution that became a hub for Polish patriotic circles. Education was a motor of integration. Men from Jewish families who had attended Polish schools such as the Real-Gymnasium developed strong ties with Polish society. At school, they not only were educated in Polish culture, but they also developed friendships with their Catholic classmates. Those ties often drew them into Polish political life. Many of their teachers were leaders in the Polish underground movement, and the students themselves became active in it as well. There were fewer than ten Jewish students in the school, but like Kraushar, "each of them later distinguished himself in some way or other in Polish national life," according to Shatzky in his study of Kraushar's life. Kraushar himself did not mention the Jewish background of classmates when he recalled the circle of students from the Warsaw Real-Gymnasium and their involvement in the Polish patriotic cause. Universities were even more influential as an integrating institution. Nearly all of the Jewish men who attended the Real-Gymnasium were later active in the conspiratorial circles of university students in the years leading up to the 1863 uprising and took part in the revolt according to Kraushar. Like Salomon, Aleksander Kraushar also attended the Rabbinic School in Warsaw.[29]

In the 1850s and 1860s, Kraushar was still optimistic about a "Polish-Jewish brotherhood." His poetry in *Jutrzenka* and *Izraelita,* Jacob Shatzky wrote, was "full of the hopefulness characteristic of that era of liberal optimism" and reflected "the glowing pathos of his faith in Polish-Jewish unity." Kraushar "identified his own life with the totality of Polish life," but that did not entail embracing Catholicism, which was "not yet seen in Polish patriotic circles as entirely integral to Polishness." At the time, Kraushar was editor of the Polish underground's newspaper and moved for a time to Leipzig. When he returned to Warsaw, he began writing historical works about Polish Jewish history even as he began studying law, but he soon found a different attitude toward Jewish involvement in Polish political and cultural life than the one he had left when he moved abroad. By the end of the 1860s, the "Polish-Jewish brotherhood," which began with patriotic demonstrations in 1861, was complicated by new antagonisms mixed with earlier economic tensions. This change was noticeable in Polish literary attitudes toward Jewish equality and possibilities for integration as early as 1868, though criticism was still restrained.[30]

This gradual shift resulted, first of all, from Russian repression of Polish political activity after the failure of the 1863 uprising. Changed attitudes were also rooted in tensions following the decrees emancipating the serfs as the old feudal economy broke down, the capitalist economy rapidly expanded, and more and more Poles moved from the countryside to the industrializing cities, where Jews were economic competitors. Complicating the situation after 1868 was the migration of Jews from further east in the Russian Empire, the so-called Litvaks, who were permitted beginning in that year to migrate to the Polish lands, where they enjoyed greater rights than in the rest of the Russian Empire. Many spoke Russian, the language of the empire that Poles viewed as an occupier. For the Lewentals and their circle, these debates were not just political, but also personal. Their belonging to the Polish national community was at stake.[31]

In the late 1860s, Aleksander Kraushar retained faith in the possibility for Jewish integration. He continued to write essays and poems for *Izraelita* and works of Jewish history. Yet upon becoming a jurist, Kraushar became a legal advisor to

A Jewish Circle in a Polish City

Polish nobles and began writing about the history and culture of the Polish aristocracy, moving away from a focus on Jewish history. He "was attracted to the castles and courts of the nobles and magnates, to the Polish wars and to the national patriotic manifestations," Shatzky wrote, and "there was a sort of spiritual identification by Kraushar with the life he was describing." He did not yet leave behind his Jewish faith, however. He continued to attend High Holy Day services with his father at the Great Synagogue on Tłomackie Street after it opened in 1878 and published a poem in *Izraelita* to mark the occasion of its opening.[32]

Jadwiga Kraushar, like her husband, Aleksander, was first drawn into Polish political life through her education, although unlike men of similar economic status, Jadwiga, together with her sister Hortensja, was taught by tutors at home rather than in a school. Among the sisters' tutors were the Polish poet Jan Chęciński and the education activist Kasylda Kulikowska, who was involved in Polish political life at a time of increasing Russian restrictions, which included restrictions on education in Polish beyond language instruction. When Jadwiga and Hortensja Bersohn were still young, Kulikowska had taken part in the failed January uprising in 1863, and the teacher later established a clandestine school for women whose students were taught in Polish. Jadwiga and Hortensja frequented a reading room for women that Kulikowska established not far from the Bersohn home.

Jadwiga's and Hortensja's education with Kulikowska had a deep influence on the sisters, instilling Polish patriotism in them through intellectual life. Polish culture had already been part of the sisters' lives, especially through their father's charitable involvement with Polish cultural institutions, but Kulikowska sought to challenge what she saw as the bourgeois values of their childhood home. Both Bersohn sisters were drawn into the clandestine education in which their teacher was involved, and Jadwiga, who was three years older than Hortensja, developed a close friendship with their tutor. "Mother said repeatedly that it would be like eating bread if not for conversations with Ms. Kasylda and the books she recommended," Jadwiga's daughter, Zuzanna Rabska, recalled in her memoirs. Jadwiga's involvement in her teacher's clandestine work led to friendships with women of her own generation who were drawn into political life. Zuzanna went on to attend university, a pursuit that one family member attributed in part to Jadwiga's desire for her family's integration through Polish intellectual life.[33]

Soon after the Kraushars' marriage, their home became a popular literary salon, with gatherings on Tuesdays. Historians, artists, and other members of Warsaw's intelligentsia engaged in heated conversations about the latest books, philosophical debates, and political disputes. It was a "salon of serious traditions," Anna Leo wrote; Shatzky described it as an "aristocratic and literary salon" that was renowned throughout the Polish lands. As in the Lewental salon, the Kraushars' guests included both Catholics and Jews, among them aristocrats, and Aleksander Kraushar's former teachers and classmates from the Szkoła Główna (the Main School), where he had studied law. So, too, did Catholic church leaders participate in the gatherings, along with descendants of the Frankists, followers of the Sabbatian leader Jacob Frank who had converted from Judaism to Catholicism en masse in the Polish-Lithuanian Commonwealth in the eighteenth century. Rabska remembered conversations among literary critics, journalists, and writers at her parents' salon. Eliza Orzeszkowa recalled the eclectic nature of the guests, not only in the diversity of their religious backgrounds, but also in their political orientations and economic status: "reactionary and liberal, millionaires and the poor, in a word, fire and water." Young writers there often wooed prospective matches, among them Alicja and her sisters. Alicja, who was a frequent visitor to the Kraushars' home, wrote in her diary about her romantic longings after evenings there, where writers sometimes charmed her with the poetry they recited. Although the backgrounds and political orientations of the Kraushars' guests were varied, their salon became known in Warsaw as a gathering place for Positivist thinkers. Among the leading Positivist writers was Aleksander Świętochowski, who was a regular guest, and his presence was largely responsible for its reputation as the "Positivist" salon. Jadwiga Kraushar developed close intellectual and personal ties with other prominent Positivist writers, especially Orzeszkowa.[34]

Jewish families like the Lewentals and Kraushars, as well as others who were not of ethnic Polish background, were conspicuous in the salon world of nineteenth-century Warsaw. "It so happened that the owners of homes who brought together writers and outstanding Polish thinkers did not have Polish last names," recalled Leo, who was raised Catholic after her grandparents had converted from Judaism to a Protestant denomination before her birth. Leo remarked on those of Jewish background such as the Kraushars and her own family, as well as others, such as a family of Italian background: "Certainly there existed noble families where people of science and letters were most warmly welcomed. I speak, however, about the homes that became a kind of hearth for these people. No one in that epoch would have thought to accuse any of the above-mentioned families of a lack of Polishness; I search, however, for a reason why there did not exist any 'natively Polish' literary salon, if name and coat of arms are supposed to determine Polishness." Shatzky had a different characterization of salon life and the place of Jewish families in it, however. Many salons, Shatzky wrote, welcomed "only those whose Polish background was 'without

66   A Jewish Circle in a Polish City

blemish.'" A few salons hosted by Catholic Poles were exceptions, he noted, including the gatherings hosted by Deotyma, who extended sought-after invitations to those of Jewish background, and the feminist poet Gabriela Żmichowska, whose guests included the Kraushars.[35]

Despite the distance between the salons of Polish culture and the Yiddish circles of Warsaw's predominantly Jewish neighborhoods, the two worlds met on Holy Cross Street, Warsaw's book row of antiquarian bookshops. There, Yiddish-speaking Jewish men wearing *peyes* (sidelocks) and the traditional *kapotes,* or kaftans, of Hasidic Jews, and sometimes women, owned shops selling Polish used books. Others hawked their wares from stalls lining the street. Ever since Gecel Zalcstein had opened Warsaw's first antiquarian bookstore on Holy Cross Street in 1818, the trade in Polish used books had been the domain of Jewish booksellers, and by the end of the nineteenth century, Jews owned at least 80 percent of the thirty-five bookshops that sold used Polish books in the city. They were the foil of bourgeois, Polish-speaking Jewish publishers such as Salomon Lewental. A Polish memoirist recalled that in many of the smaller secondhand shops, books were arranged haphazardly on shelves and in piles on the floor, not according to subject, because their owners could not read the titles. One might be tempted to dismiss such a description as a Polish stereotype of the uncultured Jew, yet the memoirist did not paint all Jewish booksellers on Holy Cross Street with the same brush. He emphasized much more so the knowledge that other Jewish owners of antiquarian Polish bookshops possessed about Polish literature. The booksellers became familiar with their clients' interests and put aside books the sellers thought they might want to read. Sometimes the booksellers surreptitiously held uncensored books behind the counter for them, risking the wrath of the tsarist police, who sometimes conducted surprise inspections.[36]

A handful of long-standing antiquarian bookshops became centers of intellectual life. Aleksander Kraushar frequented the secondhand bookstore of Arje Kleinsinger, where Kraushar spent hours deep in conversation with writers, newspaper editors, and other intellectuals. A Polish journalist recalled that Kleinsinger, whose family owned several bookshops of used Polish books, advised him about what books to read and introduced him to Prus, the Positivist writer, among the Polish intellectual luminaries who gathered regularly in Kleinsinger's bookstores. Kleinsinger, wrote the memoirist, "although he went about in a kaftan and perhaps did not express himself exactly correctly in the modern Polish language, had more expertise than more than one critic and was a greater enthusiast of Polish literature and history than much of the Warsaw intelligentsia."[37]

From Brotherhood to Disillusionment

Salomon and Hortensja Lewental, like other Polish publishers and hosts of literary salons in the second half of the nineteenth century, were mediators of culture at a time when ideas about what constituted Polish national identity and the place of Jews in it were shifting. By the time Alicja and her siblings were growing up in the 1880s, even the Positivists had become more pessimistic about the potential for Jewish integration.

The Positivists' views on the "Jewish question," asserting that Jews could become part of the Polish national community if they shed their external differences, had always contained internal contradictions. On the one hand, the Positivists praised the Jewish contribution to Polish economic development and promoted a pluralistic concept of Polish nationhood. But Positivists' views about the possibilities for Jewish belonging were in tension with their emphasis on the need to develop a "native" Polish middle class, and their views on the "Jewish question" never gained widespread traction in Polish society.[38] The contradictions within the Positivist attitude were more fundamental as well. The Positivists "saw no possibility of using [the Jews'] potential without the immediate and complete Polonization of the Jewish masses. Welcoming Jewish emancipation, the Positivists saw it as the first step toward the dissolution of a distinctly Jewish identity within Polish society." The assimilationist stance that the Positivists saw as the condition for Jewish integration into Polish society came into conflict not only with the realities of traditional Jewish life, from the Yiddish that most Jews spoke to their traditional dress and adherence to religious traditions, but also with the developing political ideologies of Jewish nationalism in the last decades of the nineteenth century.[39]

The wave of pogroms in the Russian Empire in 1881–82 "dealt a final blow to the eroded Positivist hopes for large-scale Jewish assimilation." Alicja was two when a pogrom against Jews broke out in Warsaw on Christmas Day in 1881, following a stampede that killed a parishioner in the seventeenth-century Holy Cross Church, with its Baroque façade and the heart of Poland's beloved Chopin soon to be enclosed in a pillar. It was not only the Yiddish-speaking masses that fell victim. The first article about the Warsaw pogrom in the Polish-language Jewish newspaper *Izraelita,* published five days after the events, expressed a sense of despair. Although it reported that the Polish intelligentsia and many among the lower classes had condemned the violence, the pogrom challenged one's "confidence and good faith in civic [*obywatelską*] unity," and the article ended with an appeal to maintain this sense of unity.[40]

The Warsaw pogrom hastened the disillusionment of Aleksander Kraushar. He later recalled the sense of betrayal that he experienced. He evoked the atmosphere of the early 1860s, when

Warsaw's Jews had joined the throngs of mourners at a funeral of Polish victims killed by the Russians in patriotic demonstrations. Those years became known as an era of "Polish-Jewish friendship," when, he later wrote in poetic form, "I was greeted with brotherly words, and as a symbol of eternal friendship, I received the title of 'Pole of the Mosaic persuasion.' But the memory of those days was short-lived, and God knows why, for what crimes, a few years later in December [1881], my bedding was torn into pieces by the crowd." Five years after the pogrom, Kraushar lamented the changing times that he feared would hinder his child's path. "What future awaits my poor boy?" Kraushar wrote that year about his son to the writer Józef Ignacy Kraszewski, who himself had sometimes expressed disparaging views of the "Jewish plutocracy," with his stereotypical depictions of Jewish financiers becoming influential in Polish literature. "He was born a Pole. The Russians [Muscovites] order him to be a Russian. [Jan] Jeleński forbids him from being a Pole, while he does not want to be a German and he can no longer be a Jew." A decade later, when Polish newspapers began to publish attacks on the descendants of Frankists, questioning both their Polishness and their Catholic faith, Kraushar took up their defense by publishing a book about their history.[41]

The violence in the Russian Empire contributed to a wave of Jewish immigration to the West that was driven by the impoverishment of the empire's Jewish population. The bourgeoning numbers of Jews over the course of the nineteenth century had exacerbated the effects of Russian policy, which restricted most Jews to residence in the Pale of Settlement. In the aftermath of the pogrom in Warsaw, however, the president of the city's Jewish community, Ludwik Natanson, lamented the decision of some Jews to emigrate and called for a redoubling of efforts to integrate into Polish society. In *Izraelita,* he declared that only by "becoming closer to the neighboring population,"

Hortensja Lewental, 1882–1883. Muzeum Warszawy, MD165/Fot.

A Jewish Circle in a Polish City

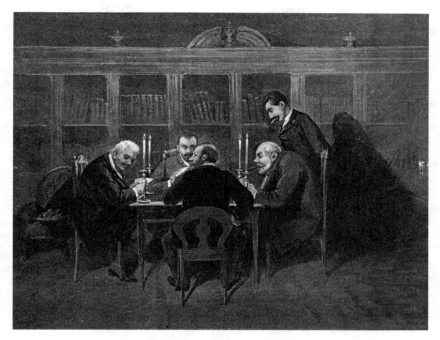

"Wint u Lewentala" [Bridge at Lewental's]. From the back is
Salomon Lewental. Straight ahead: painter Roman Szwojnicki.
At left: illustrator Franciszek Kostrzewski. By Leonard Sempoliński,
Muzeum Warsawy, MD139/Fot.

erasing external markers of difference—including the Yiddish language—could Jews remedy the dire situation.[42]

Yet the vast majority of Polish Jews remained a Yiddish-speaking, religiously observant population, and as Warsaw's Jewish population increased, they became more and more visible in economic life. With economic tensions rising at the end of the nineteenth century, the Jewish antiquarian booksellers of Holy Cross Street were among the businesses that became targets of anti-Jewish polemics. In 1895, a Polish newspaper

Mathias Bersohn, circa 1907. Muzeum Warszawy, MD140/Fot.

initiated a boycott of Jewish-owned used bookstores, accusing them of selling stolen books and moldy textbooks that made children ill. A widely used training manual for booksellers, published the following year, criticized Jewish owners as incompetent and referred to the "low moral level" of the Jewish bookstall owner: "Such a trader usually has little idea about literature, bookselling arrangement, the nobility of this profession, and its needs," the manual asserted.[43]

Alicja and Hortensja Lewental, too, would have disdained the Yiddish-speaking Jews who owned bookshops on Holy Cross Street. The polemics against "uncultured" Jews and their involvement in Polish culture did not leave the Lewental family untouched, however. For years, even as they turned their home into a literary gathering place, critics had been accusing Alicja's father of being an unscrupulous speculator and outsider whose alleged greed for profit had degraded Polish journalism. The attacks challenged the very essence of the sense of belonging that Salomon had cultivated for more than a quarter of a century as a publisher who was faithful to Polish culture.

3

The Disillusionment of a Polish Jew

As Alicja Lewental came of age, her father's place in Polish cultural circles became increasingly tenuous despite her family's immersion in the social life of that milieu. She was barely eight years old in 1887 when Salomon Lewental became co-owner of one of Warsaw's oldest and largest newspapers, *Kurjer Warszawski*, setting off a firestorm of criticism as part of anti-Jewish polemics in the following years.[1] When Alicja was eleven, he sold his prized publication, the illustrated journal *Kłosy*, whose declining circulation he blamed on years of his vilification.

Alicja's yearning for acceptance in Polish Catholic society developed against the backdrop of her father's prominence in Polish culture and attacks on that role. Although she rarely expressed awareness of how the polemics were affecting him, she hinted at their impact in 1898, in the midst of her own crisis of faith and feelings of rejection in romance that she attributed to her Jewish background. When a Polish artist whose drawings her father had published in *Kłosy* expressed gratitude

The Disillusionment of a Polish Jew 75

to him that year in public, Alicja was moved enough to describe the event in her diary. The artist, Wojciech Kossak, lived in Berlin, but during a visit to Warsaw for an exhibition of his work, he publicly paid tribute to her father. Alicja recalled:

> But what a joy to have such a father as Daddy! And how strange that I am proud of his last name, that it never bothered me that I carried Daddy's name? True, Daddy suffered a lot, worked a lot, from being so impoverished to [gaining] such colossal wealth that he left all people at his feet. And now, at this feast for Kossak . . . who appears daily before the [German] emperor, who has his studio in the emperor's palace, he himself, Kossak, raises [his glass] to Father's health and publicly remembers that Daddy was the first one who a dozen years ago supported his young talent, shaped and guided him with his influence, giving him work in *Kłosy*. And he was not ashamed to shake hands with a Jew publicly, give a toast to a Jew. . . . And Daddy is not at all proud of this! . . . I am terribly proud of my father, of my last name.[2]

It was a rare direct reference to her father's publishing work in her private musings and the only one hinting at the polemics against him. But the sense of pride that Alicja declared in reaction to the artist's tribute, together with a stronger assertion of dignity that she expressed later that year, was only a brief hiatus—though an ambiguous one—from the sense of shame about her Jewish background that permeated her diary. For now, however, Alicja proclaimed herself to be proud of her father's name even as she expressed surprise at feeling that way. She was, after all, proclaiming as a badge of honor a name that also symbolized for her a Jewish identity that had caused her anguish. Her struggle over belonging in her private world was intertwined with her father's fate in the public sphere. Salomon's professional life, like his daughter's personal life, was buffeted by heated debates about the place of Jews in the Polish national community. A central factor in the Lewentals' path at the turn of the century was the abandonment of their hope for acceptance as Poles without leaving behind a Jewish identity.[3]

Jewish Publishers, Polish Books

When Salomon Lewental took over Jan Glucksberg's publishing house and bookstore in the early 1860s, he inherited a pioneering business and a history of Jewish involvement in Polish publishing that had developed in the decades before his birth. The road that Lewental followed from modernizing Jewish circles to the center of Polish cultural life through the publishing business was one that others had trod before him. He was a successor to a circle of Jewish publishers who had been at the center of the Polish book trade and Polish culture since the first half of the nineteenth century. The Glucksberg family, into which Salomon married when he wed his first wife, Ernestyna, was among the first to follow that path.

Jan Glucksberg and his brother Natan were patriarchs of a Jewish family that spearheaded the development of the modern Polish book trade. They were the sons of a German Jew who had come to the Polish lands at the end of the eighteenth or early nineteenth century, and the family's book business began modestly when their oldest brother, Lewin, opened a French reading room in Warsaw. Natan and Jan Glucksberg transformed that venture into one of the most successful Polish publishing houses. By 1820, the Glucksbergs' business was issuing more books than the other fifteen printing houses in Warsaw combined.

Soon after the Glucksbergs entered the Polish book trade, Samuel Orgelbrand, the son of a Jewish native of Warsaw, established a competing publishing house in the city after opening a small bookstore attached to an antiquarian bookshop in 1836. Samuel's brother Maurycy followed him into the publishing business, and by the time Salomon Lewental married Ernestyna Glucksberg, Jewish publishers were a prominent force in the Polish book trade. Of the twelve largest and most prominent nineteenth-century publishers, most of whom began their publishing activity in the first half of the century and also owned bookstores, seven were Jewish, while at least two others were of ethnic German origin, including that of Gebethner and Wolff, who were dominant in the book trade. In addition to the Glucksberg and Orgelbrand brothers, the Merzbachs established a publishing dynasty that included four family members across two generations; they opened bookstores and publishing houses first in the Prussian partition and later in Warsaw. Numerous other Jewish owners operated Polish publishing and bookselling businesses on a smaller scale, comprising one-third to one-half of bookstore owners selling new Polish books between the 1830s and 1870s.[4]

Jewish publishers in the Polish lands and throughout Eastern Europe in the nineteenth century became part of the intellectual circles of their surrounding society and helped to shape cultures that began to consolidate national communities beyond local affiliations, though that shift was a gradual process. Their decisions about what books to publish were a factor in the development of ideas about nationality and culture at a time when conceptions of the Polish nation were still nascent. Book publishers influenced what literary works were circulated and transmitted from one generation to the next, shaping a shared culture and common history that became part of the literary canon. They commissioned and issued Polish translations of works from Western and Central Europe and from the United States, disseminating to Polish society evolving political ideas about nation, state, and citizenship. In the middle of the nineteenth century, the Glucksbergs and Orgelbrands published Polish dictionaries, facilitating the standardization of language. The situation was similar throughout Eastern Europe.[5] Jewish publishers and booksellers issued the first dictionaries and national encyclopedias not only in Poland, but also in Hungary; disseminated composers' musical scores in Russia and Hungary; and owned bookstores that were centers of intellectual life in Bucharest and Belgrade.[6]

Samuel Orgelbrand's publication of the first Polish encyclopedia, beginning in the 1860s, established a common narrative of the Polish past that became an element in national belonging. The twenty-eight-volume encyclopedia, which he began publishing at the same time as he was issuing volumes of the first full edition of the Babylonian Talmud in the Kingdom of Poland, was a landmark of Polish publishing. Orgelbrand had been mulling over the encyclopedia project for years when he wrote to one of the prominent Polish writers whose works he published, Józef Ignacy Kraszewski, about his plans in 1854. Kraszewski was central to the development of the Polish writer's role as a symbol of national identity in the absence of an independent Polish state in the nineteenth century, and Orgelbrand sought his support. The publisher had his eye on the monumental encyclopedia projects that his French, British, and German counterparts had initiated and carried out in the eighteenth and nineteenth centuries, from the French encyclopedia that was a milestone of the French Enlightenment; to the *Encyclopaedia Britannica*, begun in the mid-eighteenth century; to numerous German encyclopedias, including a 242-volume edition whose final installments were in preparation as Orgelbrand wrote to Kraszewski in 1854.[7]

Poland, too, must have its own universal encyclopedia, Orgelbrand asserted, one that not only translated the sum of human knowledge into the Polish language, but also incorporated the Polish past into the broader canon of history.[8] Orgelbrand's encyclopedia project was a culmination of his role at the nexus of Polish intellectual networks, drawing on the resources of the writers, historians, scientists, and other scholars whose works he published. He determined the selection of editors, who in turn decided which entries to include and how to present each topic, shaping the perspective from which history, religion, culture, and politics were synthesized to the extent that Russian censorship permitted. Orgelbrand's decisions were the starting point from which the encyclopedia determined how—and whose—history, culture, and ideas were presented to the Polish reading public as significant for the sum of knowledge about the world.[9]

In his 1854 letter to Kraszewski, Orgelbrand indicated that his vision of an encyclopedia was based on a desire to educate the Polish reading public and to assert Polish cultural and national maturity. "Other nations have long overtaken us in this regard," Orgelbrand wrote about encyclopedias published in other languages. Although a Polish encyclopedia could translate many entries from these German, French, Russian, and English works, encyclopedias in other languages neglected Polish history and culture, he asserted. A Polish encyclopedia must therefore contain original entries relating to Poland, including for Polish writers and other individuals who were significant for Polish history. The same was true for the histories and cultures of other Slavic countries, he wrote.[10]

Orgelbrand lamented that he could provide only small honoraria to the writers, journalists, and other scholars who wrote entries, and he struggled to finance the final volumes. But Orgelbrand characterized his motivations in emotional rather than economic terms. "Love for every profession can become a passion," he wrote, and it can become the "most beautiful legacy that one can leave to one's children." The encyclopedia presented a broad conception of belonging to the Polish nation, one that reflected his own identifications. A series of drawings in the 193-page entry on Poland depicted the various strata of Polish society, among them illustrations not only of members of the nobility, who had considered themselves the embodiment of the nation, but also the gentry, peasants, and Jews. The encyclopedia included numerous entries about significant rabbis and other aspects of Jewish religious and cultural history, including an entry on Nahmanides (Ramban), the thirteenth-century Spanish rabbi and biblical commentator, and the bibliography for the entry on Poland included works on Jewish history. The entry on the Catholic Church in the Polish lands, however, points to an aspect of Polish history that complicated this inclusion of Jews in a broad conception of the Polish nation. Even at a time when Catholicism was not yet a central element of Polish nationalism, the entry emphasized the political role of Catholicism, focusing on the pre-partition period at a time when censorship would have made it difficult to address the politics of the partitioned Polish lands.[11]

From the very start, the publishing activity of the Orgelbrands and the Glucksbergs both influenced and reflected the cultures of Polish intellectual life.[12] In the Glucksbergs' first decades of publishing activity, the works they issued combined a nascent Polish national identity with a broader European outlook through both the languages of their publications and the ideas they introduced to Polish readers. In addition to Polish-language translations of works by Molière, Goethe, and other European writers, Natan Glucksberg also published memoirs of Old Poland, Polish school textbooks, and travel guides that drew on ideas about attachment to land at a time

The Disillusionment of a Polish Jew 81

when Poland no longer existed as a political state, as well as dramas, novels, and poetry by the most important Polish playwrights and writers. In later decades, Jakub Mortkowicz, the son of a used Polish bookstore owner from a more traditional Jewish family in Radom, and Jakub's wife, Janina, owned a prominent Warsaw bookstore in the early twentieth century known especially for its art books, bringing knowledge of European art to Polish circles. Their bookstore became a gathering place for Polish intellectuals.[13]

Competition among publishers was fierce. They courted the most prominent Polish writers, who sometimes changed publishers from one book to the next. Natan Glucksberg was the first Polish publisher to provide a stipend to the writers whose works he published, making his publishing house more attractive to writers until other publishers adopted the same practice. The publishers' economic relationship with writers had broader implications. Publishers influenced what was written through their decisions about which writers to support financially, and they sometimes provided access to journals and books from abroad for the writers they supported, circulating to Polish writers new ideas about politics and culture that were developing in Western Europe and the United States. Sometimes competition among publishers turned to antagonism, bringing to the surface resentment on the part of non-Jewish publishers toward their Jewish competitors.[14] At other times Jewish and non-Jewish booksellers and publishers cooperated. Maurycy Orgelbrand, for example, was involved in the establishment of a Polish bookselling organization that was otherwise dominated by non-Jewish publishers.[15]

The integral role of Polish culture as a symbol of national identity drew Jewish publishers and their bookstores into conspiratorial politics opposing Russian rule, fostering a sense of national belonging. Underground newspapers and proclamations were drawn up and passed from hand to hand during literary gatherings in bookstores as well as in publishers' homes. Sometimes publishing operations and the editorial offices of newspapers were located in the same building as bookstores, so salon gatherings there had direct access to news about the latest political developments, without the filter of censorship. Some booksellers provided writers with banned books that had been smuggled into the Polish lands and that they could not display on the shelves. A handful of booksellers were more directly involved in making banned books accessible, paying smugglers to carry them illegally across borders. Books that were banned in the Polish lands and were published in L'viv and Krakow, in the Austrian partition, were sometimes sent to Leipzig, where they were disguised with covers of German-language prayer books and other publications before being transported into the Kingdom of Poland. Others were smuggled through St. Petersburg. Some booksellers paid bribes to customs officials, and a few paid a regular "salary" to censors as bribes. The Jewish owner of one of Warsaw's largest used Polish bookstores, Jakub Przeworski, was active in these operations.[16]

Polish language and literature, together with political involvement and social connections that stemmed from their publishing activity, connected Jewish publishing families to a culture in which previous generations had not been strongly rooted. Some publishers, as well as Polish society, considered publishing to be an act of patriotism. The main Polish publishing houses were based in the Kingdom of Poland within the Russian Empire but were active across borders of the partitioning empires, involving them in the preservation of a Polish culture and identity that sought to transcend divisions of empire.[17]

Individual publishers took even more direct part in the most dramatic displays of Polish patriotism in the nineteenth century. Jan Glucksberg was well respected in Polish patriotic circles; as a young man, he had fought in the failed Polish uprising that broke out in 1830. Samuel and Maurycy Orgelbrand were both active in political intrigues during the uprisings as well. Maurycy had established a branch of the family's publishing business in Vilnius, and when police raided his bookstore during the 1863 uprising, they found maps and pamphlets for the rebellion. Maurycy's wife, who was active in conspiratorial politics as well, was sent into exile in the Russian interior, and he accompanied her before the couple returned to the Polish lands. Jakób (Jakub) Gieysztor, an activist in Vilnius during the 1863 uprising, recalled that Orgelbrand agreed to publish illegal materials for the uprising after the Zawadzki publishers, who were of ethnic Polish background, declined to do so.[18]

Even as they became influential in Polish culture and drawn into Polish politics, members of the first generation of the Glucksberg and Orgelbrand families were also leaders in Jewish life. In addition to helping to establish the Rabbinic School in Warsaw, Jan Glucksberg was part of the Jewish delegation that appealed to government authorities for civil rights for Jews, while he and Samuel Orgelbrand were on Warsaw's synagogue council. After Salomon Lewental entered the publishing business, he followed in their footsteps as a leader in Jewish communal and charitable institutions. The book trade became a path by which members of the first generation of Jewish publishing families reshaped their identifications into Poles of the Mosaic faith, even as the sons of the patriarchs in the Orgelbrand and Glucksberg families, as well as Samuel Orgelbrand's younger brother, were already leaving behind that identity through baptism. The newspaper polemics that targeted Salomon Lewental at the end of the 1880s challenged the very viability of their sense of belonging as both Polish and Jewish.

84   The Disillusionment of a Polish Jew

Salomon Lewental and other Jewish publishers helped to circulate literature that opposed a narrowing conception of national belonging, especially works by Polish Positivist writers. The catalogues of publishers without Jewish background included Positivist authors as well, and a few of the most prominent Positivist writers—in particular Prus, a central literary figure in the circle—never appeared under the Lewental imprint, according to extant sources. Another leading author in the Positivist circle, Aleksander Świętochowski, published only one book with Lewental. But in the 1870s, Salomon issued nearly two dozen works by Józef Korzeniowski, considered a forerunner of Polish Positivism, and in the following decade he published or reissued all of the novels of Orzeszkowa, a leading Positivist who wrote about the "Jewish issue."[19]

Polish Positivists were not the only writers on Salomon's publishing list whose works brought new cultural ideas to Polish audiences. He also published novels and works of philosophy translated from German and French, transmitting ideas among cultures and regions. Among the translations he issued were works imbued with appeals for religious toleration and rationalist and humanistic ideas. A handful of these works dealt directly with the role of Jews in European societies. In 1877 Salomon published a Polish translation of one of the most important German works in discussions about Jewish emancipation in the last decades of the eighteenth century, when the possibility of emancipating Jews was being debated by intellectuals and government officials alike in Western and Central Europe. Published in German in 1779, the play, *Nathan the Wise*, was written by Gotthold Ephraim Lessing, a central figure of the German Enlightenment. It was set in Jerusalem during the Third Crusade but was viewed as a parable about religious toleration and German-Jewish coexistence. Two decades after publishing Lessing's play, Salomon issued a history of humanism in Italy and Germany, translated from German into Polish. He also published Polish translations of classic Greek dramas, from Homer to Sophocles, whose ideas influenced the humanistic values of the Renaissance and the Enlightenment.[20]

Salomon continued to publish such works as exclusionary ideas about the nation crept into Polish debates. The first Polish journal that espoused an overtly anti-Jewish agenda, *Rola,* began publication in 1883. Its articles sneered that Jews were not only exploiters of the peasantry, but also "infected . . . and degraded Polish culture," in Theodore Weeks's characterization. The Natansons, who were close to the Lewentals, were a frequent target of *Rola*'s vitriol. By the end of the 1880s, the attacks on Jewish involvement in Polish culture did not come only from explicitly antisemitic newspapers, which were still on the margins of Polish public life, and not only from conservative and clerical circles. The progressive journal *Głos* was sympathetic to socialism and supported the emancipation of Jews in the Russian Empire, but its suspicions that Jews were "Judaizing" Polish culture echoed *Rola*'s characterization of Jews as a threatening element. Poles must take measures to fight against that contamination, *Głos*'s editors were asserting by the mid-1880s, characterizing Jews as a racial group. By 1888, one year after Salomon had become co-owner of *Kurjer Warszawski, Głos* had "abandoned the liberal approach to the 'Jewish question.'" The author of one article, writing about French Jews, "could not imagine that a seemingly assimilated Jew could really be a Frenchman if he also belonged to an international Jewish organization," according to the historian Brian Porter. For the article's author, Porter wrote, "The only meaningful assimilation was *total* assimilation, the complete abnegation of one's former identity, allegiances, and cultural practices. There could be no 'Jewish Poles' or 'Polish Jews,' there could be no 'Poles of the faith of Moses'; there could only be Jews and Poles."[21]

The tenor of the articles marked a shift from the polemics of earlier years. In the decades since the 1863 insurrection, Polish intellectuals of all stripes had, to a certain degree, observed "an unwritten code of behavior to be followed in the public debate on the Jewish question. Regarding open expressions of anti-Jewish sentiments to be in bad taste, this convention assumed some degree of support for the idea of equality and assimilation, [to] which even the conservatives paid lip service." Now it began to seem that this "unwritten code" no longer held, and Lewental found himself at the center of the polemics.[22]

The Lewental Affair

When Salomon Lewental became co-owner of the newspaper *Kurjer Warszawski* in 1887, the deal was the talk of Polish cultural circles. It was one of the city's most widely read periodicals, established in 1821. "In the last few weeks the Warsaw journalistic world, and partly also the non-journalistic world, has taken great interest in the change that has taken place in the editorial womb of the hitherto most popular Polish journal, a tradition reaching to the distant past, that is, *Kurjer Warszawski*," an unnamed author wrote in the journal *Niwa*. The article was restrained in its criticism, yet its characterization of Salomon echoed the canard of the greedy Jew—"the known publishing speculator Mr. Lewenthal, an Israelite"—using a spelling of his name that did not conform with Polish orthography. The journalist Antoni Zaleski, founder and editor of the conservative journal *Słowo*, noted that *Kurjer Warszawski* had fallen into "semitic hands."[23]

The Jewish circles of which Salomon was a part had been responding to similar accusations for years. Economic resentments had long affected Jewish relations with their neighbors in

The Disillusionment of a Polish Jew   87

the Polish lands. Repeatedly in the 1860s and 1870s, Warsaw's Polish-language Jewish newspaper, *Izraelita*, and its precursor, *Jutrzenka*, published essays about the historical reasons for the prevalence of Jews in trade and business. The new anti-Jewishness was caused by jealousy of material wealth and economic competition, an *Izraelita* journalist declared in 1873, because "from contemptuous, repulsive beggars, they [Jews] dared to stand as people" on an equal footing with non-Jews. *Izraelita* published other articles disputing the notion of Jewish separatism.[24]

Anti-Jewish polemics rooted in the ideology of race rather than in economic competition came largely from elsewhere at that time, however, not from Polish writers. In Central Europe, racial antisemitism targeted Jewish involvement in German culture and spread to France and England, becoming a "pan-European" movement. Polish-speaking Jews in Warsaw who aspired to acceptance in Polish society looked to their French and German counterparts as their models, examples, for them, of Jews who asserted their identification with the countries in which they lived while remaining Jewish, so the attacks on Jews in Central and Western Europe were cause for alarm. In 1869, an *Izraelita* article challenged polemics against Jews in the German composer Richard Wagner's 1850 essay "Jewry in Music." It was not traditional Jews who were the target of Wagner's polemics but those who were increasingly taking part in German cultural life. *Izraelita* pointed out the contradictions in Wagner's essay, which called for Jews to prove themselves loyal Germans while decrying their involvement in German culture as a foreign contaminant.[25]

Izraelita's responses became more urgent in the 1870s. Shortly after reporting on an 1873 lecture in Warsaw by an ideologue from Central Europe who espoused anti-Jewish ideas based on racial ideology, the newspaper published three unsigned articles titled "What Are We Supposed to Do?" The author defended the devotion of Jews to the countries in which they lived despite persecution and poverty, calling the new anti-Jewish animus "an ominous ghost" of anti-Jewish hatred that had been lingering under the surface of the "brightness of a new era." Despite the article's generally pessimistic tone, it answered the question "What should we do?" with an optimistic faith in progress and learning: "The answer to this question lies with three words: patience, work and progress!" It continued:

> There dawns a horizon of better knowledge for the masses, and then the ghost of night known as "hatred" will leave for the abyss without return. In the meantime let us continue to progress unceasingly with our course, for our own good as well as for the good of the entire society. Let us not stop in endeavors toward the purification of our religion . . . in reviving in people our spirit of truth and love, laying the foundation of our faith. Let us disseminate more and more the light among our fellow citizens—let us increase simultaneously our material and moral stores, because for us they are a guarantee of further development in the future, and they can only benefit the country.
>
> The rest time and learning will accomplish![26]

By the 1880s, suspicions of Jews involved in broader European cultures intensified. The esteemed German historian Heinrich von Treitschke's 1880 tract "A Word about Our Jewry," which focused on German Jews, contained similar contradictions as those faced by Salomon Lewental and other Jews in the Polish cultural sphere. Increasingly German Jews identified with the culture of the country in which they lived, with the expectation that this would lead to acceptance as Germans. Yet when Ger-

The Disillusionment of a Polish Jew 89

man culture became central to their identities, they were accused of contaminating that culture. Von Treitschke, while couching his criticism in praise, singled out the very cultural medium in Germany—newspapers—that became central to Salomon's publishing activity. The focus of von Treitschke's complaint was journalists more than publishers and newspaper owners, but his essay echoed the ones that Salomon would encounter in the Polish lands later that decade. The "greatest danger," according to von Treitschke, "is the unjust influence of the Jews in the press—a fateful consequence of our old narrow-minded laws which kept the Jews out of most learned professions. For ten years public opinion in many German cities was 'made' mostly by Jewish pens. It was a misfortune for the Liberals, and one of the reasons of the decline of the party, that their papers gave too much scope to the Jews. The present weakness of the press is the necessary reaction against this unnatural state of things."[27]

The Polish lands were not immune to these ideas despite Polish writers' focus in the early 1880s on the accusation that Jews were to blame for the ills of capitalism, which was rapidly expanding in the Polish lands, rather than on the ideology of race. As in Central Europe, polemicists turned their attention to the involvement of Jews in Polish culture, especially journalism. By the 1880s, the Polish-language press, largely centered in Warsaw but with a readership that transcended the borders of the partitioned Polish lands, had become a "surrogate nation-space," and journalists acted as "national educators and guides." Newspapers became a forum for debates about where Jews fit into the Polish national community, and with the press rapidly expanding, Jewish ownership of Polish newspapers and journals became a target. In 1879, nine Polish-language periodicals circulating in Warsaw were owned by Jewish publishers, some of whom also served as editors. They were not a dominant presence

90   The Disillusionment of a Polish Jew

in a city with nearly sixty Polish periodicals, but conservative and clerical writers criticized what they alleged was the "Judaization" of the Polish press. Several newly established Polish newspapers began to promote an anti-Jewish agenda.[28]

When Salomon became co-owner of *Kurjer Warszawski,* the article in *Niwa* noted that he had just purchased joint ownership of the newspaper from Gebethner and Wolff. At the same time, Gebethner and Wolff bought the journal *Kurjer Codzienny* from the Orgelbrand brothers—also "Israelites," the article noted—and it "continually limped along" in the progressive spirit of its editorship. It was Salomon's co-ownership of *Kujrjer Warszawski,* not the sale of *Kurjer Codzienny* to Gebethner and Wolff, that critics cited as cause for concern. Despite *Niwa's* characterization of him as a speculator, the article reserved judgment on the fate of *Kurjer Warszawski* under his co-ownership while noting that numerous writers who had previously published in *Kurjer Warszawski* were moving to *Kurjer Codzienny:* "Will *[Kurjer] Warszawski* decline in quality? Today we do not have any right or reason to predict this; of course it is necessary to expect that the faithful will not allow the longtime tradition to go astray and that with the sincere and fervid efforts of the remaining associates it will be able to manage the difficult task."[29]

It was the introduction of paid matrimonial announcements in *Kurjer Warszawski* in 1889 that made Salomon among the first targets of heightened polemics. Critics decried the announcements as a crass attempt at profit without regard for literary quality. Among those leading the way in the criticism were journalists for *Rola,* which published explicitly anti-Jewish vitriol. Salomon was attacked in Galicia, within the Austro-Hungarian Empire, and in periodicals abroad as well. The criticism took on the "character of an antisemitic smear," a literary commentator wrote decades later. Concerned about the

The Disillusionment of a Polish Jew 91

impact of the polemics on *Kłosy*, the illustrated journal Salomon
owned whose circulation was declining, he removed his name
as publisher of the journal. The criticism did not let up.[30]

The attacks on Salomon were part of broader polemics
that targeted "assimilated" Jews, at times combining racial
ideology with economic resentments. "This entire mass seems
like one huge ant hill of exploiters . . . in a word, millionaire
exploiters on one extreme and impoverished exploiters on the
other," asserted one article in *Głos,* which had issued a "call for
tolerance" of Jews just that summer. "Between the millionaire
Jew and the impoverished Jews is only a difference of degree,
but there is no conflict of interest." The following year, an article in the newspaper argued, in the words of one historian,
that Jews' "racial bonds were so tight that even assimilated,
'enlightened individuals' were still marked by their essential
natures, differing from their 'orthodox brethren' only in form,
not substance."[31]

Salomon had been accused of being concerned above all
about money and the acquisition of property even before he
became co-owner of *Kurjer Warszawski*. His purely financial
motives, his critics alleged, were evidenced by his ownership of
journals with conflicting ideologies, proving that his motivations were purely for the sake of profit. Some critics focused on
Kłosy, the illustrated journal that he had owned since 1865,
which had a reputation of being a "Catholic" publication. "An
innate fault of *Kłosy* is that it is perhaps the only anomaly on
Warsaw soil, that a periodical which attempted always to assume
a conservative, and even Catholic, character, is the property of
a dignitary, even the president, of the Israelite community,"
wrote the journalist Zaleski in 1886. "The same Mr. Lewental
published and signed as editor of the progressive *Świat,* [which
is] the opposite of *Kłosy* in terms of direction and tendency. So
the fervent Israelite was in one journal a Catholic, in another

an atheist, and as a result of this, as it has been pointed out in our journals, in both he was supposed to be nothing, only a speculator."[32]

Świętochowski, one of the most prominent Polish Positivist writers, mocked Salomon in several of his columns in the journal he published and edited, *Prawda*. He scoffed at the fact that a Jewish publisher owned a journal, *Kłosy*, with a reputation of having a "Catholic bent." "The most fiercely Catholicizing of our journals remain in the hands of non-Catholics," he wrote earlier in the 1880s.[33] Świętochowski's disparagement of Lewental was as much anticlerical as it was about the publisher's Jewish identity: "We have numerous periodicals that stand resolutely on rules, and on Jews, who give lectures on Catholicism." Yet in 1890, Świętochowski criticized an article in *Głos* for its "misrepresentations about the Jews," and he was among the writers who sought to come to Lewental's defense.[34]

The extent of Salomon's influence on *Kłosy*'s content is unclear. While the journal was known as having a Catholic, conservative character, its articles create a more nuanced portrait. The journal published stories about the history of local churches, to be sure, and its pages regularly contained articles and drawings romanticizing the Polish landscape, but it also brought news and literature from abroad to its readers. The journal issued translations of British literature and travel stories about the United States, informing readers about its government, the streets of New York, and the Civil War; three years after the Emancipation Proclamation, it published an article about the post-emancipation impact of the enslavement of African Americans. There was little in the journal about the Polish Jewish population, but one article recounted the legend of Esterke, known in Polish and Jewish folk tradition as the mistress of the fourteenth-century Polish king Kazimierz the Great, a story that often symbolized Polish toleration toward the Jews.[35]

The Disillusionment of a Polish Jew   93

With the introduction of paid wedding announcements in *Kurjer Warszawski* in 1889, Salomon came under scrutiny not only by right-wing newspapers, but also in less vitriolic terms by more moderate writers, including Prus, who had a reputation for supporting Polish-Jewish cooperation.[36] Prus did not directly echo *Rola*'s anti-Jewish rhetoric against Salomon, but he took a swipe at the publisher by referring to his relationship with *Kłosy*'s editor, Adam Plug (pseudonym of Antoni Pietkiewicz), in which Salomon serves as the hangman of the editor, who was accused in the press of being Lewental's minion. Prus was at a crossroads in his views toward the "Jewish question" at the time. He had long had faith in assimilation as the "solution to the Jewish problem," even after the pogroms in 1881–82 shadowed his earlier optimism. In 1889, however, Prus began publishing vehement criticism about a massive donation by the German Jewish banker Baron Maurice de Hirsch to endow trade, industry, and agricultural schools for Jews in Galicia. Prus focused on the trade schools; he was concerned that such an endeavor would displace Poles. Hirsch's project led Prus to have a "crisis of faith" in assimilation, according to Agnieszka Friedrich. In 1889, Prus published a seven-part series of articles titled "For 12 Million Guldens," in which he wove stories replete with stereotypes about "Jewish avarice and nouveau-riche tendencies." Prus distinguished himself from the racial antisemitism emanating from Central Europe and from some right-wing Polish newspapers. But his polemics, from a writer with a reputation for having "philosemitic" views, lent legitimacy to sharper criticism by other writers.[37]

Eliza Orzeszkowa was deeply agitated by the anti-Jewish polemics. To be sure, Orzeszkowa's own views were not entirely devoid of some of the stereotypes that were the foundation for the vitriol. Like Świętochowski and Prus, she had been part of a shift among liberal Polish intellectuals between the 1860s

94   The Disillusionment of a Polish Jew

and the 1880s from an optimistic, pro-assimilationist stance to pessimism about its viability. In her private correspondence with other writers, she sometimes wrote sarcastically about Lewental's wealth, asserting that he had built his fortunes on the backs of writers. At times she praised the fair remuneration that Salomon paid to writers, while at other times she characterized him as a speculator. "I do not know if you know that almost the first foundations of fairy-tale auspiciousness for the publisher of *Kłosy* are midwifed by your palm," she wrote a decade earlier to Teodor Tomasz Jeż [Zygmunt Miłkowski], who noted in his own correspondence that Lewental paid him well for his publications. "The current wealth of Lewental (last year he produced officially 600,000 rubles of profit) gushed for the first time from your pen." When *Kłosy* published Jeż's writing under Lewental's stewardship, Orzeszkowa wrote to Jeż that the journal "for the first time had become popular. . . . And from there Lewental began to make a fortune. Does he remember this? He is a Jew; he should be grateful because gratitude—this is a tribal characteristic of Jews." In 1886, Orzeszkowa wrote to another writer about her appeals to Lewental to provide financial help to residents in Grodno, where she lived, after a fire destroyed buildings throughout the city, from the Jewish quarter to the city center, and left thousands homeless. "Now this is ending sadly because the cluster of our brothers is drowning and will drown in poverty. But Salomon himself would no longer be able to help them; perhaps if he would turn over the gold roof from his palace," she wrote to Michał Bałucki, a Polish poet and playwright.[38]

In her published writings and in her correspondence with other writers, however, Orzeszkowa was still one of the most vocal literary advocates for understanding toward Jews and for Polish-Jewish cooperation despite her negative literary portrayals of traditional Jewish life. Earlier in the 1880s, after the anti-

The Disillusionment of a Polish Jew 95

Jewish violence in the Russian Empire had spread to Warsaw, she wrote a pamphlet titled "About the Jews and the Jewish Question," which Salomon helped to get past the censors. The pamphlet, to be sure, reflected a shift away from her previously optimistic outlook for the possibilities of Polish-Jewish coexistence and was a "denunciation of the destructive effects of Jewish nationalism." She was dismayed when other writers took up her criticism of the nascent politics of Jewish nationalism rather than her call for understanding, since the focus of her essay was a challenge to the very canard that now characterized the attacks on Salomon: the accusation that Jews were "swindlers" in their very essence and dishonest in business. Such accusations "are not caused by any specific Jewish nature. They represent the shortcomings and imperfections of human nature in general, which are to be found in varying degrees and in various guises in the lap of other races and social groups," she wrote in the pamphlet. "If they stigmatize Jews more strongly and with greater intensity, then the greater stigma and intensity may be attributed to historical and social factors."[39]

The same year as she published the pamphlet in 1882, Orzeszkowa wrote a novel that, at least on its surface, seemed to respond to the pogroms. The novel, *Mirtala,* was set in Rome after the failure of the first-century Jewish rebellion against the Romans, and Orzeszkowa might have intended the story of tense relations between Jews and the Roman rulers of Jerusalem to stand in for antagonism between Poles and the Russian Empire after the 1863 rebellion, at a time when Russian censorship made it difficult to address those tensions directly. Orzeszkowa sent the novel to Salomon with the hope that it would be serialized in *Kłosy.* For more than a year she received no response from him, and although he finally agreed in late 1883 to publish the work, first in *Kłosy* and then in book form, the journal's editors decided to delay its publication out of concern that her

96   The Disillusionment of a Polish Jew

negative portrayal of Jewish nationalism would further incite anti-Jewish sentiment. Only in 1885 did *Kłosy* begin publishing *Mirtala* in its pages. Orzeszkowa was dismayed when one artist refused to do illustrations for it; she suspected it was because the artist "is an antisemite," she wrote to Lewental.[40]

Now, at the end of the 1880s and early 1890s, Orzeszkowa was disturbed not only by the explicitly anti-Jewish attacks, but also by polemics that were tinged with more moderate accusations against Jews written by fellow Positivist writers, among them Prus and Wiktor Gomulicki, whose poetry she admired. "It will not be news for you when I say that I am wholeheartedly and deeply opposed to antisemitic currents, which predominate in several organs of our press and have already brought out such statements that are atrocious in content and form, such as Gomulicki's statements against Lewental; such a waste of honest impulses and great talent, such as the articles by Prus on this issue," Orzeszkowa wrote to Erazm Piltz, founder and editor of the Warsaw journal *Nowiny*.[41]

Leopold Meyet, a Jewish lawyer who was active in Polish intellectual life in Warsaw, urged Orzeszkowa to mobilize Polish writers to denounce the vitriol. He was alarmed at the "danger that threatens our society from such behavior of the organs of public opinion," Meyet wrote. "Everyone is invoking Prus, who has gone completely haywire." Orzeszkowa took up his appeal. She wrote to Maria Konopnicka, a prominent poet and feminist writer who had developed a close friendship with Orzeszkowa; it was Lewental who had first connected the two writers years earlier, and Konopnicka had been editor of a short-lived journal for women that Salomon founded.[42]

Orzeszkowa encouraged Konopnicka to respond to the anti-Jewish polemics. "Yes. It is necessary to do something to help," Konopnicka responded. "I am not a great supporter of Jews, but I hate oppression and injustice. Perhaps I would not

The Disillusionment of a Polish Jew 97

be able to praise them—if they were peaceful and happy—but when they are persecuted—I stand on their side." Konopnicka's attitude toward the "Jewish question" underscored the ambivalence of some Polish Positivist writers toward the place of Jews in Polish society. The main character of Konopnicka's short story "Nasza Szkapa" (Our Nag), published the same year, was a Jewish merchant who, in Israel Bartal and Magdalena Opalski's characterization, "appears on the scene in order to deprive a debt-ridden worker's family of yet another of its few remaining necessities." The story was characteristic of Polish literary portrayals of Jews from the mid-1880s through the 1890s that "focus on the unsuccessful efforts of Polish characters to free themselves from the capitalist webs that entangle them. In all cases the 'flies' are ultimately strangled and become the prey of a swarm of Jewish 'spiders.'"[43]

Nevertheless, in 1889 and 1890, the circle of "progressive writers" in Warsaw, as they were known, including Świętochowski, was already discussing how to respond to the anti-Jewish polemics, Meyet wrote to Orzeszkowa. Like Prus, Świętochowski was shifting in the 1880s away from the Positivists' optimistic, pro-assimilationist views he had helped to develop decades earlier. By the end of the nineteenth century Świętochowski "did not hesitate to lend his support to the antisemitic movement," Bartal and Opalski wrote, citing his words from 1898: "I defended the Jews fifty years ago when they wanted to be Poles, and this is why I do not defend them today, when they are the enemies of Poles." Yet at the end of the 1880s, Świętochowski was among the writers who were concerned about the vitriol. For her part, Konopnicka published "Mendel Gdański," about a bookbinder who asserts his loyalty to Warsaw and Poland in the face of threats of anti-Jewish violence. Orzeszkowa herself wrote a short story published in *Kurjer Warszawski* about a Jewish pauper—a contrast with the story's ironic title, "Rotszyldówna" (The Rothschild Girl), implicitly challenging the characterization of Jews as wealthy speculators, or at least setting up the title character as a foil to them.[44]

In the shadow of the polemics, Salomon decided to shut down *Kłosy,* selling it to another publisher, which then ended its publication. The decision was painful for him. The illustrated journal had published the works of prominent writers and artists and was a source of particular pride in his publishing catalogue; he listed its title first, in large type, on the letterhead he used in correspondence. Salomon blamed the journal's demise on the relentless polemics against him, which he asserted were the cause of declining circulation. Some observers, including Prus, insisted that the journal's economic problems were not connected with the polemics. Prus nevertheless expressed some sympathy toward Salomon. "The Polish press is losing not only a beautiful organ, but also an honestly run one, because *Kłosy,* despite the paper bombs that were thrown at it, was an honest magazine," he wrote. But he rejected Lewental's explanation for the decline in circulation in acerbic commentary. "I am very sorry, but I would sincerely like to cite the names of 'indigenous' Poles, and even nobility, who would contribute ninety thousand rubles to run a Polish magazine," he wrote in a somewhat mocking tone. "However, no magnate would be able to do this, no nobleman, but a person at whom (or so he thought at least) 'mud was thrown because of his religion.' So S. Lewental has made an undoubted contribution to Polish literature: he made sacrifices for it. But he is mistaken if he attributes the failure of Kłosy to his [religious] 'confession.' . . . The success or failure of a magazine is determined not so much by the owner's religion, but by the number of readers in a country. So let the publisher of *Kłosy* moderate his bitterness, which is, from a human perspective, completely justified. And if he (and he does) care about the crown of civic

The Disillusionment of a Polish Jew 99

service, let him be guided in the future not by the fact that 'mud was thrown at him,' or by his [religious] 'confession,' but . . . by social benefit."[45] Orzeszkowa, too, was sharply critical of Salomon's assertion that the polemics were to blame for his closure of *Kłosy*. But she acknowledged the personal toll on him. During a trip to Warsaw from Grodno, Orzeszkowa visited him at home and assured him that numerous authors were sympathetic to him and were grateful for his "open home," sentiments that "really delighted him, noticeably," she later wrote to Bałucki, recounting the meeting. "Speaking honestly, this person did not deserve the bad treatment that he encountered, and I was glad that I was able to comfort him with some pleasant news for him." Orzeszkowa lamented Salomon's decision to shut down *Kłosy*, but he had assured her he would continue his publishing work, focusing on important literature in editions of high quality, she wrote to Bałucki.[46]

Salomon was grateful for Orzeszkowa's support. Bitter over the journal's closure, he described the attacks against him as a "plague" in a letter to her. "For your kind, warm words— God will pay you a hundred times!" he wrote. "I will never forget about them, since from them comes only a noble, humanitarian spirit, as is characteristic of all your works and deeds. The antisemitic chaos, which is nowadays of prime interest, chose me a long time ago as the target of [its] rifles, and while not being satisfied any longer with brutal imaginations and public slanders, it runs into the most visible and effective blackmails!" Despite the writers' efforts to counter the polemics, Salomon was especially hurt at what he viewed as the failure of the literary world to come to his defense. "Aside from you, not a single voice spoke against the plague, which gains ground in more and more circles. A sad and painful sign!" he wrote to her. Comparing the polemics to violence against Jews in the German states in the early nineteenth century, known as the "hep hep" riots, he continued, outraged: "This year [marks] thirty good years of my publishing work—laborious, hard work, struggling with censorship over promoting language, and everything that I got to cherish and loved in the cradle, and with the constant hep! hep! of literary thugs! This struggle exhausts my energy, and I have tough everyday responsibilities—for which I must preserve myself."[47]

Some writers who later recalled the Polish cultural life of those years did not let up in their disparagement of Salomon. The sociologist Ludwik Krzywicki, a Marxist, accused him in his memoir of earning "a huge fortune from the shameless exploitation of Polish writers." In the 1880s, the attacks had extended to disparagement of *Kłosy's* editor, Plug, whom critics accused of being a "lackey of the Jews," but Krzywicki was sympathetic to the editor. Plug had settled in Warsaw in order to become "Lewental's serf," Krzywicki wrote, "devoted, hard-working and, naturally, badly paid. I came into contact only once with this speculator [Lewental], who chose the publishing realm as his prey." Krzywicki asserted that Lewental exploited Polish writers who needed an outlet for their work and toiled while he got rich. The writer's bitterness seemed to be heightened by his personal encounters with the publisher, whom Krzywicki had approached about publishing his work. Salomon offered a pittance as payment, according to the memoirist's recollection, so Krzywicki published it himself, "earning a profit about a dozen times more than Lewental's proposal." He continued: "According to Plug, everything happened in this world in the most typical way—he worked, whereas Lewental bought buildings and expanded the reach of his influence. Each of them was content: Lewental, since he had made a fortune; Pietkiewicz [Plug]—since he worked in a useful sphere. His [Plug's] innate need was work, and he worked for ten."[48]

The Disillusionment of a Polish Jew

In later years, however, several writers challenged the accusations against Salomon about his treatment of writers. The writer Bolesław Limanowski recalled that "in conditions when I really needed a penny, I received an entirely good payment" from Salomon for publishing his work in *Kłosy*. The writer Ferdynand Hoesick, who married Salomon's daughter Zosia in 1902, painted a glowing portrait of him that was likely a reaction to the accusations of unscrupulousness in previous decades. It was, to be sure, a romanticized image written by his son-in-law. Hoesick had known Salomon from literary and journalistic circles in the 1890s before marrying his daughter, and in his memoirs, written after Salomon's death, Hoesick described him as "one of the most respected Polish publishers, a bookseller-publisher in a grand style, in a grander style even than Gebethner and Wolff." The Lewental bookstore "towered over other Polish firms," Hoesick recalled, and was known especially for the "monumental works" that his publishing house issued: an album of artwork by the Polish painter Jan Matejko and the collected works of the most renowned writers in both Polish and foreign languages. "Lewental had his glorious page in the history of Polish culture, and as the publisher of *Kurjer Warszawski*, which in the last years brought tens of thousands of rubles annually in profit, he occupied a first-tier position in Warsaw, nay, in all of Poland," Hoesick declared.[49]

Salomon's character was the exact opposite of that described in the accusations against him, according to Hoesick's portrait. He was an "exceedingly influential individual on whom everyone counted" and was a well-liked figure in Warsaw. Even as a man of "priestly fortune," Hoesick declared, Lewental was ethical in his business dealings, "which differentiated him so honorably from many great Warsaw men of means. . . . Everyone recognized him as not only a decent person, but also an exceptionally sympathetic one, gentlemanly in every respect, honest, humane, good, collegial, warm and without pretensions, completely straightforward in manners. . . . He was regarded as one of the most intelligent people in the city, to whom many came for advice, coming many times about some kind of business or decision. And his advice, always unselfish, never disappointed, because he oriented himself exceptionally easily in every situation, always finding his way in every situation to the very crux of the matter."[50]

When Salomon penned his farewell article in the last issue of *Kłosy* in 1890, he did not hide his disillusionment. He characterized his motivations in very different terms than his critics did. He was no speculator, no opportunist, and his love for Poland and Polish culture was as deep as the dedication of the writers whose works he published, he asserted. He described his motivations as being deeply personal but also patriotic and philosophical. At the root of the journal's dwindling readership and economic failure, he wrote, was the abandonment of an inclusive conception of belonging to the Polish nation. He lamented the decline of a worldview that had shaped both his personal and professional pursuits: "Setting about to publish *Kłosy,* I founded it on the basis of love for one's native country and on humanism, in all the breadth of the meaning of this word." Now, he wrote, "times and ideas have changed. The principles of humanism promoted by *Kłosy* had gone bankrupt, humanity had begun to be characterized and sorted, and various barriers created for it." Humanism, for Salomon, was not only a philosophical outlook that viewed human reason as the basis for morality and understanding of the world, but also a worldview that believed all individuals deserved dignity and equal treatment. It was a lament over the failure of liberalism. The attacks he had endured for years had done more than just economic harm, he asserted. He made only brief reference to his critics' focus on his identity as a Jewish owner of Polish

The Disillusionment of a Polish Jew 103

periodicals: "Some of those who worked with *Kłosy* held that my [religious] confession harmed the journal. I considered such a statement to be a heavy insult, directed at my society," he wrote. He would nevertheless continue to dedicate himself to Polish publishing, he promised his readers, "for the good and development of the writing of the homeland, which preserves our dearest, most beloved jewel—our language."[51]

Alicja grew up under the shadow of her father's disillusionment as he grappled with the turmoil in his professional life. Unlike Salomon and other Jewish publishers who preceded him, who followed a path to Polishness above all in the public realm of economic and then cultural life, it was mainly through the private sphere that his eldest daughter sought entrance into Polish society. And while her father believed by the end of the 1880s that his Jewish identity had become a liability to his public profile and professional success, Alicja increasingly experienced her family's Jewish background as an obstacle to private fulfillment. She felt the pressure not only of her own hopes to leave behind the burden of that background, but also of her parents' struggle for acceptance in Polish society.

4
"The Nighttime Butterfly"

On the last day of the last year of the nineteenth century, Alicja Lewental recalled the day when she first took pen in hand and confessed to the pages of her journal the turbulence that had accompanied her discovery of love and heartbreak at sixteen years old. "I remember four years ago, when I wrote in my bed and, trembling, I asked about the future, I remember how I longed for this future, how extremely, passionately, I longed for it because I believed!" she wrote as she recalled those first diary entries. "I believed in a world in which God exists and hears my pleas and that I would be happy with him. . . . I dreamed about love, about the enchanting life as a couple, about the mysterious bliss of this life."[1]

That evening, on December 31, 1899, at a New Year's Eve gathering in her aunt's home, Alicja's family and friends toasted her and wished for her to find a husband in the new year. But Alicja herself was pessimistic about her future by then. For years, she had experienced political debates about national belonging through failed romances, unrequited love, and disappointments in her search for a husband. Alicja viewed her

"The Nighttime Butterfly" 105

Jewish background as an obstacle to finding a husband who would fulfill her family's hopes for acceptance in Polish society, a stigma she must overcome. She encountered disappointment in love as a rejection of her identity as a Polish woman from a Jewish family who was being raised in the Catholic faith. Throughout her diary, love and marriage were intertwined with her romantic patriotism, love of Polish culture, and the emotions of national belonging that surrounded her—all of which were complicated by her confusion over what it meant to be Catholic, what it meant to be Jewish, and what those affiliations meant in the minds of others.

Alicja's despair at the end of 1899 had its roots in pivotal experiences nearly three years earlier, when she was seventeen. In the middle of January 1897, at an evening of dinner and dancing in the Warsaw home of a family acquaintance, she met a man, Jan Ulanicki, who had just the kind of pedigree that her mother wanted for her. In the months after their first encounter, Alicja and Ulanicki spent numerous evenings together at salons and balls, deep in conversation about the Catholic faith, the materialism of the modern world, her pessimism, and their different backgrounds. On their second meeting, they spent the night deeply engaged in conversation. "We did not see anything around us, and we did not hear anything, we were taken with our conversation, which was so engaging!" she wrote in her diary. "He talks wonderfully, and we touched exactly on such topics that one never talks about at salons: about life and our outlooks on the world and on people. A strange thing: we are both pessimists a little." Alicja was moved by Ulanicki's deeply held religious beliefs and by his tragic family history, which had left him an orphan. He was intrigued when she told him about her diary. "It must be terribly interesting," she recalled him saying as she recounted the conversation in her journal.[2]

The next day, as she was playing a Beethoven sonata on the piano in her family's apartment, Alicja heard a knock at the door: Ulanicki had come to visit and left his visiting card with her parents. She was so taken aback that she could not continue playing. Within months of their first meeting, he declared his love for her. She was elated and began to write in her diary of their impending engagement. When they attended a literary gathering together to celebrate a literary anniversary of Deotyma, the storied poet and salon hostess, Alicja marveled that Ulanicki's name appeared together with her own and the names of her parents in the guest book. She feared that her parents would be wary of what she described as his impoverished situation. But they approved of Ulanicki. He was well mannered and, more important, had a suitable lineage: he was Catholic, and he was from Volhynia, a region associated with the aristocracy in the eastern parts of the Polish-Lithuanian Commonwealth before the partitions; such a lineage outweighed their concerns about her young age and their uncertainty about whether he could support her financially. They would soon exchange rings, she wrote, and the wedding would be a year later.

Ulanicki's background and his meager financial means were not entirely uncommon for members of the Polish intelligentsia from noble families. They were often frustrated by their limited economic opportunities and an attendant lack of social advancement after having migrated to the developing urban centers of the Polish lands in the decades after the emancipation of serfs. Polish aristocrats had controlled expansive estates in the eastern Polish-Lithuanian Commonwealth for centuries, and before Poland lost its independence at the end of the eighteenth century, they had had as much power as the king. The nobles saw themselves as the embodiment of the Polish nation. But the Russian authorities had gradually eaten away at the aristocrats' hold on Polish society since the partitions, and the

"The Nighttime Butterfly" 107

tsar's emancipation of the serfs upended the old feudal way of life. The sons of the Polish aristocracy began searching for work in Warsaw and other burgeoning cities, where they were no longer at the top of the pecking order. They were disoriented by the developing capitalist economy, which prized money, not land. Some blamed their diminished status on Jews. But Jewish families like the Lewentals who sought acceptance in Polish society often still viewed the aristocracy as a symbol of the Polish nation. It was through the aristocracy that they could prove themselves to be Polish patriots.[3]

Yet with Ulanicki, Alicja steeled herself for rejection. She worried that a man from an aristocratic family, "this ideal person from the perspective of intellect, heart, soul," could not fully accept her into his world. "He cannot exist for me, he stands too high! Would he, from an old Volhynian family, a believing Catholic, tie the knot with a baptized little Jewish girl [*żydóweczka*]?" she wrote, expecting that she would convert before marrying a Catholic man. "No, this is not possible." Two weeks later, she warned herself once more to prepare for disappointment: "At dinner, [a woman] told me that he does not love me . . . well and this cannot be!" Alicja wrote, apparently recounting a conversation with an acquaintance. "How would he, 'a person with an unblemished last name, from an old ancestral line of nobility, of a splendid past, which he, however, no longer remembers,' as he himself told me, be able to love a baptized little Jewish girl, though wealthy? No, no, I cannot count on him, and nevertheless how good it would be for us together!"[4]

In the months before Alicja met Ulanicki, she had written frequently of another man, Jan Kempner, who gave her less cause for uncertainty. He was from "her circle"—from an acculturated Jewish family and close enough to Alicja's family to sit with them during a benefit concert for a Jewish charity overseen by her mother. Even when she remained somewhat optimistic about her prospects with Ulanicki, Alicja wrote that she would be content with Kempner: "I prefer Kempner now because at least here [with Kempner] I would remain a Jewish girl, and there [with Ulanicki], I would have to change religion. Why? What for?" Now as she agonized over the prospect that Ulanicki was "too high" for her, she consoled herself that at least Kempner would not reject her over her Jewish background: "I do not have anything against this [Kempner], he is from my sphere, my faith, kind-hearted, decent, very much in love with me, and that is everything that is necessary! Why push one's way among Catholics, who certainly would not want me, would reject me? Better to stay as who you are born."[5]

Still, Alicja rejected Kempner as a husband: "Ach, this name Kempner! If not for this name, I would be able to be happy that he loves me." Her rejection of him seemed to stem from her mother's refusal to accept the match. His last name—and perhaps Kempner himself—was "too Jewish" for Hortensja; she wanted husbands for her daughters with a surname ending in "ski," as one of her sons-in-law recalled years later. It was the only way to erase the symbol of difference that the name "Lewental" represented. It was not the last time that Alicja's mother would reject a suitor for her because he was "too Jewish." Alicja, on the other hand, was more ambivalent than Hortensja was about whether she should cast her fate with a Catholic husband or whether acceptance was even possible.[6]

Hortensja's aspirations for her family to become equals in Polish society through her daughters' marriages were not unique in her social circles, and her focus on last names as a symbol of aristocratic heritage was not hers alone. Anna Leo, who was descended from a Jewish family, described the values of the financier circles, of which her own family was a part, in a depiction that echoed Alicja's world. "The daughters of bankers were not educated, of course, in any public academic institutions," recalled Leo, who was just a few years older than Alicja and whose milieu overlapped with hers. "It was necessary to marry a husband in order to become a fundamental member of the Polish nation; it was necessary, therefore, in marrying, to be able to change a foreign last name for a Polish one. Snobbery, the result of ideas that surrounded them, identified 'Polish' with 'aristocratic.'" The social hierarchy, she wrote, was based "not so much on property figures as much as on service to society. One and the other drew a connection with the aristocracy, whether through social relations or through marriage of the daughters of bankers with members of the aristocracy, or half- and quarter-aristocratic heritage." Leo criticized the materialism that Alicja, too, had begun to lament: "The sin of the Warsaw financiers, as a collective concept, was the tragic superficiality of life," Leo ruminated. "The men worked, but the women, raised from their earliest years under the care of governesses, were raised as if suffering flowers, without contact with the essence of life, developing in the atmosphere of their own social circle."[7]

Alicja did not challenge her mother's rejection of Kempner, yet she remained skeptical that she could ever find acceptance in Ulanicki's world. When Ulanicki declared his love for her, she feared that his family would not accept her as a "baptized Jew": "I dreamed about this from the first time I saw him . . . but not for a moment did I suspect that this would come true, he a Catholic, I . . . a Jew!" Her anxieties about Ulanicki continued into the summer, when she and her family decamped to Zakopane in the Polish mountains, a respite from what she described as her exhaustion with salon life. She expected that the engagement to Ulanicki would be finalized upon her return to Warsaw at the end of the summer. But so, too, did she remain fearful of disappointment. She spent her time in the mountains reading, "thinking about the content of books, because otherwise dark thoughts take over me."[8]

In Zakopane, Alicja went to church, where she prayed for her family and for Ulanicki. An archbishop blessed her as she knelt, her head bowed with tears in her eyes as she prayed: "'God, allow me to belong officially to Your Church! Allow me to know his religion and his faith!' And the archbishop blessed me, and such a sense of calm, bliss entered my heart. I prayed for the entire family because I alone of the entire family know how to pray, and I understand Him." She wrote frequently in her diary, lamenting when she came to the end of another notebook. "How much each [notebook] contains, how many feelings, and thoughts, and longings. . . . In a month it will be my birthday, I will finish my eighteenth year, and it fills me with fear, and as I look at this entire pack of diaries, they tell each other how I was not able to use my childhood!"[9]

By the time the Lewentals prepared to return to Warsaw in August, Alicja longed for the city. But tension seemed to grow in the Lewental home; her father yelled at her, and she wrote vaguely of conflict with her mother. Instead of confiding to her diary about the deteriorating possibilities for marriage to Ulanicki, her entries described the resumption of her life in Warsaw: reading, gathering with friends and family, hearing news of acquaintances being married, and praying to God for the fulfillment of her hopes. Within weeks of her return from the Polish mountains, Alicja began to write once more with despair and appealed to God, though she still did not yet write about the details of her deflated hopes for her engagement. "All at once I became sad, but this was such sadness that I cried and cried without end. . . . Life is a great farce, but only a farce, so how is it worthwhile to suffer so?" She wrote once more of her first love, her second cousin, who had recently married a Jewish woman—"a Jewish hag [*żydowica*] from Odessa, with an even uglier name, Walltuch," Alicja had written about his fiancée the previous year after learning of their engagement.[10]

"The Nighttime Butterfly" 111

By early November, Alicja began fretting that what she had feared—that the stigma of her Jewish background would lead to rejection—had come true. She referred vaguely to her own behavior as a cause for the rejection and to a conflict with her mother about it. "No, Mamusia's words stand before me in my thoughts so much that I cannot get rid of them," she lamented. "God, God, how stupid I still am, how gullible! Was it possible for me to believe him, to blindly trust his every word, his glance? Doubts creep into my soul! And perhaps he only said everything without intentions, allowed himself to trick a Jew because it is not a young lady from "<u>society</u>" [underlined in the original]! This speculation makes me crazy."[11]

Alicja became ever more confused about the meaning of her family's Jewish background for her own life. As it became clear that the marriage to Ulanicki would not take place, she expressed her laments over unrequited love as anguish about the barrier of that identity. She felt humiliated and alone. "I live entirely with him, and I think and I feel that it is terrible to think that he only played with me, laughed at me, perhaps saying, 'Now, stupid Jewish girl, she thought that I would ever want to [marry her],'" she lamented. "How naive! And I lacked only the strength to keep the promise I made to myself not to engage with him, moreover, because he is not for me, and I repeated to myself, furthermore, 'You are a Jew—and he is a Catholic from a proud Volhynian family; you are not for him!'"[12]

A month later Alicja wrote in her diary, addressing herself as Lila, the diminutive of her first name:

They are all Catholics, remember this Lila, so you protect yourself in the future from what you have now encountered! . . . Remember that they are Catholics, and you are a Jew! Every day repeat to yourself, that is not enough, two, three, ten times a day! When you only begin to dream about any of them, if you glimpse some sympathy in their eyes, and you hear a warm word in their mouth, think right away, this is a Catholic, and you are a Jew! Tell this to yourself loudly, scream and silence your conscience and heart with it! They are Catholics, playing with a Jew, even liking or loving you, of course ... but then, what are the consequences? He makes jokes, jeering, makes fun of you and will go away in a cold stoicism, saying "but this is a Jew after all." Lila, Lila, experience has already taught you, life warned you so early! You discovered this bitterness, this humiliation of the seducer so young ... do you again want to fly into the light, you poor, nighttime butterfly? Oh, how I am sorry for you, Lila, that you live in this world, that you have to live apart from him. . . . They are Catholics, everyone, everyone is Catholic, so do not dream, do not believe, do not desire! Your love will continue to be derided, your heart will be trampled on, because you are a Jew. . . . So close yourself up in yourself, coat your heart with armor and always remember that this world is not yours, that you are an intruder, that you alone are a Jew, among all of these Catholics! No, this thought does not leave me now for a moment, it will always be in my heart, conscience and mind. . . . God and yet how sad to tell myself, they allowed me to live together with myself and that I must accept this mercy, but no longer asking for anything, because I am a Jew![13]

The salon life, where Alicja mingled freely with Catholic men and met prospective suitors, had been only an illusion, she now believed as she wrote in her journal that night. Alicja's

"The Nighttime Butterfly"   113

disappointments led her to tire of the materialism of her world. She yearned for meaning beyond dancing, elegant clothes, and gossip, and at times she believed she would find that meaning in marriage and children. This fulfillment was not just personal; it was also a path toward proving her identity as a Pole— a "patriot," as she had written years earlier: "I want to go further and further beyond this worthless life of a young girl and to arrive finally at the moment when I will feel needed, and this moment will be: a husband and child. To surround a husband with care and love, to raise a child to be a true patriot and a good citizen, this is my world!" Now, at eighteen, she began describing the balls and dances as a "comedy" as she grew weary of the wittiness, compliments, and empty conversations that were the basis for courtship, which had led only to loneliness, she wrote. In a series of entries in November 1897 and the following year, she lamented a loss of faith in the possibility of finding fulfillment through marriage. No matter that her family's wealth allowed her to mingle with Polish cultural circles and high society, even if her Jewish background made her family's place in that society an ambiguous kind of belonging. No matter that she believed in Jesus. The very path to success—marriage to a Catholic man of appropriate social standing—seemed to be out of reach. Perhaps God, whom she sometimes referred to as Jesus or Christ and at other times in more general terms, did not hear her because she was a Jew, she lamented in one entry.[14]

In 1898, Alicja expressed hope that she could protect another young Jewish woman, Zuzia—possibly a reference to her cousin—from the same path of despair and rejection, from believing in the illusion that the elite, wealthy world of which they were a part meant they were equals to Catholic peers in their "salon life," as Alicja described it. The poor might suffer from actual hunger, she wrote, but her own world of wealth led to an existential hunger:

People think that the salon is laughter, a game, love, heaven on earth, poor people are envious of the rich for their world of glitter and champagne, but they do not see that . . . inside there are doubts, pain, bitterness; that this glow brings to light more and more the painful side of this life, that champagne only serves to put one in a stupor, to dull one's pain, that the salon is sometimes worse than their poor, dark, and damp nights. . . . And I too was enthralled for several years by this laughter, dancing, passion. . . . Now when I see everything, I find nothing, nothing and I lost my heart . . . squandered forever. . . . So I have protected Zuzia from this because we, Jewish girls, demoralized by not having help in religion, in [religious] confession, we have to support one another, so the more experienced must share their experience with others and, at least in this way, save them. . . . So I have undertaken to guide Zuzia and to lift her in the moment of her fall. I would like so much to save her from what was lost to me. She is still a child and does not understand the simplest things.[15]

At the end of 1897, Alicja began searching for another path, however briefly, leading her to consider taking part in the Jewish philanthropic activities of her family. Alicja's search was tentative and seemed to last for only a few weeks, but it hinted at the possibility of her embracing a Jewish identity that she had previously viewed only as a barrier. Some acculturated Jews in Eastern Europe were taking that path much further in those years. In the last decades of the nineteenth century, some Jews further east in the Russian Empire who had grown up in Russian culture or had embraced it in their young adulthood, once

"The Nighttime Butterfly" 115

aspiring to acceptance by their neighbors and emancipation by the tsar, began to turn away from such hopes. Jews who were integrated into their surrounding society and culture, sometimes leaving behind religious traditions as well, were a slim minority of more than five million Jews in the Russian Empire, but they were among those who spearheaded Jewish national movements that would eventually transform Jewish life.

National groups throughout the empires of Central and Eastern Europe, from Poles and Ukrainians in the Russian Empire to Czechs and Slovaks in the Austro-Hungarian Empire, had long been challenging the rule of imperial authorities, arguing that every nation had a right to its own state, and some Jewish intellectuals were influenced by these political movements, among them Polish nationalism. Conceptions of Jewish nationalism began to consolidate in the years after the anti-Jewish violence in 1881–82, but these ideologies had deeper roots. Secular Jewish political parties that developed in the following decades—not only Zionist parties, but also the Bund, the Jewish socialist party—filled a vacuum of communal leadership caused by the breakdown in the authority of traditional Jewish institutions and religious authorities under tsarist policy in previous decades. So, too, did disappointment among some Russified Jewish economic and intellectual elites over deflated hopes for emancipation have an impact.[16]

In the years after the pogroms, new political ideas began to crystallize, envisioning new forms of Jewish community based on nationalist or socialist ideologies. Some early activists began to argue in fiery speeches and passionate political tracts that Jews were a nation like any other and that they should have their own state, one that would give them control over their own fate. Sometimes raised in Jewish families that had loosened the ties of religious traditions, they no longer believed that only God could redeem Jews from a state of exile. Only secular politics, not religious faith, could bring that about. The possibility and desirability for integration now came under attack not only by antisemites, but also by some leaders of the developing Zionist parties who viewed acceptance as an illusory goal. Nor could they count on the Russian authorities to improve their oppressive conditions, they came to believe. Unlike in Western and Central Europe, the Russian Empire had not granted its Jews the same rights as the rest of the population beyond the lifting of legal restrictions on Jews in the Kingdom of Poland. In later years, meanwhile, some Jewish intellectuals who embraced nationalism nevertheless rejected the concept of the nation-state, arguing that Jews could have a full national life in the diaspora and should have autonomy in the Russian Empire. Their ideology came to be known as diaspora nationalism, or autonomism, organizing under the name of the Folkspartey. Despite differences in their ideologies, the socialist Bundists, the Zionists, and the diaspora nationalists shared a common goal: transforming the way Jews defined community and their relationship with surrounding societies.[17]

Jewish nationalism and continued faith in integration were not necessarily mutually exclusive viewpoints. In the 1890s, for example, the same Warsaw journalist, Nahum Sokolow, was editor of the Polish-language Jewish newspaper *Izraelita,* which promoted integration, and the Hebrew-language *Ha-Tsefirah,* which supported political Zionism beginning in the late 1890s. Although Sokolow turned toward Zionism, his path is relevant for those, such as Alicja Lewental, who chose a different course. "Jewish existence in the turbulent world of fin-de-siècle Europe, when Jews felt powerful forces pulling them toward integration into their surrounding societies at the same time that other forces were rejecting them from these societies, was often accompanied by an acute sense of confusion," wrote the historian Ela Bauer. "The major Jewish ideological movements of the time

"The Nighttime Butterfly" 117

did not bring this sense of confusion to an end. Instead, they can be best understood as an expression of that confusion." Young Jewish intellectuals often moved between competing political ideologies. Jewish political paths and the impact of antisemitism on Jewish identities were not uniform across Eastern Europe, varying depending on political and cultural contexts. Even within empires, cultural and political constellations differed by region.[18]

The nascent Jewish nationalist parties gained adherents in Warsaw and elsewhere in the Polish lands, including some who had been steeped in Polish culture and had once aspired to integration. For some Polish writers, too, the anti-Jewish violence in 1881–82 was central to the disillusionment with the "liberal (or 'positivist') faith in a gradual and relatively painless merging of Polish and Jewish peoples." Elsewhere in the Russian Empire, a Jewish population that viewed itself in national terms could be viewed as one of many minority nationalities in a multinational empire. For some Polish liberals, however, the development of Jewish nationalist ideologies was considered to be a betrayal of Polishness—as it was by some in Galicia—at a time of Russian repressions against Polish culture, even as some Polonized Jews encountered their own feelings of betrayal by Polish society as a result of the pogroms.[19]

Alicja Lewental's young life unfolded against this backdrop. The same year as her romance with Ulanicki, 1897, was a turning point for Jewish nationalist movements, which coalesced that year with the First Zionist Congress. The activists gathered in Basel, Switzerland, in the Basel Municipal Casino, designed by a prominent Swiss architect—a reflection, perhaps, of the delegates' assertion of dignity for Jews, according to the historian Derek Penslar—and safe from the censorship and repressions of the tsarist authorities. Zionism was not yet a mass movement then, but the gathering in 1897 marked the beginning of a revolution that would transform Jewish politics in the coming years. "They were overwhelmed by feelings of empowerment and solidarity," wrote Penslar, "by a sense that the world as they knew it was about to undergo a sea-change, and that they would be its agents."[20]

The Zionists were not the only Jews who were overtaken by revolutionary fervor that year. Just over a month after the First Zionist Congress convened, Jewish socialists met in Vilnius in the Russian Empire and established the Bund, which sought to spread the message of Marxist revolution to the working-class, Yiddish-speaking Jewish masses. Unlike the Zionist delegates in Switzerland, the Jewish socialists in Vilnius gathered clandestinely, meeting within the borders of the Russian Empire as they promoted a revolutionary ideology. Thirteen activists—twelve men and one woman—crowded into the attic of a modest one-story home with a thatched roof and surrounded by a dilapidated wooden fence. Vilnius was an appropriate birthplace for a party that viewed itself as representing working-class Jews. With the narrow lanes of its Jewish neighborhood and its centuries-old synagogues, it was a city of religious traditions, known among Jews as the "Jerusalem of Lithuania," but it was also a city of the Yiddish-speaking Jewish masses, those who worked long hours in factories and struggled to make a living. As in Warsaw, many workers were young Jews who had recently arrived from the small towns around Vilnius, having left the *shtetl* to search for work in the factories that were opening in the big cities of the Russian Empire. The Bund's Russian-speaking, revolutionary Jews and their working-class, Yiddish-speaking comrades had been working toward that moment of the Bund's birth in 1897 for years. Since the 1880s, they had been establishing reading circles at night for factory workers, opening free libraries, and fighting for better factory conditions. Like the diaspora nationalists, they believed in the principle of *doykayt*, "hereness" in

"The Nighttime Butterfly" 119

Yiddish—a sense of rootedness and belonging where Jews lived in the diaspora rather than in an envisioned Jewish state.[21]

1897, in short, was a year of revolution on the Jewish street. But Alicja never gave any hint of affinity for the new Jewish nationalist movements or even awareness of them. Nor did she reject the capitalist system that had made her family's privileged life possible, as socialist politics would have entailed. She did not refer in her diary at all to Jewish political parties, not even in a disparaging way. The debates among Jews over secular Jewish political ideologies seemed not to register with her. The key questions with which the "new Jewish politics" grappled assumed a sense of common fate with the broader Jewish population, a feeling of kinship she did not share.[22]

Yet only days after confirming in her diary that Ulanicki would not ask for her hand in marriage, Alicja seemed to contemplate the possibility of embracing her family's involvement in Jewish life, or at least of viewing her Jewish background as more than an obstacle. "Something has changed in me a lot, and this change was caused . . . I do not know by what, but a desire to be useful in order to act," she confessed to her diary. "And anyway I cannot live any longer as I have until now, thinking only about him and about my pains because this can make one crazy! Bitterness toward people, greater and greater doubt engulfs me, I am growing old before my time, and pessimistic opinions come out of my mouth more and more often! And this cannot be allowed; I cannot allow this for myself." She would dedicate herself to helping those around her, she decided, tutoring the caretaker's son and immersing herself in the philanthropic activities of her family. Her parents never stopped being active in the Jewish charities that previous generations of Hortensja's family had founded, from a trade school for Jewish youth to the Jewish children's hospital. That day in November 1897, Alicja was scheduled to teach a class of Jewish children, though she did not go into further detail in her diary. "I will take up this work with passion, with love," she wrote, "and perhaps I will be successful in developing in their little heads some kind of thought and a passionate feeling in their little hearts."[23]

What thoughts, what feelings Alicja hoped to evoke in these Jewish children, and what she planned to teach them, she did not record in her diary. Nor did she write afterward about the experience. But if she was considering embracing a sense of Jewish belonging, she seemed to abandon the possibility only one week later after the funeral of a family friend, a woman from the Natanson family. Alicja wrote of her sympathy for the woman's daughter, but most of all, she lamented that the woman was being buried in a Jewish cemetery. That night, she was moved to ruminate once more on her own religious identity: "I would not want to die a Jew, och no, no, not for anything in the world! To live as a Jew is difficult, and to die without a priest, without a cross, and then to not even be buried in holy ground. . . . And not one prayer to God. . . . And I do not want to, I do not want to die a Jew! And today they lowered her there into the grave and everyone came, everyone, family and friends, and not even to bless this fresh grave, and" —Lewental ended the entry mid-sentence.[24]

Alicja's confusion over where she belonged and her family's multiple identities—Catholic, Polish, Jewish—was not only the result of a stigma imposed on her by others. Even as her mother raised Alicja and her siblings under the influence of her own Catholic faith, Jewish identity was both absent and ever present in her life. Her grandfather Mathias Bersohn and her father were leaders in Jewish communal institutions, and her mother remained involved in Jewish charities, but Alicja grew up with no understanding of Judaism or Jewish culture.

"The Nighttime Butterfly" 121

Her knowledge of Judaism was absent to such an extent that her belief in Jesus did not, in her own eyes, preclude identification as a Jew in the narrative that she wove of her young womanhood.

The only mention of Jewish holidays or observances in Alicja's diary is of her father's attendance at synagogue on Yom Kippur one year with their close family friends, Kazimierz and Antoni Natanson, with whom Salomon had just returned to Warsaw by train the night before in time for the service after a vacation the Natansons and Lewentals had spent together abroad. Salomon was in the synagogue all day, Alicja noted in her diary. Considering her lack of knowledge about Jewish observance, she was probably unaware of the significance, or even the irony, when she commented that her father took a break from the service midday to eat, since she might not have known that observant Jews were required to fast on Yom Kippur. Rather, it was Catholic traditions and faith that set the rhythms of Alicja's life. Christmas and Christmas Eve, New Year's Day, and Easter were spent with Hortensja's relatives at the homes of aunts and uncles and even with Hortensja's parents, who nevertheless remained Jewish leaders. A few days before Christmas one year, the Lewentals visited the home of one of Hortensja's sisters to decorate the Christmas tree. Another year, Alicja described the decorations on a Christmas tree in her own home, with a crystal ball and an angel on top. The Lewentals adopted the rituals of Catholicism that were intertwined with the marking of time in Polish culture, even before they were baptized.[25]

Alicja never explicitly mentioned being present at the Jewish cemetery in Warsaw, but she described funerals of Jewish relatives and family friends who were buried there. She might have attended the funeral there of her parents' friend from the Natanson family in November 1897, and she wrote of her father's sadness when her uncle, Salomon's brother Fabjan, died, but she does not mention attending her uncle's funeral at the Jewish cemetery, where he was buried. Unlike her closeness to her mother's sister and brother-in-law, the Kraushars, whose gradual embrace of Catholicism mirrored her mother's, Alicja rarely spent time with her father's brother, whose identity as a Jew was so different from her own upbringing. Her uncle's death "did not make a big impression on me," she wrote, "because I spent time with Uncle [only] a few times a year, and I never felt a great devotion to him, yet I felt it deeply because of Daddy, who was as if he were dead."[26]

Alicja regularly recounted attending church, sometimes alone and at other times with her mother and siblings. They visited churches while traveling in the Polish mountains and in cities throughout Europe. In Switzerland, Alicja and her family visited a church in a small town where, she wrote, "under the Latin inscription 'Gloria in excelsis Deo' [a Christian hymn] is written 'Jehovah' in Hebrew letters, a remnant from the times of religious tolerance." It is unclear who translated the phrase for Alicja, who undoubtedly could not read the language. Earlier that same day, they had visited the castle of a woman who, she noted, "was a Jew, was baptized, and became so fiercely pious that she erected a statue of Christ in her park." The statue made an impression on her as she passed it while sailing on a ship: "When this figure was already visible from afar, everything fell silent on the ship; everyone bowed their heads." She occasionally wrote of conversations with priests whom she encountered at gatherings in private homes in Warsaw or while on vacation in Zakopane, where a priest visited her mother in the home where the Lewentals stayed. Others who were close to Alicja's family—a woman who seemed to be the children's nanny, with whom she sometimes went to church, and another woman who was her mother's former teacher—also had

"The Nighttime Butterfly" 123

an influence on her faith. "She is so good and loves me so much," she wrote of her mother's teacher, "and besides, she believes so much in God. She promised me that tomorrow she will pray for me and listen with all of her attention. How much she truly restores one's unwavering faith."[27]

Only a handful of times in the nearly seven years of her journal did Alicja describe her participation in a gathering explicitly connected with Jewish communal life. She recalled being present at a concert that was organized to raise money for a charity, overseen by her mother, that provided financial support to a trade school that taught Jewish women to sew. Her mother asked Alicja to approach the wealthy parents of young women of Jewish background from her social circles to contribute funds for the event, and Alicja was proud of her success in doing so. She and her mother attended the concert with several of her cousins, an aunt, the son of her mother's closest friend, and several other friends—individuals who also attended some of the same balls as Alicja and her sister Marta did but who were now in an explicitly Jewish milieu. She recalled when one man in their group talked in a loud voice, speaking not only in Polish and French, but also in Yiddish, perhaps only a few words. In her entire journal, it was the only reference she made to Yiddish. Two years later, Alicja helped her grandmother—Hortensja Lewental's mother—raise funds for a concert benefiting the Bersohn and Bauman Jewish children's hospital, and Alicja attended the concert with her extended Bersohn family as well as the son of her mother's close friend.[28]

Alicja's comments about Jews were almost always negative. Even as she lamented the stigma of Jewish identity, she absorbed cultural stereotypes and condescension toward traditional Jews. Her views were not a racial ideology, but rather a disdain for Jews who, she felt, lacked manners and cultural sophistication. "How wonderful is the type of Jew of Aron, noble, thrilling, or even an old debt collector! What a sympathetic figure, there are no longer such types today, there are not!" she wrote about the play *Żydzi,* by Józef Korzeniowski. The drama, which premiered in 1843, portrayed Jews, according to Michael Steinlauf, as "more honorable than the unscrupulous landowners they serve; the Polish landowners are more 'Jewish' than the real Jews." Only in the following years did Polish playwrights more frequently depict Jews as "agent[s] of corruption," a precursor to the stereotypes of Jews in Alicja's lifetime.[29]

In her disdain for traditional Jewish life, Alicja was, perhaps, influenced by her mother, who occasionally expressed similar contempt in letters she wrote to family members.[30] Alicja's comments about traditional Jews also echoed the works of Polish Positivist writers whose books her father published and which she read as she came of age. She mentioned reading Orzeszkowa's work *Meir Ezofowicz,* which was critical of traditional Jewish life, in the same entry in which she referred to her second cousin's embarrassing behavior one evening. She had been appalled, she wrote in an earlier entry, when he acted in a way that did need seem befitting of a Bersohn at a gathering at her aunt's home. "No, yesterday he behaved in such a way that there was not any difference between a Berson [Bersohn] and any of those little Jews who sat there!" she wrote about her cousin. "He laughed so loudly that he could be heard throughout the salon, he spoke loudly, drank terribly, clenched his hands with one of those little Jews"; here Alicja used the word *Żydek,* a diminutive of "Jew" in Polish that can be considered a derogatory term. In another entry, she described a man whom she considered to be unrefined at one of her social gatherings as a "typical Jew," while, after another ball, she referred to several men who danced elegantly even though they were Jewish. Her only somewhat positive evaluation of "Jewish characteristics" seemed to be her use of the term *żydowski łeb* [Jewish

"The Nighttime Butterfly" 125

brains] to describe a Jewish suitor whom she considered sharp-witted, though even then her perception of his "Jewishness" was ultimately negative. "Mr. Fajans came, whom I do not like," she recounted about one suitor, "even though he is very nice, polite and [has] so-called clever Jewish brains, always, constantly, he has something funny to say, some kind of trick with money or cards to show, he entertains both the company and himself." But his behavior, she continued, still "somehow reveals [that he is] a Jew right away."[31]

Above all, Alicja's uncertainty about the meaning of her Jewish background was intertwined with a social life that revolved around hopes for marriage. Among the acquaintances with whom she mingled at dances and balls were both Catholic young people and those from Jewish families. They mixed regularly at dances and salons to such an extent, according to her chronicle, that the presence of only one Jewish man at a ball one evening warranted a comment in her diary, while she was disappointed when she found herself at a gathering she referred to as "strictly Jewish," an experience she described only once in nearly seven years. At other times, she found herself in the opposite situation: attending gatherings where her feeling of otherness was heightened by the presence of few others of Jewish background. "If they assign me some Jew, then I will simply refuse," she wrote before one prospective social gathering, wondering with which man she would be paired. The dances she attended were often in the homes of other Jewish families and those who had converted, but she also recounted evenings spent in the salons of families without any apparent Jewish background.[32]

Among the female acquaintances Alicja mentioned most frequently, however, and among her mother's most intimate friends were individuals with the last names of prominent acculturated Jewish families and those who had converted in earlier generations. Social life was not limited to those circles, either in Alicja's own home or in the homes she visited, but at least for her mother, intimate friendships—Hortensja's closest friend and the families with whom the Lewentals vacationed—often were with other Jews while her children were growing up, though Hortensja also was close to both a Catholic woman who had tutored her in childhood and to Polish writers who were not Jewish.

Alicja, on the other hand, felt the absence of any close friendship whatsoever. Despite her busy social life, the limits of her acceptance beyond the world of her family's "Jewish circle" heightened her profound loneliness. "I wish that I could finally find a good friend, after so many years of searching, and I wish that it would be wonderful together, that we would be like [Franciszka] Perlmutter and Mamusia for our entire lives," Alicja wrote when she lamented the loneliness from which her diary provided a refuge. "Then, if this happened, a diary would not be necessary!"[33]

Even as Alicja's disillusionment and lamentations began to reach their height at the beginning of 1898, in the months after Ulanicki shied away from a proposal of marriage, she also expressed her strongest rebellion against the stigma she felt from her Jewish background. In February of that year, Ulanicki passed her in the street while riding in a carriage. It had been more than three months since the devastation of her deflated hopes for marriage to him. When he passed her on the street on that snowy morning, he turned away instead of greeting her. Writing in her diary that night, Alicja expressed not only the pain of rejection, but also—despite her absorption of negative perceptions about Jews—a refusal to succumb to the feeling of inferiority. "God, why am I disappointed in every person? God, why did he turn away? Is it because he can see a reproach in my

"The Nighttime Butterfly" 127

eyes, or anger, or regret? . . . No, he cannot look in this direction, he cannot even look at me because I turned away. . . . I will show him that although I am a Jew, I have my honor, not shame, and pride, which seethes!" she wrote. "I will turn away when he wants to pay his regards [literally, bow], and with my head raised I will not even glance at him."[34]

The pride that Alicja felt during those months, when she contemplated whether her Jewish background could be more than just a stigma to overcome, was short-lived. Shame soon overtook her once more. Later that year, several months after reading an announcement of Ulanicki's engagement to another woman in the newspaper her father published, she knelt in front of her bed and resolved to dedicate herself once more to daily prayer, this time reciting prayers to the Virgin Mary, a central figure in Polish Catholicism. But she lamented that she had decided to pray in her own home, where she would not feel the stares of acquaintances, as she had written in an earlier entry: "Today for the first time I woke up at 7 and recited all of the prayers to the Virgin Mary in front of my bed, whatever I know how to, I will do this daily, but it is not the same as in church, during the service. And I feel more and more excluded, more and more foreign among all of these Catholics! They must be so foreign to me when I draw myself to them, how I would give everything in the world to have belonged to them from birth!" Yet pride occasionally reemerged, however ambivalently. It was only four months later that she expressed pride in her father's last name after Kossak, the artist who toasted him, was "not ashamed to shake hands with a Jew publicly."[35]

Alicja's encounters with the feeling of being the "other" as a result of her Jewish background were mainly in the realm of private life, though influenced by the broader world of culture and politics. She referred only a handful of times in her diary to antisemitism in the public realm. In September 1899, in one of her shortest entries, she lamented the outcome of the second trial of Alfred Dreyfus, the French army officer who had been found guilty of allegedly passing French military secrets to the Germans. It was a false accusation of disloyalty that resonated for Alicja. The guilty verdict confirmed for some the sense that Jews would always be suspect in their loyalty to the country in which they lived, no matter how much they identified with it and despite the outcry from some French intellectuals about the trial's outcome. "So Dreyfus has been sentenced!" Alicja wrote in her diary. "And this is a civilized country, but not only a country and a civilization anymore, these are also people . . . this wild, bestial greed for blood, sick, these are people! . . . In small and large things, these are people!" Only a month earlier she had described the Hebrew inscription in a church in a small Swiss town as a remnant of the "times of religious tolerance." Those times, her comment seemed to indicate, were for Alicja in the past, not in her own lifetime.[36]

Alicja recognized that her alienation was rooted at least in part in her mother's hopes for acceptance by a Polish Catholic society that Alicja felt was rejecting her. Alicja occasionally lamented Hortensja's determination to break free of their "Jewish circle." More than a year after her mother's rejection of Kempner as a husband for her because he was "too Jewish," she was still lamenting Hortensja's decision, in the same entry in which she recounted praying to the Virgin Mary in front of her bed. "Why are my parents not content with the Jewish circle of our world?" she ruminated. As for herself, she wrote:

> I would certainly be happy with Kempner, I would not have higher, idealistic dreams! Because also among Catholics we are among the top tier, yet only for fun; when it comes to more serious thoughts or conversations, the entrance closes, and the church

shouts, "Stand there, this doorstep [threshold] is not for you!" I will not marry a Jew, I cannot because I am accustomed to something else, no Catholic will want me again, so I will be uprooted, an unneeded pawn! And then, when I do not want to look at Jews, and Catholics [do not want to look] at me, what will happen then? I will remain alone, completely alone among the entire human mass.[37]

Unlike for most Polish Jews at the time, who had limited contact with Polish culture and social circles, evolving ideas about Polish national belonging challenged Alicja's very sense of self as she came of age. The years when her youthful hopes for love, connection, and acceptance in Polish society turned to bitterness were a time when skepticism was growing about the possibility for Jewish belonging to the Polish national community. Those shifts reached beyond political rhetoric and newspaper polemics into the most intimate realms of everyday life.

5
"The Sword of Damocles"

Alicja Lewental inexplicably burst into tears. It was the middle of December in 1898, and after years of romantic disappointments, she had resigned herself to a Jewish husband, despite her mother's hopes that she would marry a Catholic man, and to a life without love.

The cause of her outburst that winter evening was a response to news that her mother's closest friend, Franciszka Perlmutter, had just shared over dinner in the Lewentals' home: she and her son would soon be baptized. The news caused Alicja such anguish that she could not maintain the mask of decorum that was expected in her social world of formal dinners and polite conversation. Her mother was outraged at her behavior. That night and the following one, Alicja filled page after page of her diary recounting her despair and the quarrel with her mother that ensued after the dinner.

The argument was the culmination of years of anguish. Alicja's religious affiliation seemed to rest on who her husband would be, even as she seemed uncertain about whether baptism and marriage to a Catholic man would remove the barriers to

"The Sword of Damocles"   131

acceptance. In the year and a half after her deflated hopes for engagement to Ulanicki in 1897, Alicja was forced to resolve her confusion. The path to baptism that she eventually undertook was not a straight one.

The argument with her mother in the waning days of 1898 came in the middle of that journey. But Hortensja would not abide the despair and pessimism that often plagued Alicja; her mother seemed not to understand it. Alicja turned, instead, to her diary. "Today I told Mamusia a lot, really a lot, and Mamusia could not understand me well about my outburst yesterday," she lamented. "Because I myself also did not understand in that moment! Why did I cry so? I do not know, I know only that this is not because of a change of religion or about her [Perlmutter] in general, this despair comes from some kind of feeling of vast misfortune falling on us and not on her!"[1]

Alicja herself had declared the previous year that she would not want to "die a Jew . . . for anything in the world," but in December 1898, the Perlmutters' impending conversion caused her days of emotional turmoil. It was not news of the baptism itself that so upset her, at least not according to her own understanding of the outburst. It was, instead, her fear of an ill-fated future, though she could not explain even to herself the reason for her sense of doom. Her anxieties over belonging, which were a constant undercurrent of her coming of age, seemed to boil over. "Some kind of apparition, a black cloud of misfortune, like the last glimpse of some past blissful moments, appeared before me in the moment of Mrs. Perlmutter's saying that right after the holidays she would be baptized with [her son] Edward," she wrote, "and I, like a crazy person, began to sob in despair, I thought that my soul would break, that something that was in my heart had died forever! And after all . . . I do not terribly love her, yet I do not know what recollections it connects to, enough that I bawled in terrible, boundless disappointment."[2]

Alicja's mother was furious at her lack of composure at dinner, and their argument over her behavior continued the following night. Afterward, Alicja confessed to her diary a feeling of trepidation, not for herself but for her parents:

> It seemed to me that some kind of thread of the past is rupturing and that this bright, radiant past has disappeared forever. ... And the future? And boundless despair, terrible despair took control of me at this thought, and it seemed to me that I am immediately losing some kind of last hope and that before my eyes I have a black chasm! And my soul took fright not for myself, but for ... my parents, ... so dear to me ... for whom I would make the greatest sacrifices in order to only see them young and cheerful. And since yesterday evening I have shivered out of fear for them; it constantly seems to me that some kind of inevitable misfortune, like the sword of Damocles, hangs over them, and I am so helpless! Why, why do I experience such a feeling?

Hortensja demanded that Alicja make a decision: "Mamusia asked me, so what exactly am I? A Jew or a Catholic by conviction? ... Mamusia has not been able to understand me for a long time, and nevertheless I have expressed myself clearly. Mamusia would convert today, she is a Catholic deep in her soul, out of conviction, she prays, believes in everything, in what religion tells you to believe, believes in the Christian religion, while I do not profess any religion, any, I do not believe in it, except that Christ exists and that prayer is the highest good in the world!" It was the starkest expression of Alicja's confusion over religious identity anywhere in her diary: "I am indifferent about whether I am a Jew or a Christian," she continued, "be-

"The Sword of Damocles" 133

cause I do not believe in religion; I do not believe in anything, in mass, communion, confession, in absolution, in religion in general; from religion I take only Christ as father, guardian."[3]

Alicja's mother was furious once more. Perhaps Hortensja's anger was motivated by her own Catholic faith, which, according to Alicja, was deeply held even though Hortensja did not "know how to pray," as Alicja had commented in an entry the previous year. But her mother's Catholicism was also inextricably tied to her desire for acceptance in Polish society, and she had her eyes turned to her family's future. Whether Alicja's father had his own strong opinions about his children's religious faith and about whether a Jewish husband would be acceptable for his eldest daughter is not entirely clear. Just a few years later, when Ferdynand Hoesick was courting Alicja's younger sister Zosia before their marriage in 1902, Salomon said he would agree to the match only if Hoesick, who was Protestant, converted to Catholicism. But in 1898, Salomon was still a member of the Jewish communal leadership, and Alicja made no mention of her father's views about whether she should marry a Jewish or Catholic man.[4]

After days of discussions and arguments after the dinner with the Perlmutters, Hortensja insisted that Alicja take down the image of Jesus and the wooden cross that hung above her bed since, her mother told her, praying to Jesus was a profanation if she did not proclaim herself to be Christian. Alicja was devastated. Only months earlier, her home had been a refuge where she could pray because she felt uncomfortable at church, where, she indicated, she sat in a pew behind her friend since she was not "Catholic by birth." Now, even within her own home, she felt rejected as a result of her confusion over religious identity.[5]

What, exactly, caused Alicja to feel such dread for her parents was unclear even to her. Perhaps she viewed her own disappointments over belonging and marriage to a Catholic man as a barometer of her parents' fate and place in Polish society. The conversion of friends and family members had long evoked conflicting reactions in Alicja. Her views of others' baptisms were at times ambivalent, often ambiguous, and sometimes positive. Two days after the argument with her mother, she expressed sympathy for her cousin when he begged his parents and grandparents for permission to convert for professional reasons. And after dancing with an uncle, Alicja commented about him in her diary, "He is charming, merry, talkative, and no one would be able to tell that several years ago he was still a Jew."[6]

But Alicja viewed the conversion of Franciszka Perlmutter and her son as marking a significant transformation for them, one she considered regrettable. Days before the baptism, she wrote about Edward Perlmutter, with whom she was close, "In February, he will already be a Catholic! What a terrible shame! Ach, how much I regret this; I regret this!" The day after the ceremony, she lamented their conversions once more: "Yesterday was his [Edward's] baptism and Mrs. Perlmutter's! Just a week ago, at Stefan's [Alicja's brother's] birthday, he [Edward] was still a Jew, and he sat with us from two to four, and today he is already a Catholic, and we are separated in our entire views of the world!"[7]

Alicja's ambivalent view of baptism, both her own and the conversion of friends and family, was perhaps the greatest indication of the ambiguity of her Jewish background in her sense of belonging. She wavered in her Catholic faith at times, but never did she express Jewishness as a religious identity. Being Catholic or Jewish seemed at times to be a matter of official recognition connected with marriage, not of faith. She sometimes appeared to reject the possibility of her own baptism entirely, while at other times she embraced it, even as she lamented that conversion would still not lead to acceptance of her Catholic identity by others. After her mother rejected Kempner

"The Sword of Damocles"   135

and Alicja expected to be engaged to Ulanicki, she wrote again, "I cannot, I, baptized, throw myself into this great Catholic family, I fear it terribly, and yet, will [his family] accept me only halfway?" Months later, she confided to her diary about her first, unrequited, love, the second cousin whose behavior had been so embarrassing to her, in an entry that is ambiguous about her feelings toward baptism: "I did not want to change religion, I admit that I did not want to! . . . I loved a Jew, Edward! . . . And I would have remained a Jew, although in my heart I was a Catholic, I would have remained a Jew for him! Yet, evidently it is better how it turned out, and I will have him [Ulanicki], and religion, and God!"[8]

In the six months before her outburst that evening over the Perlmutters' impending baptism and the ensuing argument with her mother, Alicja grappled with her hopes for her future in the midst of political tensions in the Polish lands. As her parents began to search for a husband beyond their Warsaw circles following her stymied hopes for engagement to Ulanicki, her attention occasionally turned to politics. The political events that Alicja recounted were not about the so-called "Jewish question"; when she referred to political issues in her diary, her emphasis was usually on tensions between Polish nationalists and the Russian authorities. It was the summer of 1898, the centennial of the Polish poet Adam Mickiewicz's birth, and erecting monuments in his honor became a symbol of the desire for Polish independence, memorializing him as the "incarnation of the collectivity's aspirations." As usual in the partitioned Polish lands, culture and politics were intertwined. Polish culture and language were a symbol of aspirations for independence in the absence of a political state, and Mickiewicz was the bard of Polish patriotism. In poems and plays written in the first half of the nineteenth century, he dramatized Polish resistance to

Russian rule, creating characters that became part of the lore—including a Jewish tavern keeper, Jankiel, who assisted the rebels in 1830–31 and became a symbol of the patriotic Jew. Alicja's father was drawn into the Mickiewicz celebrations, helping to fund a statue of the poet that was erected in Warsaw later that year.[9]

Alicja and her family embraced the excitement of the patriotic demonstrations. At the end of June they traveled to Krakow, part of Galicia in the Austro-Hungarian Empire, for the unveiling of the city's Mickiewicz statue, which had been planned for two decades. In Krakow, with its royal route and Renaissance Hall dominating its central square, Polish political life was freer than in the Russian Empire. Decades earlier, the Austrian rulers had granted the Poles a degree of political autonomy, and Polish cultural expression in literature, newspapers, and education was allowed space to develop. Nor had the pogroms that plagued Jews in the Russian Empire in the early 1880s spread to the Austro-Hungarian Empire. But by the late 1890s, all was not well for Jews in Galicia. Just weeks before the Lewentals arrived in Krakow in 1898, anti-Jewish violence had spread through the Galician countryside, where strained relations between Catholic peasants and small-town Jews had been festering for years. The violence had begun during Mickiewicz celebrations in the small town of Kalwarya Zebrzydowska and had spread to more than four hundred towns and villages, nearly all of them in western Galicia, the region around Krakow. Fueled by antisemitic rhetoric in newspapers and from the newly formed Polish Peasant Party, rioters attacked Jewish-owned taverns, damaged homes and businesses, and plundered property. The authorities declared a state of emergency. Alicja arrived in the city with her parents only days after the pogroms had ceased, but she did not mention the violence in her diary.[10]

"The Sword of Damocles" 137

Alicja's entries from those days in Krakow focused on the celebrations surrounding the Mickiewicz monument and the feelings of Polish patriotism they evoked in her. An atmosphere of excitement pervaded the city. She was moved by the speeches, the proud singing of one of the most prominent Polish nationalist songs to the accompaniment of a large orchestra, and the crowds in front of Wawel Castle, the fourteenth-century bastion of long-ago coronations and the burial site of Polish kings. Wreaths decorated in gold and silver were laid at the foot of the castle for the celebrations. "The entire Market Square, all of the streets, echoed with the powerful melodies, the old Town Hall, the Cloth Hall [Sukiennice] repeated them, even the wide-open St. Mary's Church seemed to breathe these beseeching songs, maybe the Lord God pities the nation?" she wrote. "And it seemed then that all of Krakow wept, the Market Square and the Town Hall and the Cloth Hall with a groan of despair, and only St. Mary's Church stood calm, cheerful, unmoved. . . . Is this indifference on His [God's] part, or is it strong faith in a better future?"[11]

Alicja noted that among those who marched in the parade there were students from all of Krakow's high schools, university students and their professors, peasants from agricultural schools in the surrounding countryside, and aristocratic personages. Among those she listed, too, were representatives of the Jewish community, a fact that did not warrant further comment from her. In the evenings she attended performances of Mickiewicz's plays with her family and gathered for a private literary evening where writers read patriotic verses, an event to which her family would have gained entry through her father's connections with the literary world or through her mother's eminence as a salon hostess.[12]

Just after the Lewentals' visit to Krakow, the struggle over Alicja's religious identity and its influence on her marriage prospects came to a head. Her parents unexpectedly informed her that they would be traveling to Vienna before their summer vacation in the Polish mountains. For a historian looking back at that time, Vienna is a notable setting for the events that ensued there between Alicja and her parents. The year before the Lewentals' visit, the politician Karl Lueger, whose party espoused antisemitism as an element of its political agenda, became Vienna's mayor, the beginning of a thirteen-year stint at the city's helm. Alicja did not mention the politics of Vienna in her diary, however. She was always an avid reader during her travels, immersing herself in books and newspapers in German, French, or English that she found in the reading rooms of the hotels in which she stayed with her family, so she might have been aware of debates about the "Jewish issue" that pervaded politics in Vienna. Still, she was focused on her personal travails. She wondered why her parents had taken such a fancy apartment with a drawing room in the luxurious Grand Hotel, a sought-after spot known for its aristocratic guests. Alicja spent her first morning there writing in her diary about the events in Krakow as her parents and sister Marta slept.

At dinner with her parents, the reason for the trip became clear: the Lewentals had come to Vienna so that Alicja could meet a possible suitor. After the romantic failures of recent years, Alicja had already agreed to allow her parents to search for a husband for her. Now, in the hotel dining room, they asked her what kind of husband she would accept. They inquired whether wealth and attractive looks were important and whether she would be willing to live in Galicia. They also sought an answer to a more consequential question: did she want to marry a Catholic or a Jew?

Alicja said she would agree to whomever her parents chose for her, she later recorded in her diary, "whether handsome or ugly." She did not note down, however, how she had responded

"The Sword of Damocles" 139

when asked about whether she wanted a Catholic or Jewish man for a husband. The question her parents posed forced her to confront the internal struggle with which she had been grappling for years. She had recently expressed in her diary that she would be content with a Jewish husband after her disappointments over rejections by Catholic men; perhaps she expressed this to her parents, because they began to search for a Jewish man of wealth and status suitable to their own position. Later she understood why they wanted to know whether she would be willing to leave Warsaw for Galicia: "[My] parents are searching for a husband for me, a Jew, wealthy, with status, if possible a landowner; it is not possible to find such a one in the [Polish] Kingdom because there are not any, so they are searching in Galicia."[13]

Alicja's parents seemed to have anticipated her response, since her suitor in Vienna, a man by the name of Józef Thon, was just such a candidate. He was from Galicia and owned land in a village outside of L'viv, and his name, she wrote, "is known in all of Galicia"; his father had received the Imperial Austrian Order of Franz Joseph I, she noted, a recognition of his military service. Every day during the family's stay in Vienna, Thon had extravagant bouquets of flowers delivered to her hotel room, and she spent her days deep in conversation with him over meals and formal teas. Her parents invited him to Zakopane, where the family was headed after the visit to Vienna. Over the next few months, during the family's summer vacation in the Polish mountain resort amid the artists and writers who sojourned there, Alicja was introduced to other Jewish candidates for a husband as well.[14]

At the end of the summer the Lewentals returned to Warsaw, where Alicja resumed her busy social life of balls, dinners, and salon gatherings. The match with Thon did not work out, and a man named Rozensztok began helping her parents in

140 "The Sword of Damocles"

their search for other Jewish suitors. She dutifully met the men they arranged for her, recording in her diary their conversations, both dull and enjoyable; the waltzes they danced together; and the elegant gowns she wore when she sat with them in the drawing room of her family's apartment. By the end of the year, Alicja came to terms with what seemed to be her fate: marriage to a Jewish man. She wrote:

> But it is my destiny not to have a Catholic for a husband, or even a sympathetic person. Mr. Rozensztok is already trying for a new candidate who apparently is supposed to come here soon. I am curious about what he looks like. Admittedly I would prefer someone thin, a tall brunette, with a face tanned by the wind and with some kind of nice first name and at the same time that he be a little more educated than Mr. T[hon], [that he] speaks French or English fluently like I do, in order to be able to speak with him in these languages because I am so used to the influence of foreign languages that I would not be able to do without speaking foreign languages. But it is not possible for me to always have the dreamed-of ideal.[15]

It was just over two weeks later, in the middle of December 1898, when Alicja burst into tears during dinner with her mother's friend and wrote in her diary with trepidation about the "sword of Damocles" that she felt was hanging over her parents.

As Christmas approached in 1898, Alicja's fears came from a different direction: fears for her city. As she agonized over her personal struggles and her family's future, the "sword of Damocles" seemed, for her, to hang over the fate of Warsaw as well,

"The Sword of Damocles" 141

as political tensions between Poles and the Russian authorities escalated. A sense of dread enveloped her. A Polish patriotic demonstration was being planned just before the unveiling of the Mickiewicz monument in Warsaw, and she did not expect it to be a peaceful event. Bringing Polish national expression into the public sphere was riskier in the Polish lands of the Russian Empire than in Galicia. Political demonstrations in Warsaw risked setting off a confrontation with the tsarist authorities.[16]

Alicja's feelings about the event brought together all three identifications that shaped her life: Polish, Jewish, and Catholic. The night before the unveiling of the Mickiewicz monument, which was to take place on the day before Christmas, she prayed to God for mercy toward the demonstrators and to protect them from violence, portraying Poland in her diary as a nation of martyrs and echoing the Polish view of the country as the "Christ of nations," eternally suffering from persecution. Above all, she was moved by the assertion of Polish patriotism. But she also worried that the political demonstrations would lead to violence against Jews. Alicja had been born two years before the Christmas Day pogrom in Warsaw in 1881, and she must have grown up with an awareness of a pogrom in the very city where she lived, one that had affected members of her extended family; during the pogrom, her uncle, Aleksander Kraushar, had seen his belongings ransacked. In a diary entry that went on for pages, however, she wrote only one sentence about her fear of violence against Jews; it was her Polish patriotism that predominated.

The night before the unveiling of Warsaw's Mickiewicz monument, Alicja wrote:

How terribly I fear the night today and the day tomorrow, the day of the unveiling of the monument!

Today at 10 there was a [prayer] service at the Parish Church ... yet it was very peaceful, and there were even relatively few people. The army was there the entire day with music and drums in order to show the population that it is ready for the slightest disorder. ... I worry about antisemitic, socialist unrest, as [is] usual in such situations, even more so because apparently [Ignacy] Daszyński has arrived. ... There will be no speeches, even a nice speech by Sienkiewicz and a beautiful poem by Konopnicka, for music, only a song by Moniuszko and Müncheimer's "Cantata" will be played, and the bishop will sprinkle [holy water] on the monument. A sad celebration, in a sad city in bondage, so there are tears in my eyes, so the heart aches, the manacles seem to rattle somewhere.[17]

Alicja wondered whether it might be better to hold the unveiling without the public demonstrations and patriotic songs, in a somber mood that she felt would be more appropriate to the continued oppression of Poles by the Russian authorities. It was, after all, an unhappy occasion when Russian soldiers on the streets symbolized the absence of Polish independence, she wrote: "Until now I did not feel this heavy weight of the lack of freedom, yet in this moment, in the moment when the entire soul is hungry for a fatherland and freedom and for one's own flag, [it is] terribly difficult, and the manacles are terribly painful!" She continued with a sentiment that expressed an ancestral connection to Poland: "Today I know that because I am a Pole, tomorrow is going to be painful for me, suffering, despair, and yet God sees and has no mercy on us, so apparently the sins of our forefathers have not been erased properly. [...] Tomorrow is Christmas, the day on which Christ came

"The Sword of Damocles"   143

down to the earth in order to expiate the sins of people, only were our sins so heavy that it was not possible to expiate them?"[18]

In the end, the demonstrations did not lead to violence, though when the Russians insisted that "God Save the Tsar" be played at the ceremony, the monument's planners canceled the planned speeches to prevent the hymn from being played, and the ceremony lasted for only fifteen minutes. Private celebrations of Mickiewicz continued that evening in the home of a family whose social gatherings the Lewentals often attended. More than 150 people gathered into the early morning hours, among them luminaries of Polish culture. Alicja was in attendance, too, listening as the host recited verses by Mickiewicz and a guest played nocturnes by Chopin on the piano. At dinner she sat near the famed writer Henryk Sienkiewicz, and nearby were other writers. She could more than hold her own in literary discussions, and she would have been able to converse with them about their own books and other literature.[19]

Months after the political events in Warsaw, a different suitor emerged as a marriage prospect, a man named Edward Fajans, from a prominent Jewish family in Warsaw that was in the shipping business. Alicja's first impression of him was negative—his behavior "somehow reveals a Jew," even though she found him to be clever and entertaining—but she soon warmed to him. He is "exceptionally intelligent and speaks wonderfully," she wrote, "wealthy and handsome and has property and status in Warsaw." As Easter approached, she prayed for the match to be successful: "Yesterday evening for the first time in a month I prayed wholeheartedly! For the first time . . . I, who was already almost converted and was just rejected by a Catholic, I let myself get lost so deeply that not even one ray of God's grace reaches there. . . . But yesterday I actually prayed wholeheartedly, maybe the Lord God will listen to me, and I want this so much! . . . There is really nothing Jewish in [Fajans], he is so well raised!" When her mother initially gave tentative approval to the match, Alicja was enthusiastic about an impending engagement. But her youthful passion, the emotional highs and fears of heartbreak during her earlier romances, were gone. "It is possible," she wrote about Fajans several months later, "to live without love."[20]

With her expected engagement approaching, Alicja again prepared to end her diary. But now her mother hesitated. Alicja was sympathetic to her: she understood that marriage to a Jewish man with the last name Fajans was a disappointment to Hortensja. Within weeks, Alicja's fate was decided once more: Fajans was "too Jewish" for the Lewentals. "Mamusia considers him too much of a Jew, accustomed to life in a different milieu from ours and also to a different society," she recounted. By the end of 1899, her mother decided herself how to resolve the question she and Salomon had posed to Alicja the previous summer in Vienna: did she want to marry a Jewish or a Catholic man? "Mamusia, speaking today with Marta, said that she would like Catholics for us both," Alicja wrote in her diary after her younger sister recounted a conversation to her. Their father, it seems, went along with his wife's decision. Alicja resigned herself to what awaited her.[21]

The pressure Alicja felt because of her mother's aspirations, despite her own resignation about marrying a Jewish man, only led to the pain of rejection by Catholic men whom her mother wanted as a husband for her, she lamented. Her love of literature and music made it possible for her to converse with men of culture, but while she reveled in these conversations, they were not what made her desirable as a marriage prospect, she understood. Marriage between Jewish women and Catholic men, she came to believe, was transactional. "I do not understand how Tonia can refuse [Ludwik] Gorecki," she commented after

"The Sword of Damocles"   145

an acquaintance from a Jewish family had rejected a marriage proposal from a grandson of Mickiewicz, "even knowing that he is not very intelligent and that he wants to come into three million." She continued:

> On these occasions, after all, she should seize the opportunity because she will not have a similar one a second time in her life, in order to be able to immediately go from a Jewish family into such a Catholic one, and with such a last name, to see that in Warsaw this last name opens doors for her even to the aristocracy and not to want him, it must be either that she really is madly in love with someone else or . . . does not have sense in her head. We, wealthy Jewish women, do not need to search for a man with money but with a name, and if she has such an opportunity and does not take it, she is really doing something stupid. I know that if it came to me, I would not hesitate for one minute because if I found a Catholic, and if, in addition, a grandson of Mickiewicz would want us, you would have to hold onto him with all your might [literally, with one's arms and legs].[22]

Alicja's fateful engagement to another Catholic man, with the last name of Zaleski, was settled just two months after Hortensja decided that her daughters must marry Catholic men. Alicja confided few details about their courtship in her diary. Whether she felt a spark of passion, what kind of personality he had, or if she enjoyed his company—her innermost feelings about him did not find their way to the pages of her journal. She soon began preparations for her baptism. The wedding date was set for June 1900, shortly after her planned conversion.[23]

146 "The Sword of Damocles"

Alicja stopped writing in her diary for almost two months. When she finally returned to the journal, she wrote that she was taking classes in religion and reading the New Testament. "On the first of June I will already belong to a different faith than my parents, my family, my entire past!" she continued. "I do not want to think about the past, I want to break entirely from it, so all the threads are already broken except for the threads of religion. So when all of the bridges are burned, when there is no longer anything that I can return to in this past, then I will begin a new life."[24]

Despite her prayers to God and Christ over the past four years of diary entries, Alicja viewed her baptism as a strictly official affair, a necessity for marriage to a Catholic man. But she worried that Zaleski had begun treating her coldly in front of other people and had stopped paying frequent visits to her home. She went ahead with plans for her baptism despite the uncertainty and despite her flagging faith in God. "For after all, if I convert, then it is only for him, not out of conviction, because the question of faith does not exist for me," she confided to her diary. "I simply do not see the point of faith because there are also misfortunes whether you believe or whether you do not believe, and I feel that later there is nothing, just like there is also only emptiness, black emptiness in life. . . . I do not even have the energy to pray, I did not have the energy to go to church this morning because I do not believe."[25]

On the day of her baptism, Alicja and her family left their home and made their way along the warren of narrow lanes in the city center to the Church of the Visitation of the Blessed Virgin Mary, with its Gothic style reconstructed from the fifteenth century. Despite her uncertainty over religious belief, Alicja later described her conversion in dramatic terms. After the baptism, she wrote, "For three days I have been a Christian, and it has made such a tremendous impression on me that for

"The Sword of Damocles" 147

three days something has made me breathless, and I want to howl in pain and sorrow. I do not know why and for what! Perhaps for my entire past, belonging now to legend." Describing the conversion ceremony, she recalled:

> On the day of my baptism, when I already stood in the church and the priest read the prayer and I felt him beside me, then tears poured from my eyes like a stream to my ears, and my lips trembled from sorrow. . . . And I lost my head and the power of my voice and the power of control over myself. I did not know anything of what was happening around me, I was completely stupefied, and today, after so many days, I do not feel as calm as I should feel after completing this act, but I have such a tremendous river of tears in my soul and heart that I am veiled by all of these tears.[26]

The concrete impact of Alicja's conversion in her daily life beyond marriage to a Catholic man is unclear. After her baptism, she would have been able to take part in Catholic Church rituals that she might otherwise not have been allowed to do, such as receiving communion. She did not change her first name, as her father did when he was baptized two years later, and she already attended church regularly. Yet baptism was for Alicja the "most important act of my life," she asserted afterward, despite her flagging faith: "I would give several years of life in order to be able to believe again like long ago when I was a child, or after all like he [Zaleski] believes! And I cannot."[27]

The wedding to Zaleski was to take place less than a week later. But two days beforehand, their engagement was broken off. There had been a conflict between him and Alicja's parents, and Alicja vaguely mentioned a dispute over money. She was

148   "The Sword of Damocles"

devastated once more. "I truly can neither write, nor speak, nor pray any longer," she lamented to her diary that night. "And why, why for this entire week after the baptism, [must I] suffer like a reprobate, when it really is the Lord God who should have mercy on me! And still, as in the past when I was a Jew, God does not hear my entreaties, my wails of pain, so how am I supposed to believe that He exists?" The following month Alicja confided in her diary about Zaleski's reported comments that he had been "engaged to a woman from a different race than mine."[28]

The inescapable stigma of her Jewish background left Alicja adrift, caught between the Jewish circles that her mother wanted her family to leave behind and the Polish Catholic world in which she felt like an outsider. Alicja's parents and their friends who sought to escape from their "Jewish world" were an inverse of a subculture, with very different results, among German Jews who perceived themselves to be fully accepted as German but remained primarily connected with other Jews. Members of that subculture shared feelings of "indignity and frustration," and solidarity due to partial integration, David Sorkin wrote. If the subculture in Germany was visible to everyone but German Jews themselves, as Sorkin argued, Alicja, at least, was far from ignorant of the barriers that separated her parents' Jewish circles from the Polish Catholic society from which they sought acceptance. She was an "insider-outsider," growing up at the center of Polish literary and social life even as she felt isolated within that world. Her experiences on the margins of Polish Jewish life were more typical of the lives of Jews in Vienna and Prague, where emancipation and integration had proceeded apace in the decades before her birth.[29]

Alicja's fractured sense of self was a twist on the lament that Franz Kafka, born in Prague four years after her, would

"The Sword of Damocles" 149

write in a never-sent letter to his father twenty years after Hortensja Lewental's decision about her daughters' marriages, with echoes of the unmooring and anguish that thread through Alicja's diary. Like Alicja, Kafka grew up in an integrated Jewish family, although unlike her family's background, he was the grandson of a kosher butcher and great-grandson of a rabbi. "And there was still enough Jewishness for you," Kafka would write to his father in 1919, "but as a hand-me-down it didn't serve the child—it all vanished as you tried to pass it on. And it was impossible to grasp, for a very fearful and very observant child, how the few nothings that you held on to in the name of Judaism could produce more than nothing in the face of your own indifference."[30]

Hortensja's distance from Judaism and Jewish culture was far more complete than it was for Kafka's father, to be sure. She did not seek to retain any scraps of Jewishness beyond her family's charitable role in Jewish institutions. Nor did she want to pass those remnants on to Alicja and her siblings; she aspired to just the opposite. Alicja's life, too, differed from Kafka's path. Like her mother, she was sharply critical of traditional Jewish life; Kafka, on the other hand, was fascinated by Yiddish theater, expressing interest in the language and in the East European Jews who spoke it. Yet the alienation that Kafka described to his father echoed Alicja's experiences. All that her parents left her was the feeling of being an outsider.[31]

After her baptism and broken-off engagement, Alicja began a courtship with Zygmunt Miński, a man who fulfilled her parents' ideal: he was a Catholic suitor who lived in a manor house in the Polish countryside, the symbol of an aristocratic heritage. He was an agronomist, an engineer who studied agriculture and crops—different from the men of letters with whom she had engaged in passionate conversations about poetry and

150 "The Sword of Damocles"

literature over the years. Miński was a quiet man, and Alicja often found herself bored by their conversations. But he was kind and well respected, and although he lived outside of Warsaw, he had been courting Alicja for years during visits to the city, dancing with her at balls and other gatherings. It was said in Warsaw that he was in love with her.[32]

By the end of 1900, Alicja's engagement to Miński was being finalized. Her father met with his family, and Alicja was introduced to his mother at a lunch in the Lewental home where a priest joined them. The preparations took place at a tumultuous time for the Lewental family. Political repressions against Polish culture were reaching into their home, and Alicja was worried about her parents. A year and a half earlier, as her hopes for engagement to Edward Fajans were dashed, her father had been arrested and briefly imprisoned by the Russian authorities over the politics of the newspaper he co-owned, *Kurjer Warszawski*. Unlike some of his predecessors among Jewish publishers in the Polish book trade, Salomon had never been particularly active in politics. He expressed his patriotism, he wrote late in life, through his dedication to Polish culture. But *Kurjer Warszawski's* editor, Franciszek Nowodworski, approached his role with a political bent. He was becoming an activist for the right-wing National Democracy camp, known as the Endecja, which had been established the same year as Nowodworski had ascended to *Kurjer Warszawski's* editorship in 1897, but the Endecja had its origins in a clandestine group called the National League, founded four years earlier. Nowodworski initially enjoyed the trust of both Polish cultural circles and the Russian authorities when he was appointed the paper's editor. But *Kurjer Warszawski* was becoming increasingly political under his editorship and was popularizing the ideology of the National Democrats.[33]

In 1899, the year before Alicja's engagement to Miński, Nowodworski angered the Russian authorities with the news-

"The Sword of Damocles"   151

paper's content and was arrested. Salomon Lewental showed no sign of embracing the National Democrats' politics, but the editor's detainment drew Salomon into political intrigues. He could not steer clear of the political implications of a publisher's role as a mediator of Polish culture. When the authorities accused Salomon of defying a government order related to the conflict with Nowodworski, he, too, was arrested.

Eliza Orzeszkowa received a letter from a good friend informing her of Salomon's arrest, and she was distressed by the news. Publishers and writers were part of a literary community for which the arrest of a prominent figure in that world was in some ways an attack on all of them. At first Orzeszkowa could not believe that Salomon had been detained. Over the years, she had developed a warm bond with Hortensja, and she worried about the impact of the arrest on his family. Orzeszkowa was concerned, too, that imprisonment could endanger Salomon's already poor health. She was relieved when she soon received word that he had been released from prison several days later.[34]

The authorities' suspicions of Salomon did not let up in 1899. They would not issue him a passport to go abroad or to the countryside, and the restrictions were affecting his publishing business, for which he often traveled throughout Europe. As Alicja recounted in her diary, Salomon seemed to be largely confined to their home, whether by order or by idleness as a result of restrictions on his publishing activities. Hortensja and her close friend, Franciszka Perlmutter, traveled by train to St. Petersburg, where they appealed to the tsarist authorities to rescind the travel ban, a trip that in the end was successful. The incident made clear that Salomon's role as a publisher inevitably brought politics into his family's life. The Lewental children grew up in a home imbued with the politics of culture in the partitioned Polish lands.[35]

Now, in the midst of preparations for Alicja's wedding to Miński at the end of 1900, the Lewental family was once more drawn into politics. Nowodworski was sentenced to exile in Odessa even though he had already been removed as editor of *Kurjer Warszawski*, and Salomon was forced by government order to leave the Polish lands for Odessa as well, far from Polish nationalist circles in Warsaw. Alicja and her mother accompanied him for ten days, bidding farewell to the other Lewental siblings and family friends as they boarded the train at the Warsaw station. The morning of their departure from Warsaw, Alicja and her fiancé went to church, and they silently exchanged engagement rings that afternoon as they sat in the library of her family's home. Miński joined the group that saw the Lewentals off.[36]

During their first days in Odessa, Alicja and her parents wandered through the city with Nowodworski and his wife, visiting the busy port and the theater. It was a grand city, influenced by a cosmopolitan culture with roots far beyond the Russian Empire, a culture brought there by merchants from throughout Europe who were drawn to the Black Sea port with its international shipping trade. Alicja took pleasure in the eclectic architecture and bustling streets. But she nevertheless disliked Odessa, she wrote, because of what she described as its Russian character.[37]

Throughout the time that she and her mother spent with Salomon in Odessa, Alicja waited anxiously for letters from her new fiancé. Perhaps she was fearful that she would once again be disappointed in her hopes for marriage. Surely Alicja must have been jealous of her younger sister Marta who had been a rival for romantic prospects; earlier that year Marta had been the first Lewental sister to marry. It was only because of Alicja's broken engagement to Zaleski that Marta ended up being wed before her, to a man who fit their parents' wishes exactly: a

"The Sword of Damocles" 153

Catholic, from a noble family, with a last name ending in "-ski." Alicja wrote in her diary with pride that her own fiancé's father and sisters, as well as her sister Marta's new husband, were traveling on foot to the Polish city of Częstochowa, the traditional annual pilgrimage of Polish Catholics to a shrine to the Virgin Mary in a fourteenth-century monastery. "The Lewentals can be proud of both of their sons-in-law because one went there himself, and the father of the second is making the pilgrimage," Alicja wrote.[38]

In Odessa the Lewentals bought a wedding ring for Miński, made of thick gold with a ruby and two diamonds. Salomon was anxious about staying in Odessa on his own, but he soon became accustomed to the city, and after ten days, Alicja and her mother returned to Warsaw without him. Miński stood once more with Alicja's relatives and family friends on the train platform as they waited for their return.

Alicja and Miński were soon married in a small ceremony in a Polish church in Vienna. They took the train back to the Polish lands that same evening. Alicja seems to have stopped writing in her diary before her marriage, as custom dictated, and she left no description of the ceremony. In the wedding announcement that the new couple's parents sent to friends and colleagues, the Lewentals noted that Miński was the "owner of a manor house in Jeżewice," surely an expression of pride in the aristocratic heritage that such a home symbolized, as they had done in the announcement of Marta's wedding the previous year.[39]

Soon after the wedding, Alicja and her new husband traveled to Miński's family estate in Jeżewice, twenty-five miles from Warsaw, embarking on the life her mother had imagined for her. In the papers she kept with her were receipts for the furniture her parents had bought for the new couple and for a diamond ring purchased by her father four months before her

154 "The Sword of Damocles"

earlier engagement had abruptly been broken off. Among the papers, too, was the diary of her young womanhood—a record of the difficult path she had taken there.

The announcement of Alicja and Miński's wedding would have drawn the attention of friends and family not only because Alicja's romantic woes in recent years had been the subject of gossip in Warsaw. In the announcement, recipients would have noted, her father signed off not with the first name of Salomon, but with Franciszek Salezy, the name of a Polish bishop and Catholic saint of the sixteenth and seventeenth centuries. The change in his first name heralded a momentous event in the family's life: Alicja's parents had been baptized. The "principles of humanism"—the words Salomon had used when he had to cease publication of the journal *Kłosy* more than a decade earlier—had once made possible his dual identification as both Polish and Jewish, but now those principles, from the perspective of the end of his life path, looked to be increasingly a relic of a previous era.

Just months before the wedding in 1901, Alicja's parents had boarded a train to Rome, where they knelt in a pew at the Vatican and formally adopted the Catholic faith. It was rumored back in Warsaw that they had been blessed by the Pope himself. During the ceremony, Hortensja took the baptized name Maria, and Salomon became Franciszek Salezy. Hortensja had never had a "Jewish-sounding" first name—"Hortensja" means "hydrangea" in Polish, with roots in Greek—and she remained known that way until her death. But Salomon, the name of a biblical king in ancient Israel, had always announced his faith with his very signature. Now his baptismal name declared his departure from that identity.

Hortensja had adopted the Catholic faith long before her formal conversion, but what motivated Salomon to undertake

"The Sword of Damocles" 155

baptism is less clear. Only five years earlier, he was still attending synagogue on Yom Kippur, the holiest day in the Hebrew calendar. He was often sick in his final years. Months after his baptism, he penned the brief sketch of his life that set in sharp relief the ambiguities of his identity as a Polish publisher, as a former leader in Jewish institutions, and as a convert to Catholicism. The identity he described reflected a painting by the Polish Jewish artist Maurycy Gottlieb that Salomon had obtained for the family's private collection; it depicted Jesus in Jewish dress, "both a Jew and a universalist figure preaching brotherly love and toleration, Ezra Mendelsohn noted." Salomon wrote in his autobiographical sketch, "In all of my publishing work, the central idea is love for God and country. As a deeply believing and religious person, I tried to imbue my works with the stamp of faith, despite various criticisms and persecutions." He then described his leadership in Jewish institutions: as a member of the Jewish communal board in Warsaw and of the committee that had founded Warsaw's Great Synagogue, and as overseer of the Jewish hospital established by Hortensja's grandfather. At the end of his life, however, he noted, "[I] withdrew from all of my community honors and together with my family was christened—this was a need of my soul."[40]

In September 1902, Salomon died of a heart attack while convalescing with Hortensja in the German spa town of Wiesbaden, the German emperor's summer retreat, where hot springs drew nobles from throughout Europe. He was sixty-one years old. Urgent telegrams from Wiesbaden would have carried the tragic news to his children and to the offices of *Kurjer Warszawski*, where a journalist wrote up the news of his death. Alicja and Zygmunt; Alicja's sister Zosia and her new husband, Ferdynand Hoesick, who had recently returned from their honeymoon; and Aleksander Kraushar traveled to Wiesbaden and then accompanied Salomon's body on the train back to

Warsaw with Hortensja. They arrived before dawn at the station, where family and friends met the mourners somberly. The next day, Kraushar helped to carry the coffin through the streets of Warsaw with journalists from *Kurjer Warszawski*, arriving at the Powązki cemetery, the Catholic burial ground of luminaries of Polish culture. Hundreds of mourners gathered for the funeral, and every major Polish newspaper in the city carried an announcement about Salomon's death. The news did not appear, however, in *Izraelita*, despite Salomon's long involvement in Jewish communal life before his baptism.[41]

Salomon had witnessed the marriages of three of his daughters to Catholic men by the time of his death. The year before Alicja's marriage, her younger sister Marta had wed Feliks Mrozowski, a law graduate of Warsaw University who managed his family's countryside estate. Alicja's sister Zosia had fallen in love with Hoesick, the journalist who had been awed years earlier by his first visit to the Lewental salon, but as a Protestant and the son of a Polish publisher of ethnic German background, Hoesick was not an ideal candidate for a son-in-law. If Salomon ever wavered about whether his daughters must marry Catholic men, he had come around to his wife's preferences by then; he insisted that Hoesick be baptized in the Catholic faith because both he and his wife "did not want to have a non-Catholic son-in-law," according to Hoesick. Once that was agreed on, Salomon was favorable to the match, Hoesick recalled, but, he wrote, "I had less of a chance with his wife, who was not free of vanity, having already two sons-in-law—noblemen from the countryside, Miński and Mrozowski, and she would not have anything against it if her third daughter also would marry a person with a Polish aristocratic last name with −ski." Hoesick agreed to be baptized as a Catholic, and Salomon telephoned the Lewentals' closest family—Hortensja's sister and brother-in-law, Jadwiga and Aleksander Kraushar, and her

"The Sword of Damocles"

Alicja and Zygmunt Miński, 1901–1902. Muzeum Warszawy, MD167/Fot.

parents, Mathias and Maria Bersohn—to invite them for champagne and a toast to the engagement.[42]

After Salomon's death, Alicja's youngest sister, Helena, also married a Catholic man with the Slavic last name that their mother desired, Bronisław Gubrynowicz, a historian of Polish literature whose father was one of the most prominent booksellers in L'viv. Their younger brother, Stefan, later married as well, but marriage did not offer him the same escape: he would always carry the last name of Lewental.

Two years after Salomon died, the ornate tombstone that was placed on his grave declared pride in his long career in publishing, his attachment to his city, and the Catholic faith he had adopted; the tombstone had a sculpture of an angel with its hands wrapped around a cross, designed by a prominent Polish artist, and an engraving that read "Franciszek Salezy

The daughters of Salomon and Hortensja Lewental and their husbands and son Stefan Lewental. Standing from left: Bronisław Gubrynowicz, Zygmunt Miński, Ferdynand Hoesick, Stefan Lewental, Feliks Mrozowski. Sitting from left: Helena Gubrynowicz, Alicja Mińska, Zosia Hoesick, Marta Mrozowska. Circa 1904. Muzeum Warszawy, MD173/Fot.

Lewental, citizen of Warsaw, editor, publisher." Nowhere did Salomon, the first name of his birth and the one by which he was known until the last months of his life, appear on the gravestone.

When Alicja's grandfather Mathias Bersohn died suddenly in 1908, Ferdynand Hoesick pasted the laudatory obituaries in the diary Hoesick kept of his own life. Bersohn was a symbol of the Jewish past and present, not only for his family,

"The Sword of Damocles" 159

but also for the Polish Catholic society from which the Bersohns had sought acceptance. In lauding Bersohn, one obituary referred to the changing times and the collapse of the "Polish Jewish friendship" of the 1860s with which Mathias Bersohn and Salomon Lewental had once cast their fate. Bersohn, noted the author of the obituary, "was one of the most popular figures in Warsaw. He did not seek renown, but recognition found him. It is a loss of a decent person, a loss all the more so that with his death there has almost disappeared this type of Polish Jew from the January times [of the 1863 uprising], meaning an ardent patriot and a righteous citizen of one's native land."[43]

Years later, Ferdynand and Zosia Hoesick's daughter, Joanna Hoesick-Podolska—Alicja's niece—ruminated on her father's pride in the heritage of the Lewental and Bersohn families into which he had married. Hoesick-Podolska also hinted at the complicated relationship of other family members to the Jewish identity of their patriarch. "My mother's grandfather [Bersohn] was an eminent individual of Warsaw, of which one should be proud," she wrote, "and not ashamed of him because he was a Jew, as was the case with more than one individual in the family."[44]

6

From a Manor House in the Countryside to Interwar Poland

Traces of Alicja's life after her marriage to Zygmunt Miński surface only occasionally in surviving archival documents: a few diary entries she wrote after their wedding; family letters, including several written by Alicja to her sister Zosia; postcards she wrote to her mother; and correspondence among her friends. What her path held in the forty-two years between her last diary entry in 1902 and her death in the final months of World War II remains partly obscured in the historical record. How she fared in the turmoil of World War I and its aftermath; in the charged political atmosphere of interwar Poland, when the "Jewish question" was a constant flashpoint in political debates; and during World War II, when the Nazis considered her Jewish by race no matter how she defined herself—these are topics for which a historian seeking to reconstruct Alicja's adult life can catch only glimpses.

What is clear is that by the end of the interwar years, Alicja, her sisters, and their children had fulfilled Hortensja's hopes that their marriages to men outside of their Jewish circles

From a Manor House to Interwar Poland

would achieve her aspirations to full absorption into Polish society among her descendants. The Lewentals, their extended family, and their friends continued along an opposite path from the ones embarked upon by others of Alicja's generation from Jewish families who embraced ideologies that sought to change what it meant to be Jewish and what it meant to belong to a country: the parties of Jewish nationalism, which considered Jews to be a nation above all; and radical politics, from the Bund to communism, which sought to change the very rules of belonging and rejected entirely the economic system that had made it possible for Alicja's parents and grandparents to rise to the heights of Polish society. As the Lewentals continued their role as mediators of Polish culture through their publishing activity even after Salomon's death, the newspaper they owned, *Kurjer Warszawski,* found itself drawn into the political strife over the "Jewish issue," which had so complicated Alicja Lewental's identity and aspirations for acceptance in her youth and young adulthood.

In Jeżewice, married to an agronomist, Alicja lived far from the cultural and social circles in which she had been immersed for years before her marriage. In the diary entries she wrote after her marriage, she sometimes lamented the loneliness of her new life. In June 1901, pregnant with her first child, she took out her journal for the first time in months. "Will I always be condemned to a solitary vigil at the fire of knowledge?" she wrote while at the estate in Jeżewice, after first writing a prayer to God to grant her wish to have a son. Nearly nine months passed before she recorded another entry. In March 1902 she took her infant son for a month-long visit to her family in Warsaw, where she passed the time reading books and praying in her childhood bedroom, as she had done for years before her marriage. With her father's health declining—he had had a heart attack a few weeks earlier—and her grandmother, Maria Bersohn, on her deathbed, Alicja felt the absence of a confidante, an echo of the lamentations that had filled her diary years earlier. Once more she found solace in writing. "I am beginning a regular diary because I cannot any longer!" she wrote, noting the strangeness of her return to the pages of her journal. In her diary and the books she read, Alicja found the comfort of intellectual stimulation and emotional connection. She wrote about the many books she was reading, reflecting upon *Wodzirej*, a collection of short stories by the Positivist writer Gabriela Zapolska, published six years earlier, first in installments in *Kurjer Warszawski*. Shortly afterward, she commented on the French book *La faute de l'abbé Mouret* by Émile Zola. The pairing of the two books might have indicated Alicja's awareness of Zola's influence on Zapolska, a reflection of her continued attention to the literary trends of the day.[1]

In Jeżewice Alicja took up charity work, establishing a nursery school for the children of farm workers. She still yearned for the contentment and feeling of belonging that had eluded her since childhood. She seemed to be at home nowhere: in Jeżewice she longed for Warsaw, and while in Warsaw, she ached for the quiet of the countryside. "Two days ago I was in the countryside, and I have complete nostalgia for this life in Jeżewice. . . . I ran to kneel in the bedroom before the Virgin Mary and the Lord Jesus, and I thank them that they allowed me happily to return! . . . I forgot about everything that was, about all of Warsaw, about my parents, the little one, friends, about everything and everyone, and I thought only about this blissful life in the countryside, the two of us!"[2]

Back in Jeżewice, Alicja sat down again with her journal and tried twice to put her thoughts to paper, but she never got beyond writing down the date. Only after her father died in 1902 did she return briefly to the pages of her childhood diary

From a Manor House to Interwar Poland 163

for solace. She was distraught. Her sorrow was perhaps so overwhelming that, for the first time since she had begun her chronicle nearly seven years earlier, she forgot to write the date. "Sometimes it seems to me that Daddy is somewhere abroad and that I must write him a letter, that I will still see him," she lamented. "And later I remind myself that he lies in a cold grave at Powązki [the Warsaw cemetery], by the church, under a thick cover of white snow. Terrible was the moment when they brought us the message from Wiesbaden that Daddy was no longer alive, all the more terrible that it was unexpected!" In the last entry of the last notebook of her journal in 1902, she wrote once more about her father: "On the 15th is Daddy's birthday. . . . And now this date is constantly without Father, and that is how it will be to the end of life."[3]

In the years after Salomon's death, the Lewental siblings were scattered across the Polish lands and across empires. Of the four daughters, only Marta remained in Warsaw, where her husband took on a leading role in *Kurjer Warszawski* while she wrote for the newspaper's section for children. Zosia and her husband, Ferdynand Hoesick, settled in Krakow, where they regularly hosted journalists and musicians in their spacious apartment. Ferdynand Hoesick set to work writing a biography of Poland's beloved Chopin, living for a time with Zosia in Paris, while penning articles about culture for *Kurjer Warszawski* and co-editing the newspaper. The youngest sister, Helena, took up her role as the wife of an esteemed professor in L'viv, while Alicja settled into a quiet life in the countryside with Zygmunt, raising their two sons. Stefan, the youngest Lewental sibling, had a reputation in his family as a dilettante before he married, racing cars and borrowing money from his sisters. Later, he traveled abroad to Paris, the United States, and elsewhere as the family's emissary for its publishing business. The sisters kept in touch by letter, and they sometimes vacationed

164 From a Manor House to Interwar Poland

together in the Polish mountains or abroad. In surviving letters to Zosia, Alicja wrote about her life in Jeżewice and visits to Warsaw; in recounting her trips to the city, only a handful of times did she mention encountering acquaintances from Jewish families who had populated her diary years earlier. Hortensja frequently visited her children. She wrote long letters updating them about one another's lives and about goings-on back in Warsaw: the baptisms and Catholic confirmation ceremonies of nieces and nephews, bouts of influenza, the sisters' trips abroad, and the increasingly frequent struggles with her own health as she advanced in years. Glimpses of Hortensja's disdainful view of Jews came through occasionally in her letters. In one letter to Zosia referring to a couple who came often to Zakopane, where Hortensja was vacationing, she wrote, "He is a typical Jew—she is ugly," using the often-derogatory word *żydek*. In another, she lamented that the only people joining her in 1908 to observe the anniversary of Salomon's death were "a handful of Jews."[4]

The decade after Alicja's marriage and her father's death was a time of political upheaval in the Russian Empire. In 1905, after Russian imperial forces opened fire on demonstrating workers in St. Petersburg and killed more than one hundred, strikes broke out throughout the Russian Empire, including in Warsaw. The tsar responded by making concessions to demands for democratic reforms by establishing an elected parliament, the Duma. In the Polish lands, nationalists prevailed in elections in 1906 and 1907 before the tsar pulled back on the democratizing reforms, restricting Duma elections to parties that supported the autocracy.[5]

Accompanying the political turmoil was a wave of pogroms that shocked Jews in the Russian Empire. Thousands of Jews were killed, and thousands more were injured in nearly 650 pogroms between 1903 and 1906, eclipsing the violence of

From a Manor House to Interwar Poland 165

1881–82. Jewish emigration from the Russian Empire, especially to the United States, accelerated. Polish nationalists' disappointment in the failure of the 1905 revolution, meanwhile, was followed by an increase in antisemitism in the following years, accompanying the influence of exclusionary ethnic nationalism in Polish politics. The right-wing nationalists—the National Democrats—were nascent. The politics of National Democracy were "at its intellectual roots and from the very beginning, pervasively antisemitic," and anti-Jewish views "remained the bonding element" among internal factions, especially after the 1905 revolution, according to historian Robert Blobaum. "Unfortunately for Poland's Jews, assimilated or not," Blobaum wrote, "it would be the Endecja [National Democracy] and its ideological and political leaders who would leave the more permanent mark on the question of who and what constituted the Polish nation, which was part and parcel of their solution to the problems arising out of rapidly accelerating social and economic change."[6]

The politics of nationalism increased among Jews, too, during the 1905 revolution and its aftermath. Zionist parties, which had been gaining adherents since the 1880s, developed mass followings as the tsar's reforms opened up a public sphere and participatory politics. The Bund came into its own as well. It organized workers' demonstrations in 1905 and led the way in establishing self-defense groups during the pogroms. Its founding goal was to spread Marxist ideology to the Jewish masses in Yiddish, yet even the Bund added a call for national-cultural autonomy to its demand for socialist revolution in its party platform that year.

For Poles and Jews alike, language was becoming even more central than before in drawing boundaries around the nation, though the association with Yiddish as the language of the Bund and Hebrew as an emphasis of Zionist parties was still

166 From a Manor House to Interwar Poland

fluid in those years. It was during the 1905 revolution and the two democratic parliamentary elections that followed that the divide hardened between Polish and Jewish, with national belonging rooted in language as well as in ethnicity—an "ethnolinguistic community." In the following years, "the possibility of fusing Jews and Poles into a harmonious synthesis was overwhelmingly rejected by Polish society," wrote the historian Theodore Weeks. "It was now necessary to choose, and if an individual born as a 'Jew' decided to choose a 'Polish' identity, this entailed a nearly total separation from the community of his or her birth."[7]

In the years after the failed 1905 revolution and its aftermath, meanwhile, Polish liberals increasingly moved away from supporting Jewish equality, even if they did not explicitly embrace racial definitions of "the Jew" and left open the possibility for converts such as the Lewentals to be accepted into the Polish nation, as some historians have argued. Liberalism had failed to address economic dislocations resulting from industrialization, leaving many Polish liberals aggrieved by their economic struggles, especially during the downturn in the first decade of the twentieth century. Between 1907 and 1912, a majority of the liberal Polish intelligentsia, which had been the Lewentals' social, cultural, and professional world for decades, abandoned its support for liberal values and, with it, its support for equal rights for Jews. Some of its members became a core constituency of the National Democrats, with its exclusionary Polish nationalism, following the 1905 revolution. It is notable that journalism—the profession of many of the men with whom Alicja Lewental interacted socially as a young woman, partly because of her father's involvement in newspaper publishing—was, together with politics, a main professional outlet for Warsaw's intelligentsia as its members left behind liberalism in the midst of frustrations with their increasingly restricted opportunities.[8]

From a Manor House to Interwar Poland 167

Newspapers, including *Kurjer Warszawski*, which the Lewental family still co-owned, found themselves at the center of Polish politics about the "Jewish question" in 1912 elections to the Russian Duma, as political parties argued vehemently over whether Jews should have equal rights in plans for municipal self-government in Warsaw. The only candidate who supported those rights, a representative of the Polish Socialist Party, prevailed in the election with the backing of Jewish electors, to the ire of Polish nationalists. Polish newspapers then launched a boycott of Jewish businesses, calling the winner a "Jewish envoy." A newspaper tied to forces supporting Roman Dmowski, the leader and co-founder of the right-wing National Democrats, was the first to call for a boycott during the election, and other right-wing nationalist newspapers followed suit. Roman Catholic clergy joined most of the Polish intelligentsia in declaring its support for the action.

Kurjer Warszawski, too, had to take a stand. Though it had helped to popularize the ideology of the National Democrats under Nowodworski's editorship at the end of the nineteenth century, it was known now as part of the liberal press—although Hortensja characterized the publication years later as the city's only "apolitical" newspaper—and in the 1912 election it joined with anti-Dmowski forces. The National Democrats singled out the newspaper as a lackey of Jews in a campaign pamphlet threatening a boycott of Jewish businesses: "Countrymen! We swear that if the Jews win the election, we will not buy anything from them! Vote for the list supporting Roman Dmowski. Down with *Kurjer Warszawski*, which serves Jewish interests!" But when the anti-Dmowski candidate also lost after refusing to support equal rights for Jews, most of the liberal press and liberal politicians fell in line with the anti-Jewish action.[9]

Kurjer Warszawski came down on the side of the boycott. The Russian authorities found the antisemitism of one article in

168 From a Manor House to Interwar Poland

the newspaper so extreme in the aftermath of the elections to the Duma that they fined its editors and Hortensja Lewental as its publisher. One reader wrote to *Kurjer Warszawski*'s editor decrying its reprint of an article from *Myśl Niepodległa*, an Endek newspaper known for its antisemitic views. "If Jews actually dominate the press and control [public] opinion with its assistance, this would prove only that Jews are exceptionally skilled and intelligent," the writer, Jerzy Baumberg, wrote with sarcasm. "You would certainly agree with me that in order to control the newspapers, enjoying the support of hundreds of thousands of subscribers, capital is not enough, but also a lot of intelligence." He ended the letter, which was never published, with direct reference to Hortensja's Jewish background: "The present co-publisher of *Kurjer Warszawski*, as well as her late husband, were Jews and were not baptized until long after buying *Kurjer Warszawski*," he wrote. "Obviously the background of the Lewentals changed this circumstance. And it proves again that Jews are unconditionally the most skilled at leading newspapers. It is only a wonder that Mrs. Lewental forgets so often about her background, or perhaps does not read *Kurjer Warszawski* at all."[10]

Warsaw's secondhand bookstores owned by Jews were ensnared in the boycott. Picketers outside of the bookshops on Świętokrzyska Street roughed up clients who defied the action. Extant sources do not indicate the extent to which the boycott affected shops selling new books. But the previous decades had already seen a dramatic decline in the role of Jews in the market in new Polish books, with ethnic Poles owning nearly two-thirds of newly opened bookstores between 1880 and the turn of the twentieth century. A similar decline did not occur in the secondhand book market, in which Jewish owners continued to play a dominant role through the interwar period.[11]

A year after the boycott began, when Hortensja's son-in-law Ferdynand Hoesick sought a buyer for his Warsaw

From a Manor House to Interwar Poland 169

bookstore—a prestigious bookshop opened by his father in 1865—Hortensja lamented to her daughter Zosia, who was married to Hoesick, that "it was sad that during the boycott, the only candidate for [buying] the bookstore was a Jew." Hoesick had taken over the Lewentals' publishing house upon Salomon's death (aside from *Kurjer Warszawski*), and he had continued its publishing activity on a limited scale, issuing a dozen books as well as sheet music. Whether Hortensja's concern was about the boycott's anticipated impact on a Jewish owner or an indication of her own distaste toward a Jew taking over the bookstore is unclear. Hoesick sold the bookstore established by his father to the man, a doctor named Stanisław Markusfeld. Two years later, Hoesick recounted in his diary an essay written by a university student mocking Hoesick's sale of the business to Markusfeld. The student's professor, a literary scholar, approached Hoesick to determine "whether Markusfeld was baptized or not" before submitting the essay, in the form of a Socratic dialogue, for publication. Hoesick recalled, "Well, I explained to [the literary scholar] that I myself do not know anything definite about this issue because if, as they categorically claim, Markusfeld, [is] as Stanisław I, the primate of the Hospital of Saint Lazar, he must certainly be baptized; others doubt it, but never mind. It is enough for me to know that Markusfeld is a decent man and that he developed my father's bookstore very well /if only the war would end/ . . . and that by selling it to him I acted very wisely in every respect."[12]

In 1914, bookstores with non-Jewish owners opened a different front in the campaign against Jewish-owned bookshops when they formed a cooperative of secondhand booksellers. The cooperative opened several locations that focused on selling books for children, portraying used bookstores "of a low cultural and ethical level" as a threat to Polish youth who, they lamented, "were forced to patronize them." The initiative was

170 From a Manor House to Interwar Poland

not only the effort of the antiquarian booksellers' non-Jewish Polish competitors; the president and vice president of the cooperative's governing board were members of two nineteenth-century Polish publishing dynasties—Jan Zawadzki and Gustaw Wolff, the latter of ethnic German background—that owned prestigious bookstores selling new books and had competed with the Lewentals, Orgelbrands, Glucksbergs, and other Jewish publishing families since the mid-nineteenth century. The cooperative decided to set up its own distribution structure because the existing distributors had been "demoralized by Jewish antiquarians"; it asserted that it had to reeducate the public about the cost of books, which had been skewed by "haggling, a remnant of Jewish trade."[13]

The extended Lewental family embraced several of the National Democrats' political leaders and thinkers in their personal lives. Gubrynowicz, the historian of Polish literature who married the youngest Lewental sister, Helena, was an activist for the National Democrats, and Alicja's cousin Zuzanna Kraushar married the writer Władysław Rabski, a proponent of that political group. Circles of intellectuals who sympathized with the National Democrats were among the closest friends of Hortensja's sister and brother-in-law, Jadwiga and Aleksander Kraushar. Aleksander himself supported the National Democrats in its early period, "before it became openly antisemitic," but he never "joined the antisemitic camp." Hortensja and other family members rarely referred to politics in their letters, perhaps to avoid drawing the attention of censors. Hortensja focused instead on family matters and on business and personnel matters connected with *Kurjer Warszawski*.[14]

World War I disrupted the Lewentals' tranquil life. The Polish lands were on the war front between the Russians and Germans, and conditions were dire in Warsaw, which was plagued by air strikes and food shortages. Alicja and other

From a Manor House to Interwar Poland

members of the Lewental family established a soup kitchen in Warsaw, helping to distribute food to needy residents. Hortensja struggled to obtain basic foodstuffs while keeping the newspaper afloat amid difficulties of buying newsprint. Yet the family did not suffer the same plight as Jews further east in the Russian Empire. As the Russian Revolution brought a collapse of the empire and plunged it into a protracted civil war, a wave of violence descended upon Jews, even as the revolution brought with it their emancipation, the final one in Europe. As many as one hundred thousand Jews were killed in the pogroms in the aftermath of World War I and during the Russian Civil War. At the same time, Poland savored its victory when its newly independent state was among the nation-states established from the embers of empires throughout East Central Europe. The fighting continued even after the Treaty of Versailles brought an end to the global conflict. Poland spent years mired in border wars with neighboring Lithuania and newly established Soviet Russia. War seemed interminable.[15]

When peace finally settled over Poland, its leaders set about unifying the new state. The obstacles were enormous. Poland continued to struggle economically after years of wartime deprivations and destruction. The economic systems of regions that had been part of three different empires had to be consolidated under a common currency, while a new national railroad network labored to link the wider Russian-gauge tracks with the standard tracks in the rest of the country. Other challenges were more existential. Leaders and voters alike grappled with the question of what kind of country Poland should be: a nation-state in which the nation was rooted in Polish ethnicity, or a multiethnic state in which all residents of the country were equal members of the national community.

The League of Nations had required Poland and the other new states of East Central Europe to sign treaties committing them to protecting the rights of minorities—"without distinction of birth, nationality, language, race or religion." The Polish Minorities Treaty had major implications for the newly independent state, one-third of whose population was not ethnically Polish. Its more than three million Jews were especially visible: they were 10 percent of its citizens and one-third of urban residents. A civic model of the Polish nation was the constitutional basis for the state, and Józef Piłsudski, the leader of a political grouping (known as Sanacja) whose multiethnic vision of Poland supported an inclusive nationalism, was head of state in its early years.[16]

Yet the ideology of the National Democrats, with their right-wing ethnonationalism, was ascendant, though their political power waned after the early years of Polish independence. Even when Piłsudski staged a coup in 1926, believing that an authoritarian regime could keep the right in check, its power to instill its inclusive sense of national belonging in the political culture was limited. Even some members of Piłsudski's own regime challenged this inclusiveness. Poland withdrew from its Minorities Treaty in 1934, and when Piłsudski died in 1935, the Polish government moved further to the right. Some Polish intellectuals and other members of Polish society maintained faith in liberal political ideas, to be sure. But by the 1930s, anti-Jewish sentiments fanned by the National Democrats were prevalent. With the entire Polish population suffering from the Great Depression, boycotts of Jewish-owned stores further impoverished many Jews. Radical right-wing ideas were especially strong among young people. In the late 1920s and 1930s, universities were sites of violent attacks on Jewish students, as well as discriminatory measures such as "ghetto benches," where Jews were forced into separate seating in classrooms.[17]

Modern Jewish cultures and the secular Jewish politics that had developed in the last decades of the nineteenth cen-

From a Manor House to Interwar Poland   173

tury nevertheless flourished in interwar Poland. Jews were part of political life at all levels, from parliamentary representation to municipal elections: in the Bund and Zionist and diaspora nationalist parties, as well as in the Polish Socialist Party and the illegal Communist Party. Political and cultural life were intertwined, with new publications and circles of writers often associated with political ideologies. Jews could choose from among dozens of newspapers in Yiddish and a smaller number in Hebrew, as well as several Polish-language Jewish newspapers. They could view a Yiddish movie or play in the theaters of Jewish neighborhoods or attend a Polish cabaret with Jews among the actors. Secular and religious life coexisted: the traditional piety of Hasidism remained strong, while religious Jews established their own political party, Agudat Yisrael, with an associated network of private religious schools, including schools for girls. Young people socialized in youth groups affiliated with political movements, often moving from one to another as they developed their evolving world views.[18]

At the same time, young Jews were increasingly immersed in Polish culture. While the minority of families who had the financial means could send their children to private elementary schools, many elementary-school children attended public schools established for Jews (unlike other schools, classes did not meet on Saturday in observance of Shabbat), and Polish was the language of instruction. Educated in the classics of Polish literature and often influenced by the patriotism of political culture in the new Polish state, they lived in multiple worlds—Yiddish and Polish, secular and religious: the rituals of the Polish state and Polish culture, often the Jewish religious lives of their homes, and, for many, the varied Jewish cultures of their youth clubs. As they came of age and became more integrated into Polish culture, they encountered an exclusionary conception of the Polish nation in the political sphere that left them uncertain about how others perceived their place in the new state. Even as many Jews were drawn to political parties whose ideologies expressed optimism that they could shape their own fate, some young people also accepted the more pessimistic reality of the limits to that possibility, as Kenneth Moss has argued. Zionist youth groups gained scores of new members in the 1930s, and many were Polish-speaking young Jews who were being raised in homes where moderate integration shaped their lives.[19]

Decades earlier, in the different political context of the Russian Empire, the Lewentals and their circle had responded to these dilemmas in a different way. Their path to full absorption into Polish society continued after World War I. Alicja and her sisters raised their children in Catholic homes, and in the early years of Polish independence, Hortensja Lewental became president of an association of Catholic women. When Hortensja died in 1923, her friends, family, and intellectuals from throughout Warsaw gathered in Holy Cross Church, where opera singers joined a choir in hymns. Two priests led the prayers at her grave at the Powązki cemetery, where the editor of *Kurjer Warszawski,* Konrad Olchowicz, and her friend Lucyna Kotarbińska, a writer involved in theater circles, gave eulogies, an indication that Hortensja had at least partly broken free of the "Jewish circle" in her social life by the time of her death.[20]

Alicja spent two decades in the Polish countryside in Jeżewice before her husband died suddenly of a heart attack in 1921. Only three years later, her older son, Wacław, was killed in Algeria while serving in the French Foreign Legion. She lived out most of her remaining years in the small town of Brwinów, less than an hour by train from Warsaw, the route winding through forests dotted with homes. In Brwinów, Alicja found a quieter life than the busy social scene of Warsaw. She spent

From a Manor House to Interwar Poland

long hours in the tranquility of a garden at the villa of her close friend, the writer Zygmunt Bartkiewicz, where there were lively gatherings with writers and artists who formed a loose circle of friends in the town and surrounding area. Bartkiewicz, who had studied art in Paris and Munich, had lived in Brwinów for more than a decade by the time Alicja moved there. Among her acquaintances were individuals who shared her Jewish background, but she, like her mother, had finally broken free of her family's "Jewish circle."[21]

Alicja was not only a friend to the writers in her social circle. She also continued her family's tradition of support for Polish cultural life, establishing a fund that supported writers and artists for stays in Zakopane. Bartkiewicz was one of its first recipients, and she helped him and others find an outlet for their writing in the pages of *Kurjer Warszawski*, of which she continued to be co-owner with her sisters. Alicja, Bartkiewicz, and Bartkiewicz's wife, Eugenia, bought a property together in the seaside resort of Jastarnia, on the peninsula north of Gdańsk that juts out into the Baltic Sea, and they often spent the summer months there together. Alicja continued her charity work, funding scholarships for children to attend camps, and gave other financial support.

But Alicja continued to grapple with the emotional turmoil that had plagued her since her first diary entries decades earlier. In the 1930s she gradually withdrew from social life in Brwinów. As she periodically did in her childhood, Alicja found solace in her religious faith, praying regularly at the town's historic church, for which she funded extensive renovations and a bronze candelabra in front of the altar. She corresponded regularly with Bartkiewicz when one or the other was away from Brwinów. Their friendship was not without conflict, however. Her religiosity exasperated the writer, who was "anticlerical," as a literary scholar later described him, and as in her younger years, Alicja encountered antipathy toward Jews in this closest of relationships. "Among the closest acquaintances of Bartkiewicz were many people of semitic background," in the phrasing of Bartkiewicz's biographer. Yet in his later correspondence with Alicja, when they discussed the "Jewish question," Bartkiewicz "did not hide from his antisemitism." He did not subscribe to the ideology of race, however: "In his eyes it was not blood, but outlook on the world and people that decides the value of a person and therefore with an awareness of Alicja's roots, the writer could label this or that behavior 'Jewish.'"[22]

At least some of Bartkiewicz's views would not have been so far from Alicja's own. After all, she had spent years as a young woman anguished over a racial ideology that had caused her such confusion and alienation as she came of age.

7

The "Road to Total Assimilation"

In 1905, Alicja Lewental's grandfather, Mathias Bersohn, donated his large collection of Jewish art and antiquarian books to the Warsaw Jewish community for the establishment of the city's first Judaica museum. He did so instead of leaving the collection to his descendants because they were not interested in Jewish art, he reportedly told an acquaintance; all of his children and grandchildren, he said, had been baptized.[1]

Fifteen years later, Bersohn's son-in-law, Aleksander Kraushar, put on his uniform as a Polish military veteran and walked through the streets of Warsaw, now the capital of the newly independent state, to the Judaica museum. Kraushar himself had been baptized in the Catholic faith years earlier. Now he deposited the final parts of his own archival collection about Polish Jewish history at the museum his father-in-law had founded. It was a symbol of the family's generational shift from a dual identity as both Polish and Jewish in Mathias Bersohn's generation to the conversion of his children and grandchildren to Catholicism: the identity of an older generation deposited in a museum of the past.[2]

178   The "Road to Total Assimilation"

The Lewentals, the Kraushars, and their relatives did not follow the path from Judaism to Catholicism alone. Baptism, while marginal in the broader Polish Jewish population, was a common step for the members of Warsaw's "Jewish plutocracy" and their children. Alicja's diary is populated with the names of Warsaw's Polish-speaking Jewish economic elites, most of whom followed the path to conversion by the first years of the twentieth century. Their family trees were intertwined as a result of marriage within their circles in the generations of Alicja's parents and grandparents, as well as in her generation, sometimes even after conversion to Christianity. The Lewentals themselves were related to many of the families through uncles and aunts, cousins, and other relatives. For these families by the turn of the twentieth century, according to the historian Joseph Lichten, "the most dramatic and contentious issues were nationality (*narodowość*) and conversion to Catholicism."[3]

What led so many to the baptismal altar generations after their ancestors had begun the path of integration into Polish culture in the mid-nineteenth century? The embrace of Catholicism by the Lewentals and their circle is rooted in increasing pessimism at the turn of the twentieth century about the possibility of bridging divides between Polish Jewish and Polish Catholic societies as exclusionary nationalism questioned the possibility even for Jews who embraced Polish culture, those who considered themselves "Poles of the Mosaic faith," to belong to the Polish nation. Alicja's experiences reflect the tail end of a trajectory that unfolded across generations.

But the Lewentals' history crystallizes inconsistencies in evolving conceptions of national belonging as both ethnicity and Catholicism became increasingly important in establishing boundaries around the Polish nation. The notion of ancestry that ethnic nationalism evoked created uncertainty about the place of Jewish families that were deeply immersed in Polish

The "Road to Total Assimilation" 179

language, culture, and a sense of a shared heritage, as linguistic and cultural affiliations adopted in previous generations shaped their descendants' sense of belonging. Racial ideology, while still on the margins of Polish politics, was more clear-cut: it considered Jewish identity to be not only immutable and different in essence, but also inferior, no matter one's religion or cultural identity. Both of these conceptions of inclusion and exclusion—ethnicity and race—were in tension with an understanding of Catholicism, a community of faith that one could choose to adopt, as a key element of what it meant to be Polish. These ambiguities and tensions complicated Alicja Lewental's struggle to reconcile her family's Jewish background with her sense of belonging to the Polish nation.

While the image of the Jew as "other" was central to the development of a cohesive modern Polish national identity, definitions of the nation remained contested, and nationalism did not inevitably lead to exclusion. Exclusionary boundaries developed gradually.

Alicja's sense of belonging was shaped in part by her parents' and grandparents' identifications under the influence of shifting conceptions of the Polish nation in the decades before her birth. Polish nationalism was most inclusive between the uprising against Russian rule in 1830–31 and the 1863 rebellion, at a time when the nation was perceived in universalistic terms of patriotic action, though still only gradually expanding beyond the nobility—a definition that could include Jews in a culturally diverse national community. In the 1860s and 1870s, however, a cultural notion of national identity began to define the Polish nation as a "community of Polish speakers, inhabiting a specific territory and cultivating certain customs and norms." Yet it was a definition that did not preclude Jewish belonging as long as Jews spoke Polish and adopted other elements of

180   The "Road to Total Assimilation"

Polish culture. The Catholic Church was only one of many sites for "enacting" national belonging in the mid-nineteenth century as Polish cultural life, from newspapers and books to plays and operas, also served to cultivate a Polish national identity. Jews who promoted integration at that time understood "national integration" as the development of closer ties with Polish society in their cultural and linguistic affiliations. Cultural identity as a form of national belonging did not yet have an ethnic connotation. Salomon, born in 1841, understood his identity as a Pole through this cultural sphere. It was in those years, in the mid-nineteenth century, when he was beginning his publishing career and when Hortensja, born fifteen years after her husband, was growing up and entering adulthood.[4]

By the 1880s, however, newspaper polemics began to question whether Jews could ever fully belong to the Polish nation as the concept of an "ethno-nation" consolidated—an undercurrent of the newspaper polemics that targeted Alicja's father. Identification with Polish culture and language was viewed as only one element of ethnicity; now national identity was also perceived as being rooted in a common past. At the same time, the increasing role of Catholicism as an element of belonging to the Polish nation by the end of the nineteenth century increased pressure on Jews who identified as both Polish and Jewish, or "Poles of the Mosaic faith," to leave behind their Jewish identity entirely in order to be fully accepted as Polish. In the first years of the twentieth century, an "ideological link between faith and fatherland emerged in full force."[5]

Even as Hortensja came to believe that baptism and marriage would pave the way for her daughters' acceptance in Catholic society, however, racial conceptions about Jews were also introduced into political rhetoric and Catholic thought in the Polish lands, though still on the margins, in the very years when Alicja was writing her diary and grappling with where she belonged. To

The "Road to Total Assimilation"   181

be sure, converts from Judaism had sometimes been viewed with suspicion in the Polish lands and elsewhere long before the advent of racial antisemitism in the last decades of the nineteenth century. In the century before Alicja's birth, Warsaw was home to a community of descendants of Frankists, whose ancestors had converted from Judaism to Catholicism in the eighteenth century following the baptism of Jacob Frank. In the nineteenth century, some Christian burghers viewed the descendants of Frankists suspiciously as economic competitors. They were also a potentially disloyal element politically, in the eyes of some Christians, "as a special, separate class of people," according to Paweł Maciejko. Only in the fourth or fifth generation did descendants of Frankist families become more fully integrated into Polish Catholic society. Nevertheless, Frankists were viewed as a "group within Christianity rather than an offshoot of Judaism."[6]

Even after the advent of racial ideology in anti-Jewish thought, the Christian theological framework acted as a restraint in the Polish lands against explicitly embracing racial conceptions of the Jew. But a transition was evident in the last years of the nineteenth century and the first years of the twentieth century. As early as 1896—the year after Alicja took pen in hand to record her life—Catholic anti-Jewish thought and racial antisemitism began to converge among some writers. By 1903, indications of racial ideas about Jews could be found in Catholic texts. The turn of the twentieth century also saw racial conceptions of the nation penetrate the political sphere. Racial ideology asserted a national identity rooted in blood, providing a "scientific imprint" for preexisting prejudices. By the early twentieth century the right-wing nationalists who in 1893 had established the National League, the precursor to the National Democrats, were instrumentalizing racial theory for political ends. Grzegorz Krzywiec argues that racial antisemitism became central to Polish nationalist political rhetoric after the 1905

182   The "Road to Total Assimilation"

revolution in the Russian Empire, though there were "harbingers" in the years leading up to it.[7]

Yet even after the 1905 revolution, anti-Jewish politics did not fully embrace racial conceptions, according to other historians. Contributors to antisemitic journals, which reflected and influenced political debates, could not assert outright a racial conception of Jewish identity that would have excluded from the Polish nation converts from Judaism such as the Lewentals; doing so would have violated Catholic Church dogma. Hortensja's role as leader of a Catholic women's organization underscores the limits to the influence of racial conceptions of the Jew in Poland. Although anti-Jewish tracts increasingly used racialized language in the decade before World War I, including writings by some priests, "no Polish antisemites of the prewar period accepted the 'logic' of biological racism entirely," Theodore Weeks noted. "While they rejected assimilation as the solution to integrating Jews into Polish society, in individual cases it could be allowed—as long as these individuals embraced Polishness so fully as to become antisemites themselves."[8]

The vast majority of Jews in the Russian Empire, including in the Polish lands, did not follow the Lewentals' path. Most maintained traditional Jewish observances, while the nascent secular politics of Jewish nationalism began to question the very desire for integration. Some Jews from middle-class Polonized Jewish families became active in these Jewish nationalist movements. Others turned to leftist circles that rejected the ideology of nationalism entirely, embracing socialist and Communist politics. Members of the Toeplitz family, who had been part of Warsaw's "Jewish plutocratic circle" since the early nineteenth century, became active in socialist and Communist movements at the end of the century; previous generations of the family had been among the first Jews accepted into Polish

The "Road to Total Assimilation" 183

economic institutions while supporting *haskalah* writers and serving on the Jewish communal board. Among the founders of the Communist Party of Poland in 1918 was Maksymilian Horwitz, whose family's integration into Polish culture began after the death of his father, a Jew from Vienna. Born two years before Alicja, Horwitz first became active in the socialist movement in the mid-1890s.[9]

Yet the Lewentals and their circle doubled down on their efforts to gain acceptance from their Polish neighbors by adopting a more radical form of integration: aspirations to full absorption into Polish Catholic society. Further east in the Russian Empire, too, baptism among Russified Jews was one response to the turmoil of Jewish life in the last decades of the nineteenth century at a time when, according to Steven Zipperstein, "certainties of the past seemed to many thoroughly discredited and outdated." Nearly seventy thousand Jews converted in the nineteenth century to Russian Orthodoxy, though this was a slim minority in a population of five million Jews in the empire. Most of the twelve thousand converts from Judaism to Catholicism in the nineteenth-century Russian Empire lived in the Polish lands. In Warsaw, the number of Christian converts from Judaism decreased after the lifting of legal restrictions on Jews in the Kingdom of Poland in 1862 and then increased after the pogrom wave in 1881–82. Historians Jacob Shatzky and Alina Cała have suggested that the Warsaw pogrom in 1881 influenced the turn to "radical assimilation," as Shatzky has described conversion, among the city's Jewish economic elites— an event that Alicja Lewental's uncle, Aleksander Kraushar, emphasized as part of his disillusionment with the possibility for acceptance in Polish society as a Jew.[10]

The increase in conversions in the 1880s, however, can be seen as a response to the deterioration in the legal status of Jews in the Russian Empire in the 1880s rather than to the pogroms themselves. A rise in baptisms among Jews generally parallels an increase in political repression. This connection holds true for the years after the pogroms, when the government imposed new quotas on the admission of Jews to universities, limitations on Jews in the legal and medical professions, and other restrictions that baptism allowed them to avoid. These so-called "May Laws" did not apply to Jews in the Kingdom of Poland. Elsewhere in the Russian Empire, conversion to Christian denominations increased especially among the "most Russified, literate and urbanized segment of the Jewish community," according to Zipperstein. In her memoir of Russian Jewish life earlier in the nineteenth century, Pauline Wengeroff attributed the baptism of two sons, which she described as a tragedy, both to her husband's abandonment of Jewish religious observance and to limited opportunities for Jews in education and in professional advancement.[11]

In Warsaw, urban economic elites who were dominant in the community of "progressive" Jews were only a minority of converts to Christianity throughout the nineteenth century. Despite newspaper polemics in the 1880s calling for the conversion of "progressive" Jews as a declaration of Polishness, according to Agnieszka Jagodzińska, baptism "determined the upper limits of their 'progressiveness,' which they in no case wanted to cross. Remaining in Judaism was at the same time a touchstone of true 'enlightenment.'" Baptism—or, conversely, remaining Jewish—among the community of "progressive Jews," of which the Lewentals were part, was both a public and a private act for them.[12]

Todd Endelman's analysis of conversion in Warsaw suggests a nuanced picture of class differences among converts and their motivations in the nineteenth century until 1903. Most converts in nineteenth-century Warsaw were from the lower and lower-middle classes, "from ordinary rather than privileged backgrounds, from strata whose economic survival was most threatened by government efforts to control the Jewish popula-

The "Road to Total Assimilation" 185

tion." Their motivations for conversion were usually pragmatic: evading restrictions before the 1860s on where they could live and their ability to make a living. In the years after the 1881–82 pogroms, however, following a decline in conversions in previous decades, the number of converts to Christianity increased among professional and upper-middle classes relative to all Jewish converts. By the end of the nineteenth century these classes comprised the majority of converts.[13]

In Warsaw, conversion to Protestantism was more common than conversion to Catholicism over the course of the nineteenth century, with approximately 3,100 Jews converting to Protestant denominations. Among Jewish financiers, about fifty Jewish bankers and industrialists were baptized as Protestants between 1832 and 1855, while more than 10 percent of graduates of Warsaw's Rabbinic School converted to Protestant Christianity in the school's first two decades, the result of missionary activity. Even in the 1880s, conversion to Protestantism from Judaism remained more common than conversion to Catholicism. For Protestant converts, baptism was not about embracing Polishness. "The paradox of Jews becoming Protestants in an overwhelmingly Catholic milieu becomes less paradoxical if their change of religion is viewed more as a decision to flee membership in the Jewish community and the disabilities and disadvantages it imposed and less as a decision to embrace Christianity and Polonism," Endelman concluded. "Jews who became Christians chose Protestantism more often than Catholicism because it was less offensive to them as secularists and victims of religious intolerance. Roman Catholicism seemed idolatrous and ritualistic, while Protestantism, by comparison, appeared enlightened and rational."[14]

For most converts from Judaism in nineteenth-century Warsaw, then, baptism was not a form of "radical assimilation" into Polish Catholic society that was the context for the Lewentals' conversion. Catholic conversions increased in the 1890s and in the first years of the twentieth century, but they were still a minority of all baptisms among Jews even as the overall number of converts from Judaism to Christianity plummeted. Yet Catholic baptisms became more common among Jewish financiers and other economic elites in the early twentieth century, including some who had earlier converted to Protestant denominations. It was in those years that conversion signified a desire for acceptance in a largely Catholic Polish society.[15]

For Jews from small towns and villages in the Russian Empire, meanwhile, conversion to Christian denominations resulted not from a view of Christianity as "a model of civilization and inclusion," but rather from "a face-to-face encounter with the people and institutions of other religions," as Ellie Schainker has argued. While Schainker frames conversion among traditional Jews outside of large cities as distinct from the phenomenon of baptism among the urban bourgeoisie, her approach to conversion as a "form of cultural mobility fostered by personal encounters" expands, rather than contrasts with, an understanding of conversion among Jews from integrated families who were distanced from religious tradition. For Polonized Jews, too, "subjective factors such as love, desperation, loneliness, and spirituality" were often central for some in decisions to convert, as Alicja Lewental's diary underscores. For Alicja, these emotional and spiritual motivations were intertwined with, rather than distinct from, the increasing role of Catholicism in Polish national identity by the early twentieth century.[16]

Although conversion from Judaism to Christianity was more common among men than among women across the nineteenth century, resulting in part from the greater impact of professional restrictions on Jewish men, Alicja's road to baptism was shaped by her experiences as a woman searching

The "Road to Total Assimilation"   187

for social acceptance. Her life complicates gender differences in the Jewish confrontation with modernity, including paths both to baptism and to less radical trajectories. Alicja's history does not fit neatly into "Western" vs. "Eastern" models of the role of gender in evolving notions of Jewish belonging. In Germany, women were often central to maintaining Jewish rituals in the home in the "Western" model, what Marion Kaplan has termed "domestic Judaism" in the context of nineteenth-century German Jewry at a time when newly bourgeois Jewish families idealized the domestic role of women while men faced pressure to integrate economically and culturally in the public sphere. East European Jewish women, on the other hand, were more likely than their Western counterparts to participate in economic life in the public realm as a result of economic necessity, bringing them into contact with Christian society. The road to conversion for Hortensja and her daughters did not follow either model. The bourgeois "cult of domesticity" had the opposite impact in the Lewentals' case: whereas Alicja's father remained a leader in Jewish communal life as she was growing up, it was her mother's embrace of Catholicism that shaped the religious culture of their home and had a greater impact on the upbringing of Alicja and her siblings, facilitating rather than putting a brake on the family's absorption into Polish Catholic society. Nor did the Lewental women encounter Christian society as a result of economic necessity.[17]

Both among East European Jewish women for whom baptism was the culmination of integrating processes, as in the Lewental family, and among those raised in traditional Jewish homes, women's conversion was often connected with marriage to Christian men. For women from traditionally observant Jewish homes, the choice of baptism often stemmed from a specific relationship rather than from a general desire to leave behind Jewish identity, while for others from traditional families, baptism was a way to escape an arranged marriage.[18] Gender differences in education also shaped paths to less radical forms of integration. Neglect of formal religious education for girls in traditional East European Jewish communities meant they were more likely than boys to receive an education that exposed them to literature in non-Jewish languages and other secularizing influences, transforming them into "agents of assimilation." Wengeroff, in her memoir of nineteenth-century Russian Jewish life, was an "agent of subverting tradition," despite her narrative blaming her husband, as well as educational and professional opportunities, for her children's baptisms. It was Wengeroff, after all, who read romance novels in European languages in addition to Yiddish romances, taught her husband German, and fought for her son to continue studying at a Russian gymnasium after he was expelled for refusing to kneel before Christian icons.[19]

For Alicja, Jewish education was absent not mainly because of gender, but also because of her mother's embrace of the Catholic faith. Yet her emphasis on reading literature in Polish and other languages contains echoes of the narrative that Iris Parush traced in memoirs by maskilic men, which pointed to a connection between educated Jewish women's "passion for novels" in non-Jewish languages and relationships with Christian men. To be sure, Alicja was at least one generation removed from the "new reading woman" portrayed in maskilic memoirs as "agents of assimilation." However, her mother, Hortensja, who grew up in a reform-minded Jewish home, can be counted among readers of European literature portrayed in maskilic memoirs as "assimilated women . . . who had lost all ties to the Jewish world," though Hortensja's continued involvement in Jewish charities founded by her parents and grandfather complicates that characterization.[20]

While historians' findings on gender and conversion in modern Jewish history shed light on Alicja Lewental's life, her experiences also expand our understanding of these processes.

The "Road to Total Assimilation" 189

Her chronicle points to the conglomeration of factors in both personal and political realms that shaped religious change, not only in the specific geographic context of her life. Alicja's journal provides access to the emotional world of one convert, helping to explain "internal . . . determinants of radical assimilation." Her chronicle illuminates how she understood her personal journey to the baptismal altar, and it is a step toward filling a gap in knowledge about the "emotional makeup" of converts from Judaism in modernity.[21]

The alienation that threads through Alicja's diary transcends variations in economic class, degrees of Jewish observance before baptism, and gender roles as factors in conversion. It echoes Michael Stanislawski's characterization of the experiences of the "destitute and desperate," who were the largest group in his categorization of converts to Russian Orthodoxy in the Lithuanian area of the Russian Empire. As with Alicja, the impoverished and displaced "failed to find secure moorings in that rocky society: young people just at the point at which normal adult life begins, who could find no partner, no profession, no stable place in society." For Alicja, it was both her status at the center of Polish society—her family's immersion in Polish cultural circles, access to elite society, and social life revolving around Warsaw's salons—and at the same time her feeling of being an outsider in that society that forced her to confront antipathy to Jewish inclusion in the Polish national community and the limits to social acceptance.[22]

Alicja's chronicle further blurs the distinction between "conversions of convenience" and those driven by religious faith. The convenience of her conversion—the ability to marry a Catholic man and the desire for acceptance in her social circles—was intertwined with her convictions about cultural belonging and the role of Catholicism in Polish national identity. Unlike for converts from Judaism to Christianity in early modern Europe, conversion for Alicja did not entail concrete, "extra-spiritual" changes in identity that for traditional Jews were part of the process of leaving behind Judaism, including characteristics that were seen as part of Jews' "collective character," especially everyday language. Yet she considered her baptism to be a decisive break with the past and described it in dramatic terms, even though it did not involve a transformation in religious belief or practice, which she had already embraced before her conversion, though with ambivalence.[23]

Alicja's experiences are not marginal to East European Jewish history despite the exceptional nature of her path. The Lewental family's history, to cite Ezra Mendelsohn in reference to a convert in Galicia in the Austro-Hungarian Empire, is a "fascinating combination of success and failure, of the triumph of assimilation and its tragedy, [which] lies at the heart of the modern Jewish drama."[24]

Alicja Lewental's diary is peppered with references to the baptism of acquaintances from her generation in her family's "Jewish circle": the Rotwands, Kronenbergs, Wawelbergs, and others. Often the baptisms were connected with marriage to Catholic men, as was the case for her. Most of those whose conversions she commented on in her diary were women, but she noted in one entry that a man in her circle, Kazimierz Rotwand, had been baptized several years earlier because "he does not want a Jewish woman for a wife." Jadwiga Wawelberg, Hipolit's daughter, who had sometimes drawn Alicja's envy as they competed for suitors, married Alicja's cousin Michał Bersohn. Both were baptized as Catholics; Alicja noted in her diary that Michał had wanted to convert for professional reasons. They settled on a countryside estate near Warsaw that the Bersohn family owned, Boglewice, embracing the trappings of an aristocratic life even without the lineage of nobility.[25]

The "Road to Total Assimilation" 191

As Alicja came of age, some contemporaries of her parents, too, were leaving behind the Jewish faith. The baptism of Hortensja's closest friend, Franciszka Perlmutter, in 1899, together with that of Franciszka's son, was the cause of deep emotional turmoil for Alicja and sparked the confrontation with Hortensja about her religious identification. Antoni Natanson, a gynecologist whose father and uncle were leaders in Warsaw Jewish life for decades, was baptized the same year as Alicja was. Other members of the Natanson family converted in the first years of the twentieth century as well. Antoni's cousin Władysław, a prominent physicist, was baptized as a Catholic and later became rector of Jagiellonian University in Krakow in the 1930s, the height of success in Polish academic life. He did not escape the wrath of antisemites, however. When he opposed quotas on Jewish students, antisemites retaliated with a bombing attempt at his apartment in Krakow. Kazimierz Natanson, who had hurried back to Warsaw years earlier with Salomon Lewental to attend the Great Synagogue for Yom Kippur, was reportedly the only grandchild of Volf Zelig Natanson, who died as a Jew.[26]

Descendants of Salomon Lewental's predecessors in the Polish book trade, the Glucksbergs and Orgelbrands, had already left behind their families' dual identifications as both Polish and Jewish by the turn of the twentieth century. In the two families' first generation in the publishing business in the mid-nineteenth century, only Maurycy Orgelbrand, Samuel's younger brother, converted to Catholicism, but all of the sons in the next generation of both the Glucksberg and Orgelbrand families were baptized, mainly into Protestant denominations. Social integration was gradual; nearly all of their sons either married Jewish women and were baptized together with their spouses, or they married women who were also converts from Judaism, often from other publishing-house families or from banking circles. When Jan Glucksberg, the father of Salomon Lewental's first wife, died in 1859 and was laid to rest in the Warsaw Jewish cemetery next to his brother Natan, he was the last member of his family to be buried with the last name of Glucksberg in a Jewish cemetery.

Fewer traces of the fate of the women in the Orgelbrand and Glucksberg families have been preserved in the historical record. While all of Natan and Jan Glucksberg's sons were baptized, Jan's daughter Ernestyna, Salomon Lewental's first wife, remained Jewish until her death. In Samuel Orgelbrand's family, at least one daughter also remained Jewish and married a maskilic writer, Hershl Rundo. After Samuel Orgelbrand's sons converted, they turned over the family's Hebrew printing business to Rundo, and the Orgelbrand sons began publishing an increasing number of Christian theological works.

It was Jadwiga and Aleksander Kraushar, Hortensja Lewental's sister and brother-in-law, who most closely accompanied the Lewentals on their path from Judaism to Catholicism. Like Salomon Lewental's life story, Alexander Kraushar's road from the son of a Polonized Jew to conversion to Catholicism, described by Jakub Shatzky as his "road to total assimilation," maintained for decades a midway point between retaining a Jewish identity and cutting all ties with Judaism. Kraushar, according to Shatzky, was a "characteristic case of assimilation in the history of the Jewish intelligentsia in Poland and one which provides a picture of the process of Polonization in the latter half of the 19th century." By the 1890s, Shatzky wrote, "Kraushar had long since come to believe that Catholicism and Polonism were synonymous." The Kraushars' baptism as Catholics was "done quietly and without fanfare."[27]

One of Aleksander Kraushar's last activities in documenting the Polish Jewish past was his publication of materials from Mathias Bersohn's collection of Polish Judaica, which Bersohn had requested in his will. It was just over a decade later that Kraushar deposited the last of his own archival materials about Jewish history at the Judaica museum founded by his late father-in-law.[28]

Epilogue

One of the few remnants of Alicja Lewental's adult life is the manor house where she lived with her husband in the countryside estate in Jeżewice. The home lies in ruins now, garbage and detritus littering the rooms, and it is obscured from view by a forest that has grown up around the dilapidated building. Down a short dirt path overgrown with weeds is a gray apartment block built on the estate under the Communist authorities after World War II, with a trellis threaded with roses standing incongruously next to a clothesline outside. The apartment building's residents did not recall the Miński family. A visitor can find only faint hints of the manor house's former grandeur.

In the small town of Brwinów, near Warsaw, where Alicja lived out most of her remaining years after her husband's death, a handful of residents have preserved traces of her memory, with hints of a colorful life. It is an unremarkable town, home to about fifteen thousand residents. A few minutes' walk from the train station is a sleepy town square, and in the other direction are a handful of stores and an unadorned café. Nearby is the town hall,

Epilogue

where a young clerk on the first floor never heard of Alicja Mińska or her maiden name, Lewental. But upstairs, with the mention of Alicja's name, an employee in the town's publicity office, Mirosława Kosiata, lit up in recognition. Alicja was a well-known personality here, Kosiata responded. She added, with a slight smile, that the main character of a romance novel from the 1980s is based on Alicja, hinting at the stories that remain part of local legend among some of Brwinów's residents. The town historian, Andrzej Mączkowski, was eager to show a visitor around. He drove past the villa where Alicja had lived, seemingly modest now by the standards of her family's wealth, on a street whose past hints of refinement had faded. A few streets away is a quaint villa once owned by Alicja's close friend, the writer Zygmunt Bartkiewicz, on grounds surrounded by a garden.

The social status and privileges that the Lewentals, and the Bersohns before them, had enjoyed for a century did not allow Alicja and her family to escape the devastation of World War II. No matter how she and her siblings defined themselves, Nazi racial law defined them and other converts as Jews. In the Warsaw ghetto, three churches held services for Christians whom such laws considered Jewish, but Alicja sought to survive instead in hiding. Her sister Marta hid in Milanówek, a town near Warsaw where Polish intellectuals had vacationed in summers before the war. A family member of Marta's husband found her a hiding place in a basement there. Other Christian converts from Judaism were also hiding in the town, including children who found refuge in a convent. Marta had stereotypically "Jewish looks," according to her granddaughter, a consideration that would have made it especially dangerous for her to be seen on the streets at a time when at least one Pole was informing the Germans about Jews in hiding in Milanówek, so she emerged from her hiding place only at night. Marta lived to see the war's end. She struggled for the rest of her life with the trauma of her survival.[1]

The youngest Lewental sibling, Stefan, was on a transport of prisoners from the Pawiak Prison in Warsaw who were sent to Sachsenhausen in Germany on May 2, 1940, at a time when the Germans were arresting Polish intellectuals in German-occupied Poland. The Warsaw ghetto had not yet been established. Stefan's last name stands out in a list of more than eight hundred prisoners sent from Pawiak to Sachsenhausen that day; unlike his sisters, Stefan could never escape from a last name that marked him as Jewish. He was reportedly among the prisoners killed in Sachsenhausen in 1941 or 1942.[2]

Alicja evaded the Nazis for nearly all of the war, but her circumstances are unclear from the historical record. When war broke out, she was resting in a spa town in Czarniecka Góra, where Poles went to be treated for medical problems, and she left for the countryside estate in Jeżewice, living there at least through 1940. She remained in touch with Bartkiewicz by letter and sent food packages to him in Warsaw, where he lived in the dire material conditions of wartime. Alicja evaded the fate of the Jews in Tarczyn, the town closest to Jeżewice. After just two months during which Tarczyn's Jews were confined in an open ghetto established by the Nazis in December 1940, they were deported to the Warsaw ghetto, where many of them died of hunger. Almost all who were still alive in the summer of 1942 were killed in Treblinka during the Great Deportation beginning in July, together with hundreds of thousands of Warsaw Jews. Only a handful of Jews from Tarczyn lived to see the war's end, including a few who were hidden by Polish residents in a nearby village. Nor did Alicja share the fate of the Jews in Brwinów, most of whom found themselves in early 1941 in the nearby ghetto of Grodzisk Mazowiecki, from which the Nazis soon sent all of the Jews to the ghetto in the Polish capital. They were killed together with Warsaw Jewry.[3]

Epilogue

Alicja lived at least in the later years of the war in Warsaw under the name Maria Zawadzka in a hospital run by nuns, where she read books to patients and gave talks to them about Catholicism. In the middle of August 1944, less than two weeks after the Polish underground launched a desperate uprising against the Germans, Alicja's youngest sister, Helena, was killed when a Catholic home for individuals with paralysis in Warsaw was burned down. From the circumstances, it is likely that she was hiding in the home because of the racial laws that defined her as Jewish.[4] Alicja was reportedly killed on the same day, together with the patients in the hospital where she was hiding. It is unclear whether she was killed as a Pole or because of racial laws that defined her as a Jew.[5] A resolution to the very conundrum with which she struggled throughout her life—whether the world around her accepted her as Polish or would impose on her a Jewish identity—remains elusive to a historian, even in her death.

In early 2023, I received a message from Joanna Plucinska, a great-great-granddaughter of Alicja Lewental's sister Marta Mrozowska. Plucinska, a journalist who was writing about her family, was seeking information about Hortensja and had read an article I wrote about Alicja's diary and her family. Six months later, I met Joanna, her grandmother Hania, and her great-uncle Janek in Warsaw. We spoke over lunch in a restaurant connected with a theater, on a street named after Maria Konopnicka, the feminist Positivist writer. Hania, Janek and their two siblings lived through World War II as children and remembered their grandmother, Marta. Plucinska and her contemporary family brought me closer to Alicja's life, helping to bridge the present and past after years of my having encountered the Lewental family only through documents.

What struck me most about the history that came into sharper focus when I met with Hania and Janek was the Frankist background of their father, from the Szymanowski family, who married one of Marta Mrozowska's daughters. (Another member of the Szymanowski family married another of Marta's daughters.) The Szymanowski family was celebrated in Warsaw; Wacław Szymanowski had designed the city's Chopin monument, which was built in the 1920s. The significance of the marriage of Hortensja Lewental's grandchildren to descendants of Frankists was ambiguous. Marta remained a deeply believing Catholic throughout her life, and the Frankists had converted from Judaism to Catholicism centuries before, as Janek noted during our conversation. By the time Marta's daughters married members of the Szymanowski family in the twentieth century, Frankists no longer followed religious observances or beliefs that were different from those of other Catholics. Yet some Frankist descendants maintained distinct social circles in nineteenth-century Warsaw and were at times considered an "other," with their Polishness and their Catholicism questioned by some antisemites in the 1890s.

It was a member of the Szymanowski family who traveled to Milanówek during World War II to arrange for an apartment where Alicja's sister Marta could hide. Hania, Janek, their two siblings, and their parents remained in Warsaw, but when the uprising broke out in August 1944 and the city became a battle zone between the Germans and the Polish underground, the parents sent the four children to Jeżewice, where the Miński family's estate was located. When the war finally ended, the Szymanowskis returned to their apartment in Warsaw, and Hania recalled that her mother—Marta's daughter—gathered the few remaining family photographs that were scattered on the floor.

Alicja's son, Zbigniew, survived the war, and it was through his daughter, Barbara Bobrowska, that Alicja's diary found its way to the Museum of Printing. In the late 1980s, an archivist

Epilogue

from the museum visited Barbara in a modest Warsaw apartment crowded with the elegant nineteenth-century furniture of Hortensja and Salomon Lewental. In 1991, the museum formally acquired the furniture together with Alicja's papers, including her diary, family photographs, letters from her parents, postcards to and from Hortensja Lewental, and other family papers.

When Barbara died in 2023, her daughter, Aneta Lewandowska, discovered piles of other family papers and photographs stored away in a bag in the cellar of Barbara's apartment building: albums from Alicja's life in Jeżewice and Brwinów, postcards, a sonnet full of romantic longing that Alicja wrote in 1896 or 1897, and countless other documents. Aneta had not known about Alicja's diary and the other papers at the Museum of Printing, and Barbara, who was born in 1932, had always refused to talk about her wartime experiences. Yet Aneta had suspected that her family had Jewish roots. Months before Barbara died in 2023, she tried to talk with her mother about her suspicions, but her mother looked away, becoming agitated, and did not respond. After Barbara's death, Aneta placed on her bedroom wall a painting of Alicja that had hung in her mother's apartment, and she displayed photographs of Alicja on a side table in the living room. Aneta slept each night under an image of a woman who connected her to a past Aneta had never known.

Among the family papers were a few documents that filled in some details of Alicja's life. On August 23, 1939, nine days before Nazi Germany invaded Poland but with war looming, Alicja began writing a short journal in a small notebook that documented the first three months of wartime. Now Aneta was in possession of this coda to Alicja's coming-of-age diary. On the same day as she began the journal, Nazi Germany had signed a non-aggression pact with the Soviet Union, with a secret protocol according to which the two countries would soon divide up Poland. Most of Alicja's entries were short, comprising just a few sentences each. Over the following months, she recorded the bombardment of cities and towns, the hardships of wartime, and the uncertainty of what was to come. One night, she wrote, she dreamt of her parents. She wrote her last entry in the notebook on November 25, 1939, leaving the remaining pages blank.

Also among the papers was a detailed family history written by Zbigniew, Alicja's son, and addressed to his children and grandchildren in 1984: "Through familiarity with the past of one's family, its development and the position that it occupied and has the potential to occupy in the nation and society, a family tradition is created that very often becomes a strong incentive to future generations for a hard-working and honest life," he wrote. Zbigniew then wrote down the history of the Miński family going back generations and the family history of his wife, Janina. It detailed Alicja's life as well, noting that she was the daughter of Hortensja and Franciszek Salezy Lewental, publisher of *Kurjer Warszawski*—using Salomon's baptismal name—and that Hortensja was from the Bersohn home. In his preface to the document, Zbigniew had written that he hoped the history would allow them to "reflect on your own life and what you have contributed to the family treasury, of which the next generations could be proud, and from which they could remember their ancestors with the honor and love that is due to them." Yet his summary of Alicja's life did not detail the lives of previous generations of the Lewental and Bersohn families, as he had done with the other branches of the family. Nowhere does the document refer to the Jewish background of Alicja's family and their leadership in Jewish communal life.

Aside from Marta, the only other Lewental sibling who survived World War II was Zosia Hoesick. Hania, Marta

Epilogue

Mrozowska's granddaughter, recalled visiting the Hoesicks' elegant home in Krakow after the war. Zosia, whose husband had died during the war, was crowded into one room of the Hoesicks' prewar home and shared the apartment with other families. Communism had upended what conferred privilege, with housing perhaps its most concrete manifestation.

In postwar Poland, the Lewentals' descendants did not remain untouched by their Jewish roots. Hania and Janek, Marta's grandchildren, did not recall antisemitism as significant to their postwar lives, though one family member recounted a relative's recollection of being called a Jew as a smear. Nor were they targeted for their Jewish roots during the Polish government's antisemitic campaign in 1968, when Jews and those of Jewish background were scapegoated for anti-Communist protests. Yet one detail drew my attention: Hania attended a school run by the Society for the Friends of Children (Towarzystwo Przyjaciół Dzieci, TPD), an organization that maintained a secular curriculum at times when the Communist government allowed Catholic religious instruction in schools in the early postwar years and the mid-1950s. The TPD curriculum served to inculcate in the schools' students an inclusive conception of the Polish nation, and there were concentrations of children from Jewish families, especially those from intellectual homes, in some of the TPD's schools. Only during the antisemitic campaign in 1968 and the wave of Jewish emigration that followed, however, did some of the students learn of their Jewish roots or that many of their classmates were Jewish.[6]

Hania's attendance at a TPD school seemed significant, but its meaning was unclear. Her mother was a deeply believing Catholic, raising Hania and her siblings in the Catholic faith, so she would not have chafed at Catholic instruction for her children. It is likely that she sent Hania to the school because of its reputation as academically strong. But the TPD's inclusive conception of Polishness also protected students of Jewish background, to a greater degree than in other schools, from a feeling of otherness. The result of Hania's schooling there was that she had Jewish friends growing up. Long after she had finished university, Hania's Jewish boyfriend was part of the wave of emigration that followed the antisemitic campaign in 1968, and she sought to join him. In the end, Hania emigrated to Canada without him and has lived there ever since, though she returns to Poland regularly to visit family and friends.

The stigma of a Jewish background among the descendants of Salomon and Hortensja Lewental has an afterlife that has lasted for generations. It is partly an effort to challenge the stigma that has prompted Joanna Plucinska to write about her family's past. She grew up in Canada, to which her parents had immigrated, her father in the mid-1980s and her mother in 1981. Joanna and her brother grew up going to church, attending Polish school on the weekends, and taking part in a Polish scout troop. Even in the Polish diaspora, Jewish background remained somewhat of a taboo in her family. "It was something we knew we were not supposed to talk about," she recalled. Yet the family lived in a neighborhood with a concentration of Jewish residents, and when a Jewish friend invited Joanna to her home for Chanukah, the invitation made her father uncomfortable; he himself does not have Jewish roots, but, as Joanna understood it, he feared that his daughter's Jewish background could one day leave her open to persecution. Joanna's mother, Małgosia Plucinska, has followed her own path back to her Jewish roots in recent years, as much a spiritual journey as an exploration of her family's past.

A search for traces of the Lewental family in Warsaw ends at the Powązki cemetery, the historic Catholic graveyard that was the final resting place of Alicja's parents and husband. Wandering

Epilogue

along the cemetery lanes, a visitor passes the last names of the family's friends and acquaintances who had also been baptized before their burial there: Natanson, Wawelberg, Rotwand. The gravestone of Ferdynand Hoesick is proudly inscribed with his title as editor-in-chief of *Kurjer Warszawski* and as a "man of letters"; Feliks Mrozowski is remembered on his tombstone as a landed citizen and as publisher of *Kurjer Warszawski*. Alicja Mińska's husband, Zygmunt, was buried here in 1921 in his family's plot, as were their sons: Wacław, whose death in the French Foreign Legion is recorded in an inscription on the gravestone, and Zbigniew, who lived long enough to begin researching the life of his great-grandfather, Mathias Bersohn.[7] At the bottom of the gravestone, beneath the inscription "Grave of the Miński Family of Jeżewice," is the family's coat of arms. Alicja's death during the Warsaw Uprising is commemorated on the tombstone.

On the other side of the wall at the back of the Catholic graveyard, the Jewish cemetery of Warsaw stretches across crowded rows of graves, those of rabbis, Yiddish writers, and other luminaries of the Polish Jewish past, but mainly ordinary people. Here, in a maze of tombstones, is the final resting place of Warsaw Jewry, the world that the Lewentals sought to leave behind. There is the grave of Salomon's brother, the administrative head of *Kurjer Warszawski*, whose gravestone was inscribed in Polish with his name, Fabjan, as well as his Hebrew name, Shraga Feyvel. Buried here is I. L. Peretz, whose apartment was the gathering place for Yiddish writers as Alicja Lewental was growing up. Toward the front of the graveyard are the tombstones of Salomon Lewental's predecessors in the Polish book trade: the Glucksbergs and Samuel Orgelbrand, whose gravestone is engraved with the words "Publisher of the first Polish encyclopedia and member of the synagogue council." It was an epitaph that declared Orgelbrand's dual identity, a Pole and a Jew in equal measure.

Though a high wall hides the rows of gravestones from the street at the front of the Jewish graveyard, the stop labeled "Jewish cemetery" on the tram that carries travelers along Okopowa Street has ensured that the graveyard and the Jews who are buried there have not been forgotten by Varsovians. The burial ground has preserved a memory of the flourishing population of Warsaw Jewry before World War II in all its diversity and dynamism—and also its destruction. The Catholic graveyard of Powązki tells a different story. It is in the life paths of the Lewentals and others who lived at the border of Catholic and Jewish societies where Polish and Jewish history is perhaps most intertwined.

Notes

Introduction

1. Museum of Printing, branch of the Museum of Warsaw, papers of Salomon Lewental, Pamiętniki A. Lewentala [henceforth Pamiętniki], AR247, vol. 3, entry of April 7, 1900, and the first entry of notebook 1, which is a continuation of the last entry in vol. 3, dated May 27, 1900. The extant diary consists of three bound volumes and three loose notebooks. They are noted here as vols. 1–3 and notebooks 1–3. Notebook 1 is continuous from vol. 3. There is a gap between notebooks 1 and 2 and between notebooks 2 and 3. There are no entries between August and December 1900. It is possible, however, that some notebooks of Alicja's diary are not extant. All translations of the diary and other sources are by the author of this book except where otherwise noted.

2. Pamiętniki, notebook 1, July 18, 1900.

3. I am grateful to Thomas Robisheaux for calling my attention to the term "exceptional normal" or "normal exception," which was first used by the Italian historian Edoardo Grendi. See Edoardo Grendi, "Micro-analisi e storia sociale," *Quaderni storici* 35 (1977): 506–20. On the connection between microhistory and Grendi's concept of the "normal exception," see Matti Peltonen, "Clues, Margins, and Monads: The Micro-Macro Link in Historical Research," *History and Theory* 40, no. 3 (2001): 347–59.

4. Pamiętniki, vol. 1, March 3, 1896, and August 2, 1896.

5. The term "Jewish plutocracy" is from Stefan Kieniewicz, "The Jews of Warsaw, Polish Society and the Partitioning Powers, 1795–1861," in *The Jews of Warsaw: A History*, eds. Władysław Bartoszewski and Antony Polonsky (Oxford: Blackwell, 1991), 173. In 1897, fewer than 14 percent of the city's Jews reported Polish as their native language, and the economic elites among

them were small in number. The declaration of one's mother tongue is often, though not always, an indication of cultural affiliation.

6. The phrase "whipping boy" to describe Salomon Lewental is from Helena Datner, *Ta i tamta strona: Żydowska inteligencja Warszawy drugiej połowy XIX wieku* (Warsaw: Jewish Historical Institute, 2007), 256. For a thoughtful discussion of the concept of "belonging" to understand the ways in which individuals relate to a broader community and social change, especially in connection with a city and a nation, see Chad Bryant, *Prague: Belonging in the Modern City* (Cambridge, Mass.: Harvard University Press, 2021), 7–10, 260–61. On the concept of belonging as it relates to Jewish history, see Maria Diemling and Larry Ray, eds., *Boundaries, Identity and Belonging in Modern Judaism* (New York: Routledge, 2016); Harvey E. Goldberg et al., eds., *Dynamic Belonging: Contemporary Jewish Collective Identities* (New York: Berghahn Books, 2011); in this volume see esp. Harvey E. Goldberg, "Introduction," 1–27, and Stanley Brandes, "Religion, Ethnic Identity, and the Sense of Belonging," 31–45; Todd Endelman, "Jewish Self-Identification and West European Categories of Belonging: From the Enlightenment to World War II," in *Religion or Ethnicity?: Jewish Identities in Evolution,* ed. Zvi Gitelman (New Brunswick, N.J.: Rutgers University Press, 2009), 104–30; and Haim Fireberg, "Antisemitic Perceptions and Jewish Sense of Belonging," in *Comprehending Antisemitism through the Ages: A Historical Perspective,* ed. Armin Lange et al. (Berlin: De Gruyter, 2021), 393–410.

7. A cogent analysis of the role of the "Jew" in the development of ethnic Polish nationalism in this period can be found in Joanna Michlic, *Poland's Threatening Other: The Image of the Jew from 1880 to the Present* (Lincoln: University of Nebraska Press, 2006), 24–68, as well as in works by Theodore Weeks, Brian Porter, Agnieszka Jagodzińska, Alina Cała, Grzegorz Krzywiec, and Jerzy Jedlicki, which are discussed in chapter 7.

8. Grzegorz Krzywiec emphasizes the influence of racial ideas: "The influence and significance of racism were far greater than appears to be commonly accepted. Hence, Tomasz Kizwalter rightly points out that although racism in its purest form had for a long time been beyond the pale of the basic currents of intellectual life in nineteenth-century Europe and America, patterns of racial thinking and racial stereotypes, such as the new direction had instilled, became part of general public notions" (Krzywiec, *Chauvinism, Polish Style: The Case of Roman Dmowski,* trans. Jarosław Garliński [Beginnings, 1886–1905] [Frankfurt: Peter Lang, 2016], 95).

9. Pamiętniki, vol. 2, January 10, 1898.

10. Pamiętniki, vol. 2, May 7, 1898.

11. Romaissaa Benzizoune, "The Muslim Prom Queen and Me," *New York Times,* June 30, 2017; https://www.nytimes.com/2017/06/30/opinion/sunday/the-muslim-prom-queen-and-me.html.

Notes to Pages 15–25

1

A Coming-of-Age Chronicle

1. Pamiętniki, vol. 1, January 1, 1896.

2. Pamiętniki, vol. 2, July 4, 1898. Valerie Raoul wrote, "Girls were encouraged to keep a diary only during a period of transition during which they moved from status of child to wife. Once married, writing about themselves was perceived as an unjustifiable self-indulgence. . . . Secrecy becomes suspect, as a wife should have no secrets from her husband" (Raoul, "Women and Diaries: Gender and Genre," *Mosaic* 22, no. 3 [1987]: 57–65).

3. Pamiętniki, vol. 2, August 27, 1898.

4. Pamiętniki, vol. 2, June 9, 1898; vol. 3, October 14, 1899; vol. 1, December 1, 1896.

5. Pamiętniki, vol. 1, December 21, 1896.

6. Peter Gay, *Education of the Senses: The Bourgeois Experience, Victoria to Freud* (New York: Norton, 1999), 446; Cinthia Gannett, *Gender and the Journal: Diaries and Academic Discourse* (Albany: SUNY, 1992), 121; Kathryn Carter, "The Cultural Work of Diaries in Mid-Century Victorian Britain," *Victorian Review* 23, no. 2 (Winter 1997): 252; Jane H. Hunter, "Inscribing the Self in the Heart of the Family: Diaries and Girlhood in Late-Victorian America," *American Quarterly* 44, no. 1 (March 1992): 53.

7. Gay, *Education of the Senses*, 446–52; Philippe Lejeune, *On Diary*, eds. Jeremy D. Popkin and Julie Rak (Honolulu: University of Hawaii Press, 2009), 7, 23, 79–88; Joanne E. Cooper, "Shaping Meaning: Women's Diaries, Journals and Letters—The Old and the New," *Women's Studies International Forum* 10, no. 1 (1987): 95–99; Gannett, *Gender and the Journal*, 113.

8. Julie Rak wrote that "diarists make secret spaces within a larger social world" (Rak, "Dialogue with the Future: Philippe Lejeune's Method and Theory of Diary," in Lejeune, *On Diary*, 18. According to the literary scholar Rebecca Hogan, "The establishment of 'privacy' as one of the generic features of the diary form coincided with the increasing consignment of women and their work to the private domestic realm by industrial civilization. In the course of the nineteenth century, those aspects of culture associated with the private became the domain of women. The image of an inner life—the life of personal reflection and emotion—became increasingly bound up with the image of the private sphere (woman's sphere), and women 'continued to turn to the diary as one place where they were permitted, indeed encouraged, to indulge full self-centeredness'" (Hogan, "Engendered Autobiographies: The Diary as a Feminine Form," in *Autobiography and Questions of Gender*, 2nd ed., ed. Shirley Neuman [New York: Routledge, 2016], 99). Here Hogan cites in part Margo Culley, *A Day at a Time: The Diary Literature of American Women*

208 Notes to Pages 26–27

from 1764 to the Present (New York: Feminist Press, 1985), 3–4. On gender and the history of diaries, see also Suzanne L. Bunkers and Cynthia Anne Huff, eds., *Inscribing the Daily: Critical Essays on Women's Diaries* (Amherst: University of Massachusetts Press, 1996); Shari Benstock, ed., *The Private Self: Theory and Practice of Women's Autobiographical Writings* (Chapel Hill: University of North Carolina Press, 1988); Margo Culley, "'I Look at Me': Self as Subject in the Diaries of American Women," *Women's Studies Quarterly* 17, nos. 3–4 (1989): 15–22; Gannett, *Gender and the Journal;* Hunter, "Inscribing the Self in the Heart of the Family," 51–81.

9. Lejeune, *On Diary,* 94, 100; Carter, "The Cultural Work of Diaries in Mid-Century Victorian Britain," 251–67; Philippe Lejeune, "The 'Journal de Jeune Fille' in Nineteenth-Century France," trans. Martine Breillac, in Bunkers and Huff, *Inscribing the Daily,* 107–22; Jane Marcus, "Invincible Mediocrity: The Private Selves of Public Women," in Benstock, *The Private Self,* 114–46; Culley, "'I Look at Me,'" 19; Rosalind Debolande Roberts and Jane Roberts, eds., *Growing Up with the Impressionists: The Diary of Julie Manet* (London: Sotheby Parke Bernet, 1987). For the English translation of Bashkirtseff's diary, see Marie Bashkirtseff, *The Journal of a Young Artist, 1860–1884,* trans. Mary J. Serrano (New York: Cassell, 1889). Poliakova's diary, which goes from 1875 to the early 1950s, was published in 2019 by ChaeRan Freeze in English translation with an extensive introduction reconstructing Poliakova's biography and historical contexts; ChaeRan Freeze, *A Jewish Woman of Distinction: The Life and Diaries of Zinaida Poliakova,* trans. Gregory Freeze (Waltham, Mass.: Brandeis University Press, 2019).

10. Culley, "'I Look at Me,'" 19; Gannett, *Gender and the Journal,* 111; Marilyn Ferris Motz, "The Private Alibi: Literacy and Community in the Diaries of Two Nineteenth-Century American Women," in Bunkers and Huff, *Inscribing the Daily,* 189–206. On the genre of adolescent girls' diaries, see Jane DuPree Begos, "The Diaries of Adolescent Girls," *Women's Studies International Forum* 10, no. 1 (1987): 69–74.

11. Ida B. Wells, for example, who was born into enslavement in 1862, kept a diary for two years, from 1885 to 1887, before she became a journalist and anti-lynching activist (Wells, *The Memphis Diary of Ida B. Wells: An Intimate Portrait of the Activist as a Young Woman,* ed. Miriam Decosta-Willis [New York: Penguin Random House, 1995]). Grimké's diary is published as Charlotte L. Forten Grimké, *The Journals of Charlotte L. Forten Grimké,* ed. Brenda Stevenson (Oxford: Oxford University Press, 1988). Geneva Cobb-Moore wrote that Grimké's diary was a "hybrid mixture of diary writing, autobiography proper, and racial biography," leaving a record of her "hurtful other life" and the "daily and yearly tensions between her two worlds of inner harmony and beauty, outer racism and chaos" (Cobb-Moore, "When Meanings Meet: The Journals of Charlotte Forten Grimké," in Bunkers and

Notes to Pages 28–39

Huff, *Inscribing the Daily,* 140, 142). See also Kerri Greenidge, *The Grimkes: The Legacy of Slavery in an American Family* (New York: Liveright, 2022), and Joanne Braxton, "Charlotte Forten Grimké and the Search for a Public Voice," in Benstock, *The Private Self,* 254.

12. Raoul, "Women and Diaries," 61. See also Begos, "The Diaries of Adolescent Girls"; Cooper, "Shaping Meaning."

13. Pamiętniki, vol. 2, January 2, 1898, and vol. 1, August 29, 1896; Raoul, "Women and Diaries," 62.

14. Pamiętniki, vol. 3, January 20, 1899. On the movement for women's emancipation in the Polish lands and women's involvement in the political sphere, see Anna Żarnowska and Andrzej Szwarc, eds., *Kobieta i świat polityki: Polska na tle porównawczym w XIX i w początkach XX wieku,* vol. 3, book 1 (Warsaw: Wydawnictwo DiG, Instytut Historyczny Uniwersytetu Warszawskiego, 1994); Anna Żarnowska and Andrzej Szwarc, eds., *Kobieta i kultura: Kobiety wśród twórców kultury intelektualnej i artystycznej w dobie rozbiorów i w niepodległym państwie polskim,* vol. 4; and Anna Żarnowska, "Family and Public Life: Barriers and Interpenetration: Women in Poland at the Turn of the Century," *Women's History Review* 5, no. 4 (1996): 469–86.

15. Pamiętniki, vol. 2, July 1, 1897.

16. Pamiętniki, vol. 1, April 21, 1897, and vol. 3, February 24, 1899.

17. Pamiętniki, vol. 1, October 12 and 31, 1896.

18. Pamiętniki, vol. 2, January 19, 1898. On Eli Makower, see Ursula Phillips, "The 'Jewish Question' in the Novels and Short Stories of Eliza Orzeszkowa," *East European Jewish Affairs* 25, no. 2 (1995): 74–78.

19. Pamiętniki, vol. 1, November 11, 1896. See Isaac Deutscher, "The Non-Jewish Jew," in *The Non-Jewish Jew and Other Essays,* ed. Tamara Deutscher (New York: Oxford University Press, 1968), 26.

20. Pamiętniki, vol. 1, January 16, 1896; vol. 3, August 19, 1899; vol. 2, July 13, 1897.

21. Pamiętniki, vol. 1, November 28, 1896, and vol. 3, January 9, 1900.

22. Pamiętniki, vol. 3, October 14, 1899, and vol. 2, March 22, 1898.

23. Raoul, "Women and Diaries," 95.

24. ChaeRan Freeze, "When Chava Left Home: Gender, Conversion and the Jewish Family in Tsarist Russia," Antony Polonsky, ChaeRan Freeze and Paula Hyman, eds., *Polin: Studies in Polish Jewry* 18 ("Jewish Women in Eastern Europe") (2005): 154; Rachel Manekin, *The Rebellion of the Daughters: Jewish Women Runaways in Habsburg Galicia* (Princeton, N.J.: Princeton University Press, 2020). Todd Endelman notes, "I do not want to argue that their conversions were inauthentic but, rather, that they were driven by a complex of motives, needs and perceptions. The fact that Jews saw Judaism in a negative light and Christianity in a positive light was the outcome of historical

210   Notes to Pages 41–46

circumstances, not spiritual yearning and speculation alone" (Endelman, *Leaving the Jewish Fold: Conversion and Radical Assimilation in Modern Jewish History* [Princeton, N.J.: Princeton University Press, 2015], 11).

2
A Jewish Circle in a Polish City

1. Ferdynand Hoesick, *Powieść mojego życia: Dom rodzicielski*, vol. 2 (Wrocław and Krakow: Zakład Narodowy im. Ossolińskich, 1959), 468; Anna Leo, *Wczoraj: Gawęda o niedawnej przeszłości* (Warsaw: Księgarnia F. Hoesicka, 1929), 58.

2. Hoesick, *Powieść mojego życia*, 2:12–14. Several invitations can be found in the archive of Władysław Korotyński, a journalist who was editor of *Kurjer Warszawski* (the newspaper co-owned by Salomon Lewental); State Archive of the Capital City of Warsaw, *Zbiór Korotyńskich*, 72/201/o. The lane once named for Hortensja is now named for Wojciech Gorski, a Polish pedagogue.

3. Here and in the following paragraph quotes are from Stanisław Baliński, *Trzy poematy o Warszawie* (London: Ognisko Polskie, 1945), 6, 11.

4. Quotations are from David Mazower, "Peretz's Worlds: Separating the Man from the Myth," *Pakn Treger* 72 (Fall 2015); https://www.yiddishbook center.org/language-literature-culture/pakn-treger/peretzs-worlds-separating -man-myth; accessed November 8, 2021. On Peretz, see Ruth R. Wisse, ed., *The I. L. Peretz Reader* (New York: Schocken, 1990); Ken Frieden, *Classic Yiddish Fiction: Abramovitsh, Sholem Aleichem, and Peretz* (Albany: SUNY, 1995); Nathan Cohen, "I. L. Peretz's Part in the Warsaw Publishing Arena," in *The Trilingual Literature of Polish Jews from Different Perspectives: In Memory of I. L. Peretz*, eds. Alina Molisak and Shoshana Ronen (Newcastle upon Tyne: Cambridge Scholars Publishing, 2017), 254–67; Michael Steinlauf: "Hope and Fear: Y. L. Peretz and the Dialectics of Diaspora Nationalism, 1905–1912," in *Warsaw, The Jewish Metropolis: Essays in Honor of the 75th Birthday of Professor Antony Polonsky*, eds. Glenn Dynner and François Guesnet (Leiden: Brill, 2015), 227–51; and "Fear of Purim: Y. L. Peretz and the Canonization of Yiddish Theater," *Jewish Social Studies* 1, no. 3 (1995): 44–65.

5. Mazower, "Peretz's Worlds"; Ruth R. Wisse, "Peretz, Yitskhok Leybush," in *YIVO Encyclopedia of Jews in Eastern Europe*, ed. Gershon Hundert (New Haven: Yale University Press and YIVO, 2008). I am grateful to Kalman Weiser for his comments in this context.

6. On Mathias Bersohn, his brother Jan, and their father, see the State Archive of the Capital City of Warsaw, *Zbiór Korotyńskich*, 72/201/o, micro-film 20637, zespół 201, archival number XI/127, pp. 1–2; François Guesnet, *Polnische Juden im 19. Jahrhundert: Lebensbedingungen, Rechtsnormen und*

Notes to Pages 46–47

Organisation im Wandel (Vienna: Böhlau, 1998), 326, 374; Alina Cała, *Asymilacja Żydów w Królestwie Polskim (1864–1897): Postawy, konflikty, stereotypy* (Warsaw: Państwowy Instytut Wydawniczy, 1989), 138–39; Jacob Shatzky, *Geshikhte fun Yidn in Varshe*, vol. 3 (New York: YIVO, 1953), esp. 328–32. See also Mateusz Mieses, *Polacy-chrześcijanie pochodzenia żydowskiego* (Warsaw: M. Fruchtman, 1938), 25–28; information about the family in this source contains errors.

7. In 1826, seventy families in Warsaw, 1.3 percent of the Jewish population, had permission to live outside the area where Jews were allowed to reside. Artur Eisenbach asserts that by seeking exemptions, these assimilated Jews (as he refers to them), who had petitioned unsuccessfully for equal rights for Jews, were accepting the argument that Jews must assimilate, as they themselves had, before gaining equal rights. The Craftsmen's Assembly formally admitted Jews into guilds in March 1861, even though they were excluded in practice (Eisenbach, *The Emancipation of the Jews in Poland, 1780–1870*, ed. Antony Polonsky [Oxford: Basil Blackwell, 1991], 209–12, 225–28). On the history of these families as part of a broader European network, see Cornelia Aust, *The Jewish Economic Elite: Making Modern Europe* (Bloomington: Indiana University Press, 2018).

8. Jacob Shatzky, "Alexander Kraushar and His Road to Total Assimilation," *YIVO Annual of Jewish Social Studies* 7 (1952): 146–74. Kraushar's first name is spelled "Aleksander" in Polish, whereas Shatzky used the English spelling. Shatzky, in his study of Kraushar, used the term "total assimilation" to distinguish between acculturation, which could be measured by objective changes such as dress and language, and a more subjective feeling of affinity with the surrounding culture. "Total assimilation," he wrote in a still useful definition, "is the organic identification by an individual with the spiritual and cultural life around him and the kind that cannot be ascribed to careerist designs or utilitarian motives." Historians such as Shatzky and others in previous decades used the term "assimilated" and "assimilation" to refer to the processes of identity change that these families underwent. In recent decades some historians have criticized the use of the terms in Jewish historical writing, arguing that they impose a narrative that simplifies a complicated, nonlinear process. However, other words, such as "integration" or "acculturation," do not capture the full extent of the process by which the Jewish families in this book gradually underwent a more thorough transformation in the relationship between the individual and society across generations. I occasionally use the term "assimilationist" to refer to Jews and others who self-identified with this term as a particular ideology. I use the terms "assimilation" and "assimilated" sparingly in order to avoid muddying the discussion of these historical developments. When I use the term "assimilation," it is not intended to necessitate a one-way process. Todd Endelman's entry on assimilation in the

212 Notes to Pages 48–50

YIVO Encyclopedia of Jews in Eastern Europe, which includes secularization as part of the processes that historians have used the term "assimilation" to describe, is the most nuanced analysis of terminology. Without rejecting use of the term, he points to the need to qualify it in analysis in order to avoid generalizations. See Endelman, "Assimilation," in Hundert, *YIVO Encyclopedia of Jews in Eastern Europe*.

9. On the Natanson family, see YIVO Institute for Jewish Research, RG356, Shatzky collection, box 11, folder 149: "History of the Jews in Warsaw, vol. 4, Biographical information"; Guesnet, *Polnische Juden im 19. Jahrhundert*, 288–93; Cała, *Asymilacja Żydów w Królestwie Polskim*, 138; Eisenbach, *The Emancipation of the Jews in Poland;* Shatzky, *Geshikhte fun Yidn in Varshe*, esp. 3:72–73, 123–29; Datner, *Ta i tamta strona*, 124–25, 176–87; Alina Cała and Marcos Silber, "Natanson Family," in Hundert, *YIVO Encyclopedia of Jews in Eastern Europe;* Mieses, *Polacy-chrześcijanie pochodzenia żydowskiego*, 141–52 (as noted, with errors).

10. *Pamiętniki*, vol. 3, February 14, 1899. Hipolit Wawelberg financed the publication of works by Adam Mickiewicz, Eliza Orzeszkowa, and other authors, and he contributed funds toward the construction of the Mickiewicz monument in Warsaw. At the same time, Wawelberg provided assistance to victims of the pogroms in 1881–82 and a decade later helped to fund the Jewish Colonization Association.

11. Samuel Kronenberg founded a bank in the early nineteenth century. He had permission to live outside the Jewish district, had social connections with Polish aristocrats, and was one of an increasing though still small number of Jews who were admitted to Polish Masonic lodges in the early nineteenth century. Yet he also was part of Jewish leadership circles and attended the reform-minded synagogue on Daniłowiczowska Street. Of Kronenberg's eight children who survived into adulthood, only one remained Jewish, according to sources. Some converted to Protestant denominations, while others were baptized as Catholics. Among his children, several remained involved in Jewish life even after their conversion. These conversions might have been intended to overcome obstacles to business interests. In 1845, when Kronenberg's son Leopold married Róża Leo, the daughter of a wealthy family that had converted to Evangelical Christianity, he was baptized as well but remained active in Jewish life, funding Jewish charities and the Polish-language Jewish newspaper founded by Henryk Natanson. Leopold joined the Jewish community's protest in 1859 against accusations in the press of a "Jewish invasion" of Polish culture during the so-called "Jewish War." He reportedly found it difficult to find Polish husbands for his daughters. Leopold's children, like other members of their generation whose parents had been baptized, maintained a distance from their Jewish background. By the time Leopold's third son, Leopold Juljan Kronenberg, published his memoirs

Notes to Pages 50-55

in 1933, he made no reference to his family's Jewish origins. He noted that "for religious education, we, Evangelicals, went to the [minister] of the Evangelical-Reformed church, Pastor Spleszyński" (Leopold Juljan Kronenberg, *Wspomnienia* [Warsaw: F. Hoesick, 1933], 9–10). See also Todd Endelman, "Jewish Converts in Nineteenth-Century Warsaw: A Quantitative Analysis," *Jewish Social Studies* 4, no. 1 (1997): 50; Eisenbach, *The Emancipation of the Jews in Poland*, 261; and Ryszard Kołodziejczyk, *Portret warszawskiego milionera* (Warsaw: Książka i Wiedza, 1968).

12. Pamiętniki, vol. 2, May 7, 1898.

13. On the role of bookstores as salons, see Kazimierz Pollack, *Ze wspomnień starego dziennikarza warszawskiego* (Warsaw: Państwowy Instytut Wydawniczy, 1961), 150–51; Zuzanna Rabska, *Moje życie z książką: Wspomnienia*, vol. 1 (Wrocław: Zakład Narodowy im. Ossolińskich, 1959), 202–3; Klaudia Kowalczyk, *Księgarstwo warszawskie w drugiej połowie XIX wieku* (Warsaw: Historical Museum of the Capital City of Warsaw, 2004). On Yiddish and Hebrew publishing in Warsaw, see Nathan Cohen, "Distributing Knowledge: Warsaw as a Center of Jewish Publishing, 1850–1914," in Dynner and Guesnet, *Warsaw, The Jewish Metropolis*, 180–206.

14. Isaiah Trunk, "Geshikhte fun Yidn in Vloclavek biz dem ershtn velt-krig (1802–1914)," in *Vloclavek un umgegnt: Yizkor bukh*, eds. Katri'el F. Tkhorsh and Me'ir Kozen (Tel Aviv: Irgun yots'e Vlotslavek veha-sevivah be-Yisra'el uve-Artsot ha-Berit, 1967), 49–85; and Marcin Wodziński, "Włocławek," trans. Christina Manetti, in Hundert, *YIVO Encyclopedia of Jews in Eastern Europe*.

15. Trunk, "Geshikhte fun Yidn in Vloclavek," 63–64.

16. Salomon Lewental's son-in-law Ferdynand Hoesick published Salomon's autobiographical sketch as a footnote in the first edition of Hoesick's memoirs in 1935. Ferdynand Hoesick, *Dom rodzicielski*, vol. 4 (Krakow: W. L. Anczyc i Spółka, 1935), 337. The sketch is not in the 1959 edition of Hoesick's memoir, which was published under the title *Powieść mojego życia* (cited in n. 1 above).

17. On the Rabbinic School in Warsaw, including a list of its graduates, see [no author listed], *Z dziejów gminy starozakonnych w warszawie w XIX stuleciu*, vol. 1: *Szkolnictwo* (Krakow: W. L. Anczyc, 1907). See also Marcin Wodziński, "Language, Ideology and the Beginnings of the Integrationist Movement in the Kingdom of Poland in the 1860s," *East European Jewish Affairs* 34, no. 2 (2004): 21–40; and Agnieszka Jagodzińska, "Warszawska Szkoła Rabinów w świetle źródeł misyjnych," *Kwartalnik Historii Żydów* 1 (249) (2014): 142–61. In the 1850s and 1860s, Wodziński found, maskilic circles in Poland split into three groups: the pro-Russian maskilim, who wrote largely in Hebrew; the radical assimilationists; and the Polonized integrationists, who saw themselves as the "middle way" of the three groups. Marcin Wodziński, *Haskalah and Hasidism in the Kingdom of Poland: A History of Conflict*, trans.

214 Notes to Pages 55–58

Sarah Cozens and Agnieszka Mirowska (Portland, Ore.: Littman Library of Jewish Civilization, 2009), 5.

18. Alexander Guterman, "The Origins of the Great Synagogue in Warsaw on Tłomackie Street," in *The Jews in Warsaw: A History,* eds. Władsław T. Bartoszewski and Antony Polonsky (Oxford: Basil Blackwell, 1991), 195; Eleonora Bergman, *"Nie masz bożnicy powszechnej": Synagogi i domy modlitwy w Warszawie od końca XVIII do początku XXI wieku* (Warsaw: Wydawnictwo DiG, 2007).

19. The number of subscribers to *Izraelita* is from *Izraelita,* December 4 (December 16), 1870. In 1862, the two "progressive" synagogues in Warsaw, on Daniłowiczowska Street and Nalewki Street, had room for 300 and 216 people respectively. Guterman, "The Origins of the Great Synagogue," 195.

20. Agnieszka Jagodzińska: *Pomiędzy: Akulturacja Żydów Warszawy w drugiej połowie XIX wieku* (Wrocław: Wydawnictwo Uniwersytetu Wrocławskiego, 2008), 36, 154, and "Reformers, Missionaries, and Converts: Interactions between the London Society and Jews in Warsaw in the First Half of the Nineteenth Century," in *Converts of Conviction: Faith and Scepticism in Nineteenth Century European Jewish Society,* ed. David B. Ruderman (Berlin: De Gruyter, 2018), 12.

21. On the spread of Hasidism in Poland, see Glenn Dynner, *Men of Silk: The Hasidic Conquest of Polish Jewish Society* (Oxford: Oxford University Press, 2008).

22. In addition to Salomon Lewental, Jewish publishers of Polish books who graduated from the Rabbinic School included Samuel and Maurycy Orgelbrand, Henryk Natanson, Józef Unger, Jan Breslauer, and members of the Merzbach family. The father of the publisher Gabriel Centnerszwer was a math lecturer at the seminary. See *Z dziejów gminy starozakonnych* and Henryk Kroszczor, *Kartki z historii Żydów w Warszawie, XIX–XX w.* (Warsaw: Jewish Historical Institute, 1979), 56–144.

23. *Kurjer Warszawski,* October 27 (November 8), 1878, 4. Reference to Ernestyna Glucksberg's death and funeral is in the State Archive of the Capital City of Warsaw, *Zbiór Korotyńskich,* 72/201/0, archival number XI 1314, k. 1–3, p. 4. Her continued involvement in Jewish life after her marriage to Lewental is documented in Jacob Shatzky's notes for his multivolume history of Jews in Warsaw, and they include lists of charitable contributions to Jewish organizations after 1863. YIVO Institute for Jewish Research, RG356, box 6, folder 70.

24. See Salomon Lewental's autobiographical sketch in Hoesick, *Dom rodzicielski,* 4:337.

25. On the history and physical layout of bookstores in Warsaw, see Marianna Mlekicka, *Wydawcy książek w Warszawie w okresie zaborów* (Warsaw: PWN, 1987), and Kowalczyk, *Księgarstwo warszawskie w drugiej połowie XIX wieku.*

Notes to Pages 59–62

26. Rabska, *Moje życie z książką*, 1: 202. Another member of the Merzbach family, Ludwik, was a publisher and bookseller in Poznań. On the Merzbach family, see Irena Treichel, ed., *Słownik pracowników książki Polskiej* (Lodz: Państwowe Wydawnictwo Naukowe, 1972), 577–78; Kowalczyk, *Księgarstwo warszawskie w drugiej połowie XIX wieku*, 100, 103, 120, 207; Mlekicka, *Wydawcy książek w Warszawie w okresie zaborów*, 176–78; Rabska, *Moje życie z książką*, 1:202–6; *Bibliographie Nationale: Dictionnaire des écrivains belges et catalogue de leurs publications, 1830–1880*, vol. 2 (Brussels: P. Weissenbruch, 1892), 665; *Lexikon des gesamten Buchwesens, Zweite, völlig neu bearbeitete Auflage*, vol. 5 (Stuttgart: Anton Hiersemann, 1999); Stanisław Burkot, "Józef Ignacy Kraszewski i wydawcy (po roku 1863)," *Pamiętnik Literacki* 49, no. 1 (1958): 209–325; Aleksander Kraushar, "Księgarz-poeta (Henryk Merzbach)," in Kraushar, *Obrazy i wizerunki historyczne* (Warsaw: Jan Fiszer, 1906), 403–12; Idesbald Goddeeris, *La Grande Émigration polonaise en Belgique (1831–1870): Élites et masses en exile à l'époque romantique* (Frankfurt: Peter Lang, 2013). In response to anti-Jewish polemics in *Gazeta Warszawska* in 1859, the Polish historian Joachim Lelewel wrote a pamphlet in defense of Jews in the form of a letter to Ludwik Merzbach, who published it under the title *Sprawa Żydowska w 1859 w liście do Ludwika Merzbacha* (Poznań: Ludwik Merzbach, 1860).

27. Shatzky, "Alexander Kraushar and His Road to Total Assimilation," 162; Leo, *Wczoraj*, 115. On the history of Warsaw's literary salons, see Janina Kulczycka-Saloni, *Życie literackie Warszawy (1864–1892)* (Warsaw: Państwowy Instytut Wydawniczy, 1970); Piotr Łopuszański, *Warszawa literacka przełomu XIX i XX wieku* (Warsaw: Pruszyński, 2019); Julian Krzyżanowski, "Kultura literacka Warszawy lat 1895–1905," in *Z dziejów książek i bibliotek w warszawie*, ed. Stanisław Tazbir (Warsaw: Państwowy Instytut Wydawniczy, 1961), 223–29.

28. On Deotyma's salon, see Olaf Krysowski, "Deotyma—'Dziesiąta muza' Norwida," *Studia Norwidiana* 38 (2020): 5–20; Kulczycka-Saloni, *Życie literackie Warszawy*, 90–99. Letters from Łuszczewska to Hortensja are in the archives of Biblioteka Narodowa, collection of Bronisław Gubrynowicz, sygnatura 7152 II, fragment korespondencji Hortensji z Bersohnów Lewentalowej z lat 1886–1914, pp. 12–13.

29. Eisenbach, *The Emancipation of the Jews in Poland*, 242, 247; Shatzky, "Alexander Kraushar and His Road to Total Assimilation," 146–74; quote is on p. 151; Aleksander Kraushar, "Roman Rogiński" and "Rodzina Męczenników (ze wspomnień szkolnych)," in Kraushar, *Echa przeszłości: Szkice, wizerunki i wspomnienia historyczne* (Warsaw: Tow. Akc. S. Orgelbranda Synów, 1917), 127–48; Datner, *Ta i tamta strona*, 117–21.

30. Shatzky, "Alexander Kraushar and His Road to Total Assimilation," 154–55; Aleksander Kraushar, *Kartki z pamiętnika Alkara z lat 1858–1865*, vol. 2 (Krakow: G. Gebethner i Spółka, 1913), 149–50; Magdalena Opalski and

216 Notes to Pages 62–68

Israel Bartal, *Poles and Jews: A Failed Brotherhood* (Waltham, Mass.: Brandeis University Press, 1992), 100.

31. Stanislaus A. Blejwas, "Polish Positivism and the Jews," *Jewish Social Studies* 46, no. 1 (1984): 21–36; Robert Blobaum, "The Politics of Antisemitism in Fin-de-Siècle Warsaw," *Journal of Modern History* 73, no. 2 (2001).

32. Shatzky, "Alexander Kraushar and His Road to Total Assimilation," 163.

33. Rabska, *Moje życie z książką,* 1:52; Maria Wierzbicka, "Z burżuazji do inteligencji: Jadwiga Kràusharowa," in *Kobieta i edukacja na ziemiach polskich w XIX i XX w.: Zbiór studiów,* vol. 2, eds. Anna Żarnowska and Andrzej Szwarc (Warsaw: Instytut Historyczny Uniwersytetu Warszawskiego, 1992), 217–27. Jadwiga became especially close with Maria Wysłouchawa, a political and social activist among peasants, and the two friends became involved in an organization that sought to bring education to women in the countryside.

34. Leo, *Wczoraj,* 116–17; Shatzky, "Alexander Kraushar and His Road to Total Assimilation," 162–63; Rabska, *Moje życie z książką,* 103–4. Orzeszkowa is cited in Shatzky, "Alexander Kraushar and His Road to Total Assimilation," 163. On the Frankists, see Paweł Maciejko, *The Mixed Multitude: Jacob Frank and the Frankist Movement, 1755–1816* (Philadelphia: University of Pennsylvania Press, 2011).

35. Leo, *Wczoraj,* 115; Shatzky, "Alexander Kraushar and His Road to Total Assimilation," 162.

36. Pollack, *Ze wspomnień starego dziennikarza warszawskiego,* 32–33. The numbers mentioned are based on my analysis of lists of publishers and booksellers in Kowalczyk, *Księgarstwo warszawskie w drugiej połowie XIX wieku,* supplemented by entries in Treichel, *Słownik pracowników książki Polskiej* and the *Polish Biographical Dictionary.* Gecel Zalcstein's last name also appears as Salcstein or Salzstein.

37. Pollack, *Ze wspomnień starego dziennikarza warszawskiego,* 32–33.

38. Robert Blobaum, *Boycott! The Politics of Anti-Semitism in Poland, 1912–1914* (Washington, D.C.: National Council for Eurasian and East European Research, 1998), 6.

39. Opalski and Bartal, *Poles and Jews,* 99, 105–11. About Polish Positivist attitudes toward Jewish integration, see also Stanislaus Blejwas: *Realism in Polish Politics: Warsaw Positivism and National Survival in Nineteenth Century Poland* (New Haven: Yale University Press, 1984), and "Polish Positivism and the Jews"; Cała, *Asymilacja Żydów w Królestwie Polskim,* 216–67; Theodore Weeks, *From Assimilation to Antisemitism: The "Jewish Question" in Poland, 1850–1914* (DeKalb: Northern Illinois University Press, 2005); Agnieszka Friedrich, *Bolesław Prus and the Jews* (Boston: Academic Studies Press, 2021).

40. Opalski and Bartal, *Poles and Jews,* 103; "The Recent Events," *Izraelita,* no. 50, year 16, December 18 (December 30) 1881, 409. On the 1881 pogrom

Notes to Pages 69–76

in Warsaw, see Cała, *Asymilacja Żydów w Królestwie Polskim*, 268–78; Shatzky, *Geshikhte fun Yidn in Varshe*, 3:99–109.

41. Shatzky, *Geshikhte fun Yidn in Varshe*, 3:107; Opalski and Bartal, *Poles and Jews*, 135; letter from Kraushar to Kraszewski, August 2, 1886; cited in Wierzbicka, "Z burżuazji do inteligencji," 223–24; Aleksander Kraushar, *Frank i Frankiści Polscy (1726–1816)* (Krakow: Gebethner, 1895). See also "Introduction," in François Guesnet, Howard Lupovitch, and Antony Polonsky, eds., *Polin: Studies in Polish Jewry* 31 ("Poland and Hungary: Jewish Realities Compared") (2019): 3–4. Alina Cała noted that Kraszewski "was the first one to introduce a later popularized image of a nouveau-riche, materialistically oriented Jew who clumsily imitated the behavior of the Polish nobility." Cała asserts, however, that although he sometimes portrayed Jews stereotypically, he also "tried to depict them realistically, as distinct persons with individual features" (Cała, *Jew: The Eternal Enemy? The History of Antisemitism in Poland*, trans. Jan Burzyński, ed. Mikołaj Gołubiewski [Berlin: Peter Lang, 2018], 125). Weeks wrote, "Conservatives such as Józef Ignacy Kraszewski criticized the Jewish plutocracy, expressing fears about the negative influence on age-old, Polish noble traditions of a new, often Jewish (at least by origin) class of men, such as Leopold Kronenberg and Matthias Rosen, whose wealth was based on commerce and finance" (Weeks, *From Assimilation to Antisemitism*, 318). Jan Jeleński was the founder and editor of the antisemitic newspaper *Rola*.

42. "The Recent Events," 409. See also Shatzky, *Geshikhte fun Yidn in Varshe*, 3:106–8, and Izaak Cylkow, "To One's Own," *Izraelita*, no. 4, year 17, January 15 (27), 1882, 25–26. By World War I, about 3.5 million Jews had emigrated from Eastern Europe, the majority to the United States. In the last two decades of the nineteenth century, about 760,000 Jews from Eastern Europe came to the United States, and from 1900 to the beginning of World War I, another 1.6 million Jews arrived. See Hasia Diner, *The Jews of the United States, 1654–2000* (Berkeley: University of California Press, 2004), 71–111.

43. *Podręcznik księgarski: Przewodnik praktyczny dla wydawców, księgarzy, pomocników i praktykantów księgarskich na podstawie swojskich i obcych źródeł opracowany* (Warsaw: T. Paprocki i S-ka, 1896), 191–92.

3

The Disillusionment of a Polish Jew

1. The newspaper at the time was spelled *Kurjer Warszawski*. I have referred to it using that spelling instead of the contemporary spelling of *Kurier*.

2. *Pamiętniki*, vol. 2, September 21, 1898.

3. The negative view of a "Jewish" name, apparent in Alicja's diary and in recollections of Hortensja's views, as well as in Anna Leo's reference in her

218　　　　　　　　　　　　　　　　　　　　　　　Notes to Pages 77–78

memoirs to the desire to change a "foreign last name" for a "Polish" one, is in striking contrast with a finding by Alexander Guterman that "a remarkable characteristic of assimilating Jews in Warsaw, including those who moved away and finally converted to Christianity, was their unwillingness to abandon their Jewishness completely. They tended to keep their Jewish names, and even emphasized with pride their Jewish origin, out of a sense of historical continuity" (Guterman, "The Origins of the Great Synagogue," 204). Gender and generational change might account for the difference.

4. Mlekicka, *Wydawcy książek w Warszawie w okresie zaborów*, 128. In Mlekicka's analysis of the national background of Warsaw booksellers, she counts an equal number of five booksellers of Polish and Jewish background between 1795 and 1831, with none of German background and one of unknown origin; in the period between 1832 and 1864, Jews comprised half of the twenty-six sellers of new Polish books, while six were of ethnic Polish background and seven of German background, according to her statistics. Between the 1830s and the 1870s, nearly two-thirds of newly opened bookstores in Warsaw selling new Polish-language books were owned by Jews, according to my analysis of lists of publishers and booksellers collected by Kowalczyk, *Księgarstwo warszawskie w drugiej połowie XIX wieku*, and supplemented by *Przewodnik bibliograficzny*; Treichel, *Słownik pracowników książki Polskiej*; and the *Polish Biographical Dictionary*.

5. On the gradual nature of the spread of national identity beyond the elites, see Tara Zahra, "Imagined Non-Communities: National Indifference as a Category of Analysis," *Slavic Review* 69 (Spring 2010): 93–119. The involvement of Jews in East European publishing has been noted in histories of literature and printing in individual countries, but these references have been mainly factual, without an exploration of the relevance of the publishers' backgrounds. Histories of Jewish publishing activity, meanwhile, have focused either on Jewish publishing in non-Jewish languages in Germany, Western Europe, the United States, and South America or on publishing in Jewish languages. Research into Jewish publishing in Eastern Europe has focused mainly on Yiddish and Hebrew. In a history of the book in Jewish life, Ze'ev Gries argues that the history of printing in Russia had little significance for Jewish printing in the Polish lands during the partitions, and he implicitly defines such printing as printing in Jewish languages (Gries, *The Book in the Jewish World, 1700–1900* [Liverpool: Littman Library of Jewish Civilization, 2007]). For a detailed history of Jewish publishing in Eastern Europe, including publishers of books in Polish and Russian, see Kenneth B. Moss, "Printing and Publishing," in Hundert, *YIVO Encyclopedia of Jews in Eastern Europe*. In a chapter on Jews in Polish cultural life in his history of Jews in Warsaw, Shatzky also noted the role of Jewish publishers in the Polish book trade, including Lewental, the Orgelbrands, and the Glucksbergs

Notes to Page 78

219

(Shatzky, *Geshikhte fun Yidn in Varshe*, 3:406–23). On the role of publishers more broadly in cultural life and politics in Western and Central Europe in the eighteenth and nineteenth centuries, see Robert Darnton, *The Literary Underground of the Old Regime* (Cambridge, Mass.: Harvard University, Press, 1985); Pamela E. Selwyn, *Everyday Life in the German Book Trade: Friedrich Nicolai as Bookseller and Publisher in the Age of Enlightenment, 1750–1810* (University Park: Pennsylvania State University Press, 2000); Gary Stark, *Banned in Berlin: Literary Censorship in Imperial Germany, 1871–1918* (New York: Berghahn Books, 2009); Lynne Tatlock, ed., *Publishing Culture and the "Reading Nation": German Book History in the Long Nineteenth Century* (Rochester, N.Y.: Camden House, 2010).

6. See, for example, Alex Drace-Francis, *The Making of Modern Romanian Culture: Literacy and the Development of National Identity* (London: Tauris Academic Studies, 2006), 114–23, 160–69, on the Samitca publishers of Romanian books; Shmuel Spector, "Efron, Ilya," in *Encyclopaedia Judaica*, 2nd ed., vol. 6, on the founder of a Russian-language publishing house that published an eighty-six-volume Russian encyclopedia as well as a sixteen-volume Russian Jewish encyclopedia, *Yevreyskaya Entsiklopediya;* Marcel Cornis-Pope and John Neubauer, eds., *History of the Literary Cultures of East-Central Europe: Junctures and Disjunctures in the 19th and 20th Centuries*, vol. 3: *The Making and Remaking of Literary Institutions* (Amsterdam: J. Benjamins, 2004), 40–41; Isidore Singer and Ludwig Venetianer, "Révai, Mór," *Jewish Encyclopedia*, vol. 10 (New York: Funk and Wagnalls, 1906), 390, on the Révai publishers of a Hungarian encyclopedia and books. On Jewish publishers in non-Jewish East European languages in the first decades of the twentieth century, see, among others, Michael Biggins and Janet Crayne, eds., *Publishing in Yugoslavia's Successor States* (New York: Haworth Information Press, 2000), on the Kon and Svarc publishers of Serbian books; Uri Toeplitz, "Koussevitzky, Serge," in *Encyclopaedia Judaica*, vol. 12 (Farmington Hills, Mich.: Thomson Gale, and Detroit: Macmillan Reference, 2006); and A. Lourie, *Sergei Koussevitzky and His Epoch* (Charleston, S.C.: Nabu Press, 2011; reproduced from the original 1931 edition), on a publisher of works by Russian composers.

7. Burkot, "Józef Ignacy Kraszewski i wydawcy (po roku 1863)," 209. Kraszewski had been corresponding with Orgelbrand regularly at least since the early 1840s about the publication of Kraszewski's novels and short stories. Their correspondence is in the archives of the library of Jagiellonian University in Krakow, special collections, manuscript section, archival numbers 6457 IV and 6524 IV. Unlike Orgelbrand's encyclopedia, encyclopedia projects in other countries were often initiated by a group of scholars, as in France, rather than by a publisher. On the French encyclopedia, see Philipp Blom, *Enlightening the World: Encyclopedie, the Book That Changed the Course of History* (New York: St. Martin's Press, 2004), and Joanna Stalnaker, *The*

220 Notes to Page 79

Unfinished Enlightenment: Description in the Age of the Encyclopedia (Ithaca: Cornell University Press, 2010). Orgelbrand was not the first one to attempt the monumental undertaking of publishing a multivolume encyclopedia. Two other publishers also sought to publish a Polish encyclopedia: the Glucksbergs, who issued a handful of volumes before the project was cut short, and Daniel Friedlein, a Krakow publisher whose project did not progress beyond the planning stage. Friedlein's ancestor opened one of the first bookstores in the Polish lands, in Krakow in 1796, and began publishing activity in 1828. See Ludwik Fiszer, *Wspomnienia starego księgarza* (Warsaw: Czytelnik, 1959), 162. Orgelbrand published the Babylonian Talmud between 1860 and 1864. He was an exception in this regard; no other major Jewish publisher of Polish books in the nineteenth century issued works in Jewish languages as well, although the publishing catalogue of the Jewish publisher Gabriel Centnerszwer included Polish-language books on Jewish topics, especially children's books, and Henryk Natanson published both general Polish journals and Polish-language works on Jewish life. Catalogues of books issued by the Centnerszwer, Glucksberg, Orgelbrand, Lewental, and other publishing houses are located in the Ossolineum Library and archive in Wrocław and the National Library in Warsaw.

8. Letter from Samuel Orgelbrand to Kraszewski, August 20, 1856; in Jacek Kajtoch, "Z korespondencji Kraszewskiego (Wybór listów Samuela Orgelbranda)," *Pamiętnik Literacki* 49, no. 1 (1958): 205–6. It is unclear how Kraszewski responded to Orgelbrand since Orgelbrand's personal papers are not extant, and Orgelbrand's letters to Kraszewski from the 1850s and 1860s are missing from the collection of Kraszewski's correspondence in the library of Jagiellonian University, special collections, manuscript section, even though an entry on Orgelbrand in the *Polish Biographical Dictionary*, vol. 24, from 1979, refers to letters from the 1850s and 1860s in the Kraszewski collection.

9. The entry for Hasidism, for example, was written by Daniel Neufeld, editor of *Izraelita;* the newspaper represented the community of Polish Jews who, unlike Hasidim, sought to integrate into Polish culture. The entry was heavily edited, with large sections cut out. The manuscript is located in the archives of the Muzeum Narodowe in Warsaw, collection of the Archives of Institutions and Editorial Boards of Publications: "Orgelbrand Encyclopedia. Publishing House. Materials from editorial folders," folder 65421 (950). Although maskilim in Central Europe viewed Hasidism as insular and backward in culture, education, and religious practice, Wodziński emphasizes the distinctiveness of maskilic attitudes toward the Hasidic movement in the Kingdom of Poland compared with the *haskalah* in other parts of Europe, despite some similarities. Only in the 1860s did the moderate successors to the Polish *haskalah* begin to take up Hasidism as an ideological challenge, according to Wodziński. Even then, however, their attitude was not uniformly

Notes to Pages 79–81   221

negative, he argues; the integrationist successors to the maskilim, while critical of Hasidism as a representative of traditional Judaism, at times sought a kind of alliance with the Hasidic movement in order to initiate educational and other reforms (Wodziński, *Haskalah and Hasidism in the Kingdom of Poland*, 1–7). See also Raphael Mahler, *Hasidism and the Jewish Enlightenment: Their Confrontation in Galicia and Poland in the First Half of the Nineteenth Century*, trans. Eugene Orenstein, Aaron Klein, and Jenny Machlowitz Klein (Philadelphia: Jewish Publication Society, 1985).

10. Letter from Orgelbrand to Kraszewski, August 20, 1856, in Kajtoch, "Z korespondencji Kraszewskiego," 205–6.

11. Letter from Orgelbrand to Kraszewski, August 20, 1856, in Kajtoch, "Z korespondencji Kraszewskiego," 206. The citation is from Irena Treichel, "Samuel Orgelbrand," *Polish Biographical Dictionary*, vol. 24, 188. Orgelbrand had trouble finding a single editor, he wrote to Kraszewski, so he established an editorial board comprised of six historians, literary critics, and other scholars, several of whose works he had previously published. Only fragments of documents from the Orgelbrand publishing house and the encyclopedia project are extant. Documents from subsequent editions of the encyclopedia published after his death are contained in the library of the Institute for Literary Studies of the Polish Academy of Sciences, Warsaw branch, Archives of Societies, Publishing Houses, and Editorial Boards of Periodicals, collection of Encyklopedia Powszechna S. Orgelbranda. Supplementa. Materiały z lat 1899–1912, archival number 365, folders 1–103. Other partial collections of documents from the encyclopedia project's editorial board are located in the archives of the Muzeum Narodowe and the library archives of the Krakow branch of the Polish Academy of Sciences. The encyclopedia entry for Poland is in *Encyklopedia Powszechna*, vol. 21 (Warsaw: S. Orgelbrand, 1865), 5–198.

12. Catalogues from the Glucksbergs' publishing house are located in the library of Zakład Archiwum im. Ossolińskich in Wrocław.

13. "Great Polish booksellers of Jewish origin are a tradition that reaches from Glucksberg to Jakub Mortkowicz," wrote Aleksander Hertz (*Jews in Polish Culture* [Evanston, Ill.: Northwestern University Press, 1988], 229). About the Mortkowicz family, see the memoir by a granddaughter, Joanna Olczak-Ronikier, *W ogrodzie pamięci* (Krakow: Znak, 2001). The languages in which the Glucksbergs printed and published changed as Warsaw fell under successive political authorities during the early period of partition. The first Glucksberg involved in Poland's book trade, Lewin, lent and sold books in French. Only after Lewin's younger brother, Natan, took over Lewin's bookstore in 1817 did the family begin printing and publishing in Polish, almost exclusively so by the 1830s. During the second generation of the Glucksbergs' publishing activity, the family also occasionally printed decrees of the Russian partitioning authorities. Natan Glucksberg maintained trade contacts in

Kiev, while the publishing house of Jan Glucksberg issued a handful of works in Russian as well as a collection in Polish titled "Hymns and Prayers on the Occasion of the Coronation of [Tsar] Nicholas I."

14. Józef Zawadzki, for example, the most prominent publisher of ethnic Polish background from the 1830s to the 1870s, complained to Kraszewski about newly opened bookstores owned by Jews in Vilnius, where he was based, and lamented in his letters to Kraszewski the latter's decision to publish his works with the Glucksberg family. Tadeusz Turkowski, ed., *Materiały do dziejów literatury i oświaty na Litwie i Rusi: Z archiwum drukarni i księgarni Józefa Zawadzkiego z lat 1805–1865*, vol. 3, part 1 (Wilno: Towarzystwo Przyjaciół Nauk w Wilnie, 1937), 109, 119.

15. See, for example, letters from Michał Glucksberg to the ethnographer and musicologist Jan Karłowicz, in which Glucksberg refers to newspapers and books that he sent to Karłowicz. Zakład Archiwum im. Ossolińskich, Wrocław, manuscript division, collection 58, archival number DE-9378 (29/4), letter from Michał Glucksberg, March 6, 1876; and letters from Maurycy Orgelbrand to Jan Karłowicz, Ossolineum, DE-9550 (120). See also numerous letters from the Orgelbrands, Glucksbergs, and Salomon Lewental to Józef Ignacy Kraszewski in the library of Jagiellonian University in Krakow, special collections, manuscript section, archival numbers 6457/IV, 6456/IV, 6459/IV, 6473/IV, 6503/IV, 6516/IV.

16. Kowalczyk, *Księgarstwo warszawskie w drugiej połowie XIX wieku;* Fiszer, *Wspomnienia starego księgarza,* 25, 72–73; Zbysław Arct, *Gawędy o księgarzach* (Wrocław: Zakład Narodowy im. Ossolińskich, 1972), 88; "Jakub Przeworski," in Treichel, *Słownik pracowników książki Polskiej,* 722–23. A member of the Arct family in an earlier generation, Michał Arct, had a prestigious bookstore on Nowy Świat, not far from Salomon Lewental's. Arct was from a Jewish family from Zamość and Lublin and converted to Christianity in 1857.

17. On the role of language in nationalist movements and ideologies, see Joshua Fishman, *Language and Nationalism: Two Integrative Essays* (Rowley, Mass.: Newbury House, 1973).

18. Tadeusz Korzon, ed., *Pamiętniki Jakoba Gieysztora z lat 1857–1865* (Wilno: Biblioteka Pamiętników, 1913), 55.

19. Shatzky, *Geshikhte fun Yidn in Varshe,* 3:406–23. Shatzky's assertion that Jewish publishers were important in circulating Polish Positivist literature is supported by my analysis of Lewental's publishing output based on annual publishing catalogues, held in the Biblioteka Narodowa in Warsaw; his correspondence with Orzeszkowa and other writers; and the trade journal for publishers and booksellers, *Przewodnik Bibliograficzny,* which published lists of new books.

20. The history of humanism in Italy and Germany in the original German is Ludwig Geiger, *Renaissance und Humanismus in Italien und Deutschland*

Notes to Pages 85–86

(Berlin: G. Grote, 1882). Geiger's father was one of the founders of the German movement of Reform Judaism, Abraham Geiger. In addition to being a historian of humanism and the Renaissance, Geiger also helped to found a journal for German Jewish history and wrote books about Goethe, German Jews, Jews in Berlin, and a biography of his father, among other works.

21. Weeks, *From Assimilation to Antisemitism*, 94, 100; Brian Porter, *When Nationalism Began to Hate* (New York: Oxford University Press, 2000), 178. About the Natansons as targets of anti-Jewish polemics in *Rola*, see Agnieszka Friedrich, "'The Natansons as an Embodiment of the Evils of Assimilation in the Anti-Semitic Weekly *Rola*,'" *Scripta Judaica Cracoviensia* 16 (2018): 55–64.

22. Opalski and Bartal, *Poles and Jews*, 101

23. "Sprawy bieżące," *Niwa*, vol. 31 (1887): 794–95; Antoni Zaleski, "List szósty: Cenzury i dziennikarstwo," in Antoni Zaleski, *Towarzystwo Warszawskie: Listy do przyjaciółki przez Baronowa XYZ*, ed. Ryszard Kołodziejczyk (Warsaw: Państwowy Instytut Wydawniczy, 1971), 356; cited also in Datner, *Ta i tamta strona*, 256. (Datner and a few other academic sources use the spelling "Lewenthal" as well.) While historians have often characterized *Niwa* as an antisemitic journal, its reputation was not entirely justified, according to Theodore Weeks. Such a characterization, Weeks noted, often refers to the newspaper's criticism of the "Stock Exchange Memorandum," a report written in 1885 by Jan Bloch and Henryk Natanson, chairman and vice chairman of the Warsaw Stock Exchange, to "defend Jews from accusations that they exploited the Christian population and exerted a negative influence on the economy" at a time when government authorities were considering whether to extend the restrictive "May Laws" of 1882 to Jews in the Kingdom of Poland. The report emphasized the economic role of Jews in order to assert that restrictions would damage the economy of the Polish lands. *Niwa* published the report with critical commentary. However, Weeks wrote, the newspaper "did not explicitly deny the possibility of assimilation" and still "recognized Jews as fellow citizens" (Weeks, *From Assimilation to Antisemitism*, 96–98). Elżbieta Malinowska wrote the following about *Niwa*: "The apogee of the fight [between the 'old' and 'new' press] came in 1872. The movement of the 'young,' developed up until that point by *Przegląd Tygodniowy* and *Opiekuń Domowy*, was strengthened by two new journals: *Niwa* and *Przyroda i Przemysł*. They were united by common ideological positions, by a scientific, secular, and rational outlook on the world, as well as by a social program promoting the economic revival of the country in the areas of agriculture, industry, and trade" (Malinowska, *Problematyka Literacka "Kłosów"* [Katowice: Uniwersytet Śląski 1992], 18). Datner's excellent study of Jewish intellectuals in nineteenth-century Warsaw drew my attention to the "Lewental affair" (*Ta i tamta strona*, 256–58).

24. "Co mamy czynic?" part 2, *Izraelita* no. 15, year 8, March 30 (April 11) 1873, 113. See also, for example, "Jew and Israelite," *Jutrzenka*, no. 44, October 31, 1862, 366–67. Wodziński notes, "From the late 1870s the debate with antisemitism became *Izraelita*'s most important theme, and religious discussions between Jews became secondary" (*Haskalah and Hasidism in the Kingdom of Poland*, 224). See also Zuzanna Kołodziejska, *Izraelita, 1866–1915: Znaczenie kulturowe i literackie czasopisma* (Krakow: Wydawnictwo Uniwersytetu Jagiellońskiego, 2014).

25. Richard Wagner, "Jewry in Music (1850)," in *The Jew in the Modern World: A Documentary History*, 3rd edition, eds. Paul Mendes-Flohr and Jehuda Reinharz (New York: Oxford University Press, 2010), 302–5; "A Few Words about the Brochure of Richard Wagner, 'Judaism in Music,'" *Izraelita* no. 16, year 4, April 11 (April 23), 1869, 137–38. Grzegorz Krzywiec, on the other hand, emphasizes the influence of racial ideas earlier than when other historians date the development (*Chauvinism, Polish Style*, 93–140); Weeks, *From Assimilation to Antisemitism*, 178.

26. "Rasa Semicka," *Izraelita*, no. 12, year 8, March 9 (March 21), 1873, 89–91; *Izraelita* no. 14, year 8, March 23 (April 4), 1873, 105–7; *Izraelita*, no. 15, March 30 (April 11), 1873, 113–14; *Izraelita*, no. 17, April 20 (May 2), 1873, 133–35; "Co mamy czynić?," 113–14.

27. Von Treitschke wrote the following: "It cannot be denied that the Jews have contributed their part to the promoting of business with its dishonesty and bold cupidity, that they share heavily in the guilt for the contemptible materialism of our age that regards every kind of work only as business and threatens to suffocate the old simple pride and joy the German felt in his work. . . . What we have to demand from our Jewish fellow-citizens is simple: that they become Germans, regard themselves simply and justly as Germans, without prejudice to their faith and their old sacred past, which all of us hold in reverence; for we do not want an era of German-Jewish mixed culture to follow after thousands of years of German civilization. It would be a sin to forget that a great number of Jews, baptized and unbaptized, . . . were Germans in the best sense of the word, men in whom we revere the noble and fine traits of the German spirit. At the same time it cannot be denied that there are numerous and powerful groups among our Jews who definitely do not have the good will to become simply Germans" (Heinrich von Treitschke, "A Word about Our Jewry," in Mendes-Flohr and Reinharz, *The Jew in the Modern World*, 319–22). Von Treitschke's accusations against Jews were intertwined with criticism of the capitalist system, which was disorienting social and economic elites whose status was rooted in the old feudal system. There is a large historiography about the origins of modern antisemitism in nineteenth-century Europe. For an overview of the historiography and key issues, see Sol Goldberg, Keith Kalman Weiser, and Scott Ury, eds., *Key Concepts in the*

Notes to Pages 90–92

Study of Antisemitism (London: Palgrave Macmillan, 2021). For an anthology of key texts, see Scott Ury and Guy Miron, eds., *Antisemitism and the Politics of History* (Waltham, Mass.: Brandeis University Press, 2023). Especially helpful is David Engel, "Away from a Definition of Anti-Semitism: An Essay in the Semantics of Historical Description," in *Rethinking European Jewish History*, eds. Jeremy Cohen and Moshe Rosman (Liverpool: Littman Library of Jewish Civilization and Liverpool University Press, 2014); republished in Ury and Miron, *Antisemitism and the Politics of History*.

28. Beth Holmgren, *Rewriting Capitalism: Literature and the Market in Tsarist Russia and the Kingdom of Poland* (Pittsburgh: University of Pittsburgh Press, 1998); Datner, *Ta i tamta strona*, 234.

29. "Sprawy bieżące."

30. Bartłomiej Szyndler, *Tygodnik ilustrowany "Kłosy" (1865–1890)* (Wrocław: Zakład Narodowy im. Ossolińskich, 1981), 36–37. The characterization of the attacks on Lewental as an "anti-Semitic smear" is by Edmund Jankowski, editor of Eliza Orzeszkowa's papers, *Listy zebrane*, vol. 6 (Wrocław: Zakład Narodowy im. Ossolińskich, 1958), 415ff.

31. "Bez Obłudy," *Głos* 4, November 11 (November 23), 1889, 592–93; cited in Porter, *When Nationalism Began to Hate*, 179. According to Jerzy Jedlicki, the antisemitism in the press in the 1880s "was virulent enough but limited itself mainly to economic struggle and moral slander and did not manage to influence mainstream public opinion" (Jedlicki, "Resisting the Wave: Intellectuals against Antisemitism in the Last Years of the 'Polish Kingdom,'" in *Antisemitism and Its Opponents in Modern Poland,* ed. Robert Blobaum ([Ithaca: Cornell University Press, 2005], 61).

32. Zaleski, "List szósty," 378. See also Szyndler, *Tygodnik ilustrowany "Kłosy,"* 37.

33. Aleksander Świętochowski, "Liberum Veto," *Prawda*, no. 41, October 11 (September 28) 1884; reprinted in Aleksander Świętochowski, *Liberum Veto*, vol. 1, ed. Samuel Sandler (Warsaw: Państwowy Instytut Wydawniczy, 1976), 445.

34. Świętochowski, *Liberum Veto*, 1:119; cited also in Datner, *Ta i tamta strona*, 257; Porter, *When Nationalism Began to Hate*, 179. Many of the journalists who wrote for *Prawda* were Jewish, according to Datner.

35. *Kłosy* 1, June 23 (July 5), 1865; *Kłosy* 1, no. 2, June 30 (July 12), 1865; *Kłosy* 1, no. 3, July 7 (July 19); *Kłosy* 1, no. 5, July 14 (July 26), 1865; *Kłosy* 1, no. 7, August 4 (August 16), 1865; *Kłosy* 1, no. 9, August 18 (August 30), 1865. On the pages of *Kłosy*, Lewental also reproduced paintings of the Polish Jewish painter Maurycy Gottlieb, who, as noted by Ezra Mendelsohn, was "perhaps the first to aspire to be both a 'Polish' and a 'Jewish' artist" (Mendelsohn, *Painting a People: Maurycy Gottlieb and Jewish Art* [Hanover, N.H.: University Press of New England, 2002]). Datner asserts that Lewental had limited influence on the journal's content (*Ta i tamta strona*, 234).

226   Notes to Pages 93–95

36. Numerous writers have sought to characterize Prus's attitudes toward Jews, often in conflicting ways, as Agnieszka Friedrich has pointed out. He had a reputation among some observers as being "philosemitic," while Alina Cała refers to Prus's later positions as antisemitic, noting that he was among those Positivists who "succumbed to the stereotypical way of viewing Jews and could not really free themselves from it" (Cała, *Asymilacja Żydów w Królestwie Polskim*, 257–66). Friedrich traces the evolution of Prus's views on the "Jewish question" and finds that he eschewed the conspiracy element of modern antisemitism, focusing, instead, on social and economic factors. However, Friedrich notes, "We can certainly say that . . . in 1889–1890, a Prus disillusioned by assimilation was using terms that brought him closer than ever to anti-Semitism" (*Bolesław Prus and the Jews*, 262). Prus eventually embraced the view of Jews as a nation. In 1892, in response to an accusation in *Izraelita*, Prus wrote that he was accused by the newspaper of changing his views "because in 1881 I stated that Jews are not a 'nation,' only a 'caste,' whereas in 1892 I called them 'a nation separate to the highest degree.' In fact my attitude toward Jews did change a lot: earlier I believed that Jews could be assimilated and wanted to assimilate with European societies; today I do not believe this. I made a mistake, looking at individuals who obscured from me the population of millions" ("Kroniki tygodniowe," *Kurier Codzienny*, no. 141, May 22, 1892; reprinted in Bolesław Prus, *Kroniki*, vol. 13, ed. Zygmunt Szweykowski, [Warsaw: Państwowy Instytut Wydawniczy, 1963], 215).

37. Friedrich, *Bolesław Prus and the Jews*, 262. In a column referring to a new exhibition at the Museum of Industry and Agriculture, Prus wrote sarcastically, "Finally a separate shelf is reserved for Mr. Lewental and Mr. Plug, who have received strong knocks for 'wedding announcements' for several weeks. . . . This shelf will have the following inscription: 'Much law, but little justice [the locksmith is to blame, and the blacksmith hanged],' the blacksmith—Lewental, tap-tap—Plug. . . . This one even goes splat [falls flat]" (Prus, "Kroniki tygodniowe," *Kurjer Codzienny*, no. 27, January 27, 1890; reprinted in Bolesław Prus, *Kroniki*, vol. 12, ed. Zygmunt Szweykowski [Warsaw: Państwowy Instytut Wydawniczy, 1962], 131).

38. Letters from November 7, 1879, and September 18, 1886, in Orzeszkowa, *Listy zebrane*, 6:80, 232; Opalski and Bartal, *Poles and Jews*, 105–11; Weeks, *From Assimilation to Antisemitism*, 83–85. Friedrich, in *Bolesław Prus and the Jews*, notes that Orzeszkowa and Świętochowski never embraced a conception of Jews as a nation as Prus eventually did. On Orzeszkowa's writing about the "Jewish issue," see also Gabriella Safran, *Rewriting the Jew: Assimilation Narratives in the Russian Empire* (Palo Alto: Stanford University Press, 2000), 63–107.

39. Eliza Orzeszkowa, *O Żydach i kwestyi żydowskiej* (Wilno: E. Orzeszkowa, 1882); Opalski and Bartal, *Poles and Jews*, 102; Orzeszkowa, *O Żydach*,

Notes to Pages 96–100

227

cited in Ursula Phillips, "The 'Jewish Question' in the Novels and Short Stories of Eliza Orzeszkowa," *East European Jewish Affairs* 25, no. 2 (1995): 72–74. The bookstore that Orzeszkowa co-owned published the pamphlet, but she refers to Lewental's role in getting the pamphlet past the censors in a letter to him on April 1, 1882, in Orzeszkowa, *Listy zebrane*, vol. 1 (Wrocław: Zakład Narodowy im. Ossolińskich, 1954), 119.

40. Opalski and Bartal, *Poles and Jews*, 127; letter from Orzeszkowa to Lewental, March 12, 1884, in Orzeszkowa, *Listy zebrane*, 1:131–33.

41. Letter from Orzeszkowa to Piltz, February 8, 1890, in Orzeszkowa, *Listy zebrane*, 1:217–18.

42. Letter from Meyet to Orzeszkowa, November 11, 1889, cited in Orzeszkowa, *Listy zebrane*, 6:415-16, fn. 1; Malgorzata Fidelis, "Participation in the Creative Work of the Nation: Polish Women Intellectuals in the Cultural Construction of Female Gender Roles, 1864–1890," *Journal of Women's History* 13, no. 1 (Spring 2001): 108.

43. Letter from Konopnicka to Orzeszkowa, March 17, 1890, cited in Orzeszkowa, *Listy zebrane*,6:418, fn. 1; Opalski and Bartal, *Poles and Jews*, 108.

44. Letter from Meyet to Orzeszkowa, March 11, 1890, cited in Orzeszkowa, *Listy zebrane*, 6:415, fn. 1. Orzeszkowa had encouraged Konopnicka to write "Mendel Gdański" at the time of their efforts to counter the anti-Jewish polemics in the press. It was published in 1890. Friedrich characterizes the story as a late response to the 1881 pogrom in Warsaw (*Bolesław Prus and the Jews*, 83). Other writers who were seeking to coordinate a response to the polemics, according to Meyet, were Jan Karłowicz; Samuel Dickstein, a mathematician; and Piotr Chmielowski, a literary critic and editor of the journal *Ateneum*. On Świętochowski, see Opalski and Bartal, *Poles and Jews*, 102–3. Despite Świętochowski's shift in views about the "Jewish question," he was "a long way from accepting any forms of limitations to the Jewish population's freedoms," Friedrich noted (*Bolesław Prus and the Jews*), 56.

45. *Kurjer Codzienny*, issue 157, June 29, 1890, 246–48; reprinted in Prus, *Kroniki*, 12:246–48. Gebethner and Wolff bought *Kłosy* and then ceased its publication.

46. Letter from Orzeszkowa to Bałucki, April 30, 1890, in Orzeszkowa, *Listy zebrane*, 6: Datner, *Ta i tamta strona*, 257.

47. Archive of Eliza Orzeszkowa, library of the Institute of Literary Research of the Polish Academy of Sciences in Warsaw, manuscript number 374, letter from Salomon Lewental to Eliza Orzeszkowa, February 25, 1890, pp. 54 and 54v, translated by Oskar Czendze and the author. On the "hep hep" riots, see Stefan Rohrbacher, "The 'Hep Hep' Riots of 1819: Anti-Jewish Ideology, Agitation, and Violence," in *Exclusionary Violence: Antisemitic Riots in Modern German History*, eds. Christhard Hoffmann, Werner Bergmann, and Helmut Walser Smith (Ann Arbor: University of Michigan Press, 2002).

228   Notes to Pages 100–115

48. Ludwik Krzywicki, *Wspomnienia*, vol. 2 (Warsaw: Czytelnik, 1958), 508.

49. Bolesław Limanowski, *Pamiętniki (1835–1870)* (Warsaw: Towarzystwo Wydawnicze "Rój," 1937), 271; Hoesick, *Powieść mojego życia*, 2:471.

50. Hoesick, *Powieść mojego życia*, 2:472.

51. Salomon Lewental, "Ostatnie słowo," *Kłosy: Czasopismo illustrowane tygodniowe*, no. 1304, June 14 (June 26), 1890, 407.

4

"The Nighttime Butterfly"

1. *Pamiętniki*, vol. 3, December 31, 1899.

2. *Pamiętniki*, vol. 1, January 19, 1897.

3. For an analysis of the relationship between Jews and the *szlachta*, the Polish nobility, in the nineteenth century after the partitions of the Polish-Lithuanian Commonwealth, and the more gradual nature of the uprooting of the nobility's hold on Polish society than many previous historians have assumed, see Glenn Dynner, *Yankel's Tavern: Jews, Liquor and Life in the Kingdom of Poland* (Oxford: Oxford University Press, 2014).

4. *Pamiętniki*, vol. 1, May 14, April 12, and April 26, 1897.

5. *Pamiętniki*, vol. 1, March 20 and April 17, 1897.

6. *Pamiętniki*, vol. 1, April 8, 1897. Hoesick refers to Hortensja Lewental's preference for sons-in-law with a Slavic last name (*Powieść mojego życia*, 2:474). See also Karolina Beylin, *W Warszawie w latach 1900–1914* (Warsaw: Państwowy Instytut Wydawniczy, 1972), 65. For a thorough analysis of the legal, historical, and cultural context of first and last names in the process of Jewish integration, see Jagodzińska, *Pomiędzy*, 203–53.

7. Leo, *Wczoraj*, 253.

8. *Pamiętniki*, vol. 1, May 11, 1897, and vol. 2, July 1, 1897.

9. *Pamiętniki*, vol. 2, July 23 and 24, 1897.

10. *Pamiętniki*, vol. 1, September 3, 1897, and December 10, 1896.

11. *Pamiętniki*, vol. 2, November 5, 1897

12. *Pamiętniki*, vol. 2, December 1, 1897.

13. *Pamiętniki*, vol. 2, January 10, 1898.

14. *Pamiętniki*, vol. 1, January 11, 1896.

15. *Pamiętniki*, vol. 2, October 20, 1898.

16. There is a large historiography about the origins of Jewish nationalist movements and the role of antisemitism in their development. Scott Ury notes that early scholarship on the origins of Zionism took up the views of early Zionist thinkers who interpreted antisemitism in the context of Zionist ideology; successive generations of scholars have shifted in a cyclical way between an emphasis on anti-Jewish hatred as a specific phenomenon and situating

Notes to Pages 116–119

antisemitism within the context of, and in comparison with, racial ideologies and other forms of hatred. Ury argues that the later approach would free the study of antisemitism from contemporary political considerations regarding the Israeli-Palestinian conflict. Ury, "Strange Bedfellows? Anti-Semitism, Zionism, and the Fate of 'the Jews,'" *American Historical Review* 123, no. 4 (October 2018): 1151–71. For a concise summary of varied interpretations in the study of Zionism, see Omer Bartov, "Introduction: Lands and Peoples: Attachment, Conflict and Reconciliation," in *Israel-Palestine: Lands and Peoples,* ed. Omer Bartov (New York: Berghahn Books, 2021), 1–20.

17. The Folkspartey was established in 1906 in the Russian Empire, merging in 1916 with another party by the same name established by Yiddishists and leading to other parties with similar names in later years. See Kalman Weiser, *Jewish People, Yiddish Nation* (Toronto: University of Toronto Press, 2011); Simon Rabinovitch, *Jewish Rights, National Rites: Nationalism and Autonomy in Late Imperial and Revolutionary Russia* (Palo Alto: Stanford University Press, 2014); and Simon Rabinovitch, ed., *Jews and Diaspora Nationalism: Writings on Jewish Peoplehood in Europe and the United States* (Waltham, Mass.: Brandeis University Press, 2012). The writings of Simon Dubnow, the historian of Jewish history who developed the concept of diaspora nationalism, are translated and compiled in Koppel S. Pinson, ed., *Nationalism and History: Essays on Old and New Judaism* (Philadelphia: Jewish Publication Society of America, 1958). On diaspora nationalism in Galicia, see Joshua Shanes, *Diaspora Nationalism and Jewish Identity in Habsburg Galicia* (New York: Cambridge University Press, 2012).

18. Ela Bauer, *Between Poles and Jews: The Development of Nahum Sokolow's Political Thought* (Jerusalem: Magnes Press, 2005), 15–17, 149; Bauer argues that Sokolow's search for common ground between integrationists and nationalists challenges historians' "bipolar model of modern Jewish identity" (17).

19. Weeks, *From Assimilation to Antisemitism,* 86; Jedlicki, "Resisting the Wave," 62.

20. Derek Penslar, "1897: The Year of Jewish Revolutions?," *Jewish Quarterly Review* 108, no. 4 (Fall 2018): 520–25. See also Derek Penslar, *Zionism: An Emotional State* (New Brunswick, N.J.: Rutgers University Press, 2023).

21. On the history of the Bund, see Joshua Zimmerman, *Poles, Jews and the Politics of Nationality: The Bund and the Polish Socialist Party in Late Tsarist Russia, 1892–1914* (Madison: University of Wisconsin Press, 2004); Jack Jacobs, ed., *Jewish Politics in Eastern Europe: The Bund at 100* (New York: New York University Press, 2001); Scott Ury, *Barricades and Banners: The Revolution of 1905 and the Transformation of Warsaw Jewry* (Palo Alto: Stanford University Press, 2012); Zvi Gitelman, ed., *The Emergence of Modern Jewish Politics: Zionism and Bundism in Eastern Europe* (Pittsburgh: University of Pittsburgh Press, 2003). On the principle of *doykayt,* see Madeleine Cohen,

230 Notes to Pages 119–134

"*Do'ikayt* and the Spaces of Politics in An-sky's Novella *In Shtrom*," *East European Jewish Affairs* 50, nos. 1–2 (2020): 7–11.

22. Penslar, "1897," 520.

23. Pamiętniki, vol. 2, November 22, 1897.

24. Pamiętniki, vol. 2, November 29, 1897.

25. Pamiętniki, vol. 3, December 21 and 29, 1899.

26. Pamiętniki, vol. 3, January 12 and November 9, 1899.

27. Pamiętniki, vol. 3, August 25, 1899, and vol. 1, May 20, 1897. Literally, "Gloria in excelsis Deo" is "Glory to God in the highest." Alicja wrote "Jehovah," a Hebrew name for God, as "Jehowa," in Polish transliteration.

28. Pamiętniki, vol. 1, February 28, 1897, and vol. 3, March 29, April 1, April 18, and April 19, 1899, in a series of entries written as letters from Alicja to her mother. It is unclear whether the man mentioned, Tadeusz, was her cousin, Aleksander Kraushar's son.

29. Pamiętniki, vol. 1, March 16, 1896; Michael Steinlauf: "Jews and Polish Theater in Nineteenth Century Warsaw," *Polish Review* 32, no. 4 (1987): 439; and "'Theater," in Hundert, *YIVO Encyclopedia of Jews in Eastern Europe*.

30. See, for example, Archiwum Biblioteki Naukowej PAU i PAN in Krakow, archival number 3955, folder 1, letters from Hortensja Lewental to Zosia Lewental, September 26, 1908, and July 4, 1912.

31. Pamiętniki, vol. 1, November 12, 1896, and vol. 3, January 8, 1899. Alicja spelled the name Bersohn here as "Berson."

32. Pamiętniki, vol. 1, February 7, 1897.

33. Pamiętniki, vol. 3, December 25, 1899.

34. Pamiętniki, vol. 2, February 23, 1898.

35. Pamiętniki, vol. 2, May 7 and September 21, 1898.

36. Pamiętniki, vol. 3, September 9, 1899. Dreyfus was later pardoned and then exonerated.

37. Pamiętniki, vol. 2, May 7, 1898.

5

"The Sword of Damocles"

1. Pamiętniki, vol. 3, December 17, 1898.

2. Pamiętniki, vol. 3, December 16, 1898.

3. Pamiętniki, vol. 3, December 17, 1898.

4. Hoesick, *Powieść mojego życia*, 2:476–77.

5. Pamiętniki, vol. 2, August 25, 1898.

6. Pamiętniki vol. 3, December 18, 1898, and February 15, 1899. The latter entry, about the uncle, probably refers to Aleksander Kraushar. Sources give various years for the Kraushars' baptism. Jacob Shatzky indicated that

Notes to Pages 134–139

Aleksander and Jadwiga Kraushar were baptized in 1895. However, other sources give the year of their conversion as 1902 or 1903. See Wierzbicka, "Z burżuazji do inteligencji," 224; Shatzky, "Alexander Kraushar and His Road to Total Assimilation," 170; Antony Polonsky, "Aleksander Kraushar," in Hundert, *YIVO Encyclopedia of Jews in Eastern Europe*.

7. Pamiętniki vol. 3, January 31 and February 3, 1899.

8. Pamiętniki vol. 1, June 3, 1897, and vol. 2, September 27, 1897.

9. Patrice Dabrowski, *Commemorations and the Shaping of Modern Poland* (Bloomington: Indiana University Press, 2004), 135. After Salomon Lewental's death, obituaries referred to his financial contributions to the Mickiewicz monument. See, among others, *Kurjer Warszawski*, September 24 and 27, 1902. Salomon mentioned his role in raising funds for the Warsaw monument in the short autobiographical sketch he wrote shortly before his death in 1902 that was published in Hoesick, *Dom rodzicielski*, 4:337. On the Mickiewicz monuments erected in Warsaw and Krakow in 1898, see Dabrowski, *Commemorations and the Shaping of Modern Poland*, 133–56.

10. On the anti-Jewish violence in Galicia in 1898, see Daniel Unowsky, *The Plunder: The 1898 Anti-Jewish Riots in Habsburg Galicia* (Palo Alto: Stanford University Press, 2018), and Keely Stauter-Halsted, "Jews as Middleman Minorities in Rural Poland: Understanding the Galician Pogroms of 1898," in Blobaum, *Antisemitism and Its Opponents in Modern Poland*, 39–59. Dabrowski notes that "coincidentally," on the same day as a state of emergency was declared "ostensibly because of a 'Jewish problem,'" socialists who had been prevented from taking part in the unveiling ceremony for the Krakow Mickiewicz monument held their own celebrations. "Even then," according to Dabrowski, "despite the fact that this anti-Semitic outburst was attributable in part to [the populist Stanisław] Stojałowski's agitation, socialists and Jews found themselves linked in the public mind" (*Commemorations and the Shaping of Modern Poland*, 145).

11. Pamiętniki, vol. 2, June 27, 1898

12. Pamiętniki, vol. 2, June 28, 1898.

13. Pamiętniki, vol. 2, July 7, 1898. Jews had been allowed to own land after the emancipation decrees in the Kingdom of Poland within the Russian Empire in the 1860s and in the Habsburg Empire, including Galicia, in 1867. In the Habsburg Empire, however, there were already nineteen Jewish landowners in the 1850s, after some had purchased estates during the revolutionary years of 1848–49, and the number of Jews owning estates in Galicia rose rapidly in the 1870s. By the beginning of the twentieth century, more than five hundred Jews owned estates in Galicia. Tomasz Gąsowski, "From Austeria to the Manor: Jewish Landowners in Autonomous Galicia," in Israel Bartal and Antony Polonsky, eds., *Polin: Studies in Polish Jewry* 12 ("Focusing on Galicia: Jews, Poles and Ukrainians, 1772–1918") (2009): 120–36.

232 Notes to Pages 139–147

14. Pamiętniki, vol. 2, July 4, 1898. The diary gave no indication of whether Józef Thon was a relative of Ozjasz Thon, a Zionist leader and rabbi from L'viv who had been appointed rabbi of the Tempel Synagogue in Krakow the previous year. The synagogue followed modernizing practices of "progressive Judaism," as it was known, similar to those observed in the synagogue Alicja's father, uncle, and others in the Lewental family's circle attended in Warsaw. Alicja did not make any reference to Ozjasz Thon in her diary, however, and she did not record the names of her suitor's relatives. By this time, the Kingdom of Poland was officially known as the Vistula Land. However, the region often continued to be called the Kingdom of Poland or Congress Poland, referring to its establishment according to the Congress of Vienna in 1815.

15. Pamiętniki, vol. 3, December 1, 1898. Alicja's relative Julia—the daughter of her great-uncle Jan Bersohn—was married to a man named Maurycy Rozensztok, who was a member of legislative bodies in Galicia. It is not clear whether the man who was looking for suitors for Alicja in Galicia was related to him.

16. According to Dabrowski, the Russian authorities had conceded to the monument in Warsaw in exchange for Polish conservatives showing loyalty to the tsar with a gift of one million rubles during his visit to Warsaw the previous year. The planning committee raised more than 200,000 rubles for the Warsaw monument in just two months, with all strata of Polish society—peasants and workers in addition to the middle and upper classes—contributing, a show of national unity that prompted the tsarist authorities to impose restrictions on the ceremony and the lead-up to it (Commemorations and the Shaping of Modern Poland, 151–52).

17. Pamiętniki, vol. 3, December 23, 1898. Daszyński was a co-founder of the Polish Social Democratic Party in Galicia. Stanisław Moniuszko was a nineteenth-century Polish composer of opera music.

18. Pamiętniki, vol. 3, December 23, 1898.

19. Dabrowski, Commemorations and the Shaping of Modern Poland, 151–52.

20. Pamiętniki, vol. 3, February 3, April 2, and June 4, 1899. Maurycy Fajans was in the shipping business, and Maksymilian Fajans was a well-known painter. Alicja refers in her diary to the family's shipping business.

21. Pamiętniki, vol. 3, June 9 and December 13, 1899.

22. Pamiętniki, vol. 3, January 25, 1899.

23. Alicja did not note Zaleski's first name. There is no indication that he was related to the journalist of the same last name who lamented in 1887 that Kurjer Warszawski had fallen into "Semitic hands" and who referred to Salomon Lewental as a speculator.

24. Pamiętniki, vol. 3, April 7, 1900.

25. Pamiętniki, vol. 3 and notebook 1 (continuation), May 27, 1900.

26. Pamiętniki, notebook 1, June 1, 1900.

Notes to Pages 147–152   233

27. *Pamiętniki*, notebook 1, June 4, 1900.

28. *Pamiętniki*, notebook 1, June 7 and July 18, 1900.

29. David Sorkin, *The Transformation of German Jewry, 1780–1840* (New York: Oxford University Press, 1987).

30. Franz Kafka, *Letter to Father*, trans. Karen Reppin (Prague: Vitalis, 1999).

31. See, among others, Scott Spector, *Prague Territories: National Conflict and Cultural Innovation in Franz Kafka's Fin de Siècle* (Berkeley: University of California Press, 2000), 36–67. I am grateful to Kata Gellen and Saskia Ziolkowski for their comments about Kafka's relationship to Yiddish and East European Jews. On Kafka and Yiddish, see Dan Miron, *From Continuity to Contiguity: Toward a New Jewish Literary Thinking* (Palo Alto: Stanford University Press, 2010), 336–50; Vivian Liska, *When Kafka Says We: Uncommon Communities in German Jewish Literature* (Bloomington: Indiana University Press, 2009), 15–46; and Kata Gellen, "'Ein spanischer Dichter in deutscher Sprache.' Monolanguage and *mame-loshn* in Canetti, Kafka, and Derrida," in *Sprache, Erkenntnis und Bedeutung—Deutsch in der judischen Wiessenskultur*, eds. Arndt Engelhardt and Susanne Zepp (Leipzig: Leipzig University, 2015), 307–8.

32. On the family of Zygmunt Miński, see Seweryn Uruski, ed., *Rodzina Herbarz Szlachty Polskiej*, vol. 11 (Warsaw: Gebethner i Wolff, 1914), 107–8. Hoesick refers to Miński's aristocratic background in his memoirs, *Powieść mojego życia*.

33. Porter, *When Nationalism Began to Hate*, 10. According to Zbigniew Anculewicz, *Kurjer Warszawski* had become a "shaper of public opinion with aspirations for influencing the outlook of its readers in agreement with the national interest of Poles, articulated by the national-democratic camp" (Anculewicz, *Świat i ziemie polskie w oczach redaktorów i współpracowników "Kuriera Warszawskiego" w latach 1868–1915* [Warsaw: Oficyna Wydawnicza ASPRA-JR, 2002], 13).

34. Letters from Orzeszkowa to Leopold Meyet, May 24 [error in date], 1899, and May 11, 1899, in Eliza Orzeszkowa, *Listy Elizy Orzeszkowej* (Wrocław: Zakład Narodowy im. Ossolińskich, 1954), 196–97. The editor of Orzeszkowa's letters notes that the date of the first letter must have been a mistake and preceded the letter from May 11. Correspondence from Orzeszkowa to Hortensja is in the archives of Biblioteka Narodowa, collection of Bronisław Gubrynowicz, sygnatura 7152 II, fragment korespondencji Hortensji z Bersohnów Lewentalowej z lat 1886–1914, pp. 16–25.

35. *Pamiętniki*, vol. 3, June 4, 5, and 11, 1899.

36. *Pamiętniki*, notebook 1, December 9, 1900.

37. *Pamiętniki*, notebook 1, December 10–18, 1900. Alicja Lewental did not refer to the 140,000 Jews who lived in Odessa, the second-largest Jewish population in the Russian Empire, comprising more than a third of the city's population. It is unclear how long Salomon's exile lasted. One source indicates

234   Notes to Pages 153–162

that he was in Odessa for a year, and he remained there at least through mid-January 1901, when Alicja mentioned his absence just before filling up the rest of the notebook in which she was writing. Nowodworski was allowed to return to Warsaw only in 1903, but when Alicja began keeping a journal again after a year's hiatus, in 1902, there was no mention of her father's exile. See Pollack, *Ze wspomnień starego dziennikarza warszawskiego,* 127–28; Ignacy Baliński, *Wspomnienie o Warszawie* (Edinburgh: Składnica Księgarska, 1946); "Lewental Salomon (Franciszek Salezy)," *Polski Słownik Biograficzny,* vol. 17/1, notebook 72 (Wrocław: Zakład Narodowy im. Ossolińskich, 1972), 220–21; Herman Rosenthal and W. Perkowski, "Lewental, Francis de Sales (Salomon)," in the *Jewish Encyclopedia* (1901–1906), ed. Isidore Singer (New York: Funk and Wagnalls, 1901–1906); accessed at http://www.jewishencyclopedia.com/articles/9916-lewental-francis-de-sales-solomon, October 4, 2024.

38. Pamiętniki, notebook 1, December 17, 1900.

39. Several memoirists indicate Alicja's wedding was held in Vienna because of Salomon Lewental's exile from the Polish lands of the Russian Empire. Both Alicja's and Marta's wedding announcements are in the State Archive of the Capital City of Warsaw, *Zbiór Korotyńskich,* archival number XI 1314, pp. 16–19. Alicja's marriage certificate is in the State Archive of the Capital City of Warsaw, Akta stanu cywilnego parafii rzymskokatolickiej św. Krzyża w Warszawie, zespół 158, archival number 182, p. 236.

40. Salomon is quoted in a footnote in Hoesick, *Dom Rodzicielski,* 4:337; Mendelsohn, *Painting a People.* The painting was titled "Christ Preaching at Capernaum" and was one of Gottlieb's best-known works, according to Mendelsohn.

41. State Archive of the Capital City of Warsaw, *Zbiór Korotyńskich,* 72/201/0, microfilm 21824, archival number XI 1314, k. 1–3, pp. 20–21; library of Jagiellonian University in Krakow, special collections, manuscript section, archival number 63/60, collection of Jadwiga Hoesick-Podolska.

42. Hoesick, *Powieść mojego życia,* 2:476–77. Maria Bersohn's first name is spelled "Marya" on her gravestone, but most sources refer to her as Maria.

43. State Archive of the Capital City of Warsaw, *Zbiór Korotyńskich,* 72/201/0, microfilm 20637, archival number 127 (1134 gr. XI698).

44. Library of Jagiellonian University in Krakow, special collections, manuscript section, archival number 63/60, collection of Jadwiga Hoesick-Podolska, p. 136.

6

From a Manor House in the Countryside to Interwar Poland

1. Pamiętniki, notebook 3, June 22, 1901, and March 14, 1902.

2. Pamiętniki, notebook 3, April 21, 1902.

Notes to Pages 163–166 235

3. Pamiętniki, notebook 3, June 5 and December 1, 1902.

4. These two letters can be found in Archiwum Biblioteki Naukowej PAU i PAN in Krakow, collection of Ferdynand Hoesick, archival number 3955, folder 1, letter from Hortensja Lewental to Zosia Lewental, July 4, 1912; and archival number 3958, September 26, 1908. Alicja's letters to Zosia Hoesick are in this collection under archival number 3944. The collection chronicles in detail the lives of Zosia and Ferdynand Hoesick under archival numbers 3928–61, 4030–33, and 4380–83. On Ferdynand Hoesick, see also his *Powieść mojego życia*, vols. 1–2, and the library of Jagiellonian University, special collections, manuscript section, archival number 63/60: Jadwiga Hoesick-Podolska, "Czesc II: Pamiętnik Ferdynanda Hoesicka; Materiał do kroniki życia 1900–1920," as well as archival numbers 126/56, 64/57, 77/57, and 114/60. Other extant correspondence from Hortensa includes letters from her to Bronisław and Helena Gubrynowicz (her daughter and son-in-law), which are held in the Biblioteka Narodowa in Warsaw, microfilm 50392, archival number 7152; microfilm 50393, archival number 7153; microfilm 50394, archival number 7143; and microfilm 50397, archival number 7157. See also the entry on Bronisław Gubrynowicz in *Polski Słownik Biograficzny*, vol. 9 (Warsaw: Zakład Narodowy Imienia Ossolińskich, 1960–61), 128–29. Stefan Lewental sold his share of *Kurjer Warszawski* in 1909. Library of Jagiellonian University in Krakow, special collections, manuscript section, archival number 63/60, p. 218.

5. On the 1905–7 revolution in the Polish lands, see Blobaum, *Rewolucja: Russian Poland, 1904–1907* (Ithaca: Cornell University Press, 2016), and Ury, *Barricades and Banners*.

6. Blobaum, *Rewolucja*, 291–92.

7. Weeks, *From Assimilation to Antisemitism*, 152. On the role of language and urbanization in Jewish politics in Warsaw and the development of ethnolinguistic communities, see Ury, *Barricades and Banners*.

8. Blobaum, "The Politics of Antisemitism in Fin-de-Siècle Warsaw," 280, 285–87. Blobaum notes that these dislocations as a result of industrialization "were visited on a social structure that only recently had been modified by peasant emancipation." Grzegorz Krzywiec, *Chauvinism, Polish Style*, emphasizes the penetration of racial conceptions of the Jew into exclusionary Polish nationalism in this period. However, Theodore Weeks and other historians have argued that the influence of racial ideology was more limited. Jerzy Jedlicki, too, noted that while some Polish liberals "went over to a stance of 'progressive antisemitism'" in the years before World War I, they "did not recognize openly the determinism of ancestry as something that would hinder at least their declarative approval for the Polonization of Jews, which nonetheless was saddled with increasingly rigorous conditions" ("Resisting the Wave," 66).

236   Notes to Pages 167–169

9. The campaign pamphlet is quoted in Blobaum, *Boycott!*, 11n32. Hortensja's characterization of the newspaper as apolitical is in a letter from Hortensja Lewental to Ferdynand Hoesick on September 19, 1918, in Archiwum Biblioteki Naukowej PAU i PAN in Krakow, archival number 3958, correspondence of Ferdynand Hoesick, letters from Hortensja Lewentalowa from 1902 to 1921, and without date. The strike "was Polish liberalism's capitulation to anti-Semitism, to modern Polish nationalism's definition of the Jews and their role, that made the boycott a momentous watershed in Polish-Jewish relations, and in the subsequent formation of both Polish and Jewish political cultures," according to Blobaum. He continues: "Betrayed by the Polish liberals, assimilationism in Jewish politics was dealt a final, devastating blow. Zionism, which had not positioned itself as a popular political alternative in Warsaw and other Polish cities before 1912, became the principal alternative, in its many variations, as a consequence of the boycott" (*Boycott!*, 7, 15). See also Stephen D. Corrsin, *Warsaw before the First World War: Poles and Jews in the Third City of the Russian Empire, 1880–1914* [Boulder, Colo.: East European Monographs, 1989].

10. *Kurjer Warszawski,* no. 322, November 20, 1912, 2; Blobaum, *Boycott!,* 12. The letter from Baumberg is in the State Archive of the Capital City of Warsaw, *Zbiór Korotyńskich,* 72/201/0, archival number XI 1314, k. 1–3, letter dated March 11, 1915, pp. 27–29. On the case against Hortensja Lewental, see Archiwum Główne Akt Dawnych, Kanceleria General Gubernatora Warszawskiego, zespół 247, archival number 1592. On the history and politics of *Kurjer Warszawski* in this period, see Anculewicz, *Świat i ziemie polskie;* Zenon Kmiecik, *Prasa Warszawska w latach 1908–1918* (Warsaw: Państwowe Wydawnictwo Naukowe, 1981); and Konrad Olchowicz, *Ćwierć wieku z Kurierem Warszawskim* (Krakow: Wydawnictwo Literackie, 1974).

11. These estimates are based on my analysis of lists of publishers and booksellers in Kowalczyk, *Księgarstwo warszawskie w drugiej połowie XIX wieku,* and Polish book trade publications of the nineteenth century, as well as entries in Treichel, *Słownik pracowników książki Polskiej,* and the *Polish Biographical Dictionary.* Mlekicka dates the beginning of this shift to 1865; by 1918, according to Mlekicka, the number of ethnic Polish booksellers was over twice the number of Jewish booksellers—twenty-nine compared to twelve—and nine were of German origin (*Wydawcy książek,* 128). As evident from my analysis of newly opened bookstores, the shift away from Jewish dominance in the Polish book trade began in earnest in the 1880s.

12. Archiwum Biblioteki Naukowej PAU i PAN in Krakow, archival number 3955, folder 2, Korespondencja Zofii z Lewentalów Hoesickowej, letter from Hortensja Lewental to Zosia Hoesick, November 6, 1913; "Hoesick," in Treichel, *Słownik pracowników książki Polskiej,* 333–34; library of Jagiellonian University in Krakow, special collections, manuscript section, archival num-

Notes to Pages 170–172

ber 63/60, collection of Jadwiga Hoesick-Podolska, pp. 584–86. Despite the change in ownership, the bookstore continued to operate under the Hoesick name until 1940. During World War II, Markusfeld was most likely a doctor by that name in the Warsaw ghetto and did not survive.

13. State Archive of the Capital City of Warsaw, *Zbiór Korotyńskich*, 72/201/0, VII/28, pp. 55–57, "Sprawozdanie z okresu organizacyjnego." See also Kowalczyk, *Księgarstwo warszawskie w drugiej połowie XIX wieku*, 169.

14. Polonsky, "Aleksander Kraushar"; Shatzky, "Alexander Kraushar and His Road to Total Assimilation," 172.

15. Robert Blobaum, *A Minor Apocalypse: Warsaw during the First World War* (Ithaca: Cornell University, Press, 2017); Archiwum Biblioteki Naukowej PAU i PAN in Krakow, archival number 3955, folder 2, letter from Hortensja Lewental to Zosia Lewental, September 7, 1915. On the pogroms in the aftermath of World War I and the Russian Civil War, see Jeffrey Veidlinger, *In the Midst of Civilized Europe: The 1918–1921 Pogroms in Ukraine and the Onset of the Holocaust* (New York: Metropolitan, 2022); Eugene Avrutin and Elissa Bemporad, eds., *Pogroms: A Documentary History* (New York: Oxford University Press, 2021); and Henry Abramson, *A Prayer for the Government: Ukrainians and Jews in Revolutionary Times, 1917–1920* (Cambridge, Mass.: Harvard University Press, 1999). Avrutin and Bemporad note that unlike in previous pogrom waves, the pogroms in this period "emerged under the auspices of organized military activity carried out by different troops and armies" (*Pogroms*, 11). Tens of thousands more Jews died from their wounds and from disease during the pogroms, while approximately five hundred thousand were left homeless. Alicja's involvement in the soup kitchen was described in a biographical sketch in the archives of the Warsaw Uprising Museum, which obtained it from Alicja's grandson. The sketch is probably based on a text written by Alicja's son, Zbigniew.

16. On the minorities treaties, see Gershon Bacon, "Polish Jews and the Minorities Treaties Obligations, 1925: The View from Geneva," *Gal-Ed* 18 (2002): 145–76; Mark Levene, "Britain, a British Jew, and Jewish Relations with the New Poland: The Making of the Polish Minorities Treaty of 1919," in Antony Polonsky, Jerzy Tomaszewski, and Ezra Mendelsohn, eds., *Polin: Studies in Polish Jewry* 8 ("Jews in Independent Poland, 1918–1939") (1994): 14–41; and Carole Fink, *Defending the Rights of Others: The Great Powers, the Jews, and International Minority Protection, 1878–1938* (Cambridge: Cambridge University Press, 2004).

17. On antisemitism and anti-Jewish violence in interwar Poland, see Jolanta Żyndul, *Zajścia antyżydowskie w Polsce w latach 1935–1937* (Warsaw: Fundacja im. K. Kelles-Krauza, 1994); Adam Penkalla, "The 'Przytyk Incidents' of 9 March 1936 from Archival Documents," in Antony Polonsky, ed., *Polin: Studies in Polish Jewry* 5 ("New Research, New Views") (1990): 326–59;

238   Notes to Pages 173–174

Monika Natkowska, *Numerus clausus, getto ławkowe, numerus nullus, "paragraf aryjski": Antisemityzm na uniwersytecie Warszawskim 1931–39* (Warsaw: Jewish Historical Institute, 1999); Antony Polonsky, "A Failed Pogrom: The Demonstrations Following the Corpus Christi Procession in Lwów in June 1929," in *The Jews of Poland between Two World Wars*, ed. Yisrael Gutman et al. (Waltham, Mass.: Brandeis University Press 1989), 109–25; Szymon Rudnicki: "From 'Numerus Clausus' to 'Numerus Nullus,'" in Antony Polonsky, ed., *Polin: Studies in Polish Jewry* 2 ("Jews and the Emerging Polish State") (1987): 246–68, and "Economic Struggle or Antisemitism?" in Eliyana R. Adler and Antony Polonsky, eds., *Polin: Studies in Polish Jewry* 30 ("Jewish Education in Eastern Europe") (2018): 397–406.

    18. On Jewish life and politics in interwar Poland, see, among others, Kenneth B. Moss, *An Unchosen People: Jewish Political Reckoning in Interwar Poland* (Cambridge, Mass.: Harvard University Press, 2021); Antony Polonsky, Jerzy Tomaszewski, and Ezra Mendelsohn, eds., *Polin: Studies in Polish Jewry* 8 ("Jews in Independent Poland, 1918–1939") (1994); Gutman et al., *The Jews of Poland between Two World Wars*; Natalia Aleksiun, *Conscious History: Polish Jewish Historians before the Holocaust* (Liverpool: Littman Library of Jewish Civilization, 2021); Emanuel Melzer, *No Way Out: The Politics of Polish Jewry* (Cincinnati: Hebrew Union College Press, 1997); Jack Jacobs, *Bundist Counterculture in Interwar Poland* (Syracuse, N.Y.: Syracuse University Press, 2009). On Jewish integration in the interwar period, see Anna Landau-Czajka, *Syn będzie Lech . . . Asymilacja Żydów w Polsce międzywojennej* (Warsaw: Neriton, 2006); Ezra Mendelsohn, "Interwar Poland: Good for the Jews or Bad for the Jews?," in *The Jews in Poland*, ed. Chimen Abramsky, Maciej Jachimczyk, and Antony Polonsky (Oxford: Basil Blackwell, 1986), 130–39. On Jewish religious life between the world wars, see Glenn Dynner, *The Light of Learning: Hasidism in Poland on the Eve of the Holocaust* (Oxford: Oxford University Press, 2024); Naomi Seidman, *Sarah Schenirer and the Bais Yaakov Movement: A Revolution in the Name of Tradition* (Liverpool: Littman Library of Jewish Civilization, 2019); Gershon Bacon, *The Politics of Tradition: Agudat Yisrael in Poland, 1916–1939* (Jerusalem: Magnes Press, 1996).

    19. Moss, *An Unchosen People*, 1–7. The impact of these developments on young Jews is particularly evident in autobiographies written by Polish youth in the 1930s; a selection of these is translated in Jeffrey Shandler, ed., *Awakening Lives: Autobiographies of Jewish Youth in Poland before the Holocaust* (New Haven: Yale University Press, 2002). See also Kamil Kijek, *Dzieci modernizmu: Świadomość, kultura i socjalizacja polityczna młodzieży żydowskiej w II Rzeczypospolitej* (Wrocław: University of Wrocław Press, 2017); Jolanta Mickute, "Modern, Jewish and Female: The Politics of Culture, Ethnicity and Sexuality in Interwar Poland, 1918–1939," PhD diss., Indiana

Notes to Pages 174–177   239

University, 2011, xiii, 241–42. On the multilingual world of interwar Polish Jewish life, see Chone Shmeruk, "Hebrew-Yiddish-Polish: A Trilingual Jewish Culture," in Gutman et al., *The Jews of Poland between Two World Wars*, 285–311. On Zionism among young Jews in the interwar years, see especially Daniel Heller, *Jabotinsky's Children: Jews and the Rise of Right-Wing Zionism* (Princeton, N.J.: Princeton University Press, 2017).

20. Pollack, *Ze wspomnień starego dziennikarza warszawskiego,* 97; State Archive of the Capital City of Warsaw, *Zbiór Korotyńskich,* 72/201/0, archival number XI 1315, Lewentalowa Hortensja, 1900–1923. microfilm 21825.

21. Sources for reconstructing Alicja Mińska's life in Brwinów and her social circles there include documents and correspondence among Alicja Mińska, Zygmunt Bartkiewicz, and Zygmunt's wife, Eugenia; these were provided by Andrzej Mączkowski, a local historian in Brwinów; Museum of Literature in Warsaw, Literatura polska XIX w., part 4, archival number 310, letters from Zygmunt Bartkiewicz to Alicja Mińska, pp. 1–78; Teresa Listek-Gorczyca, "Nad korespondencją Zygmunta Bartkiewicza," *Prace Polonistyczne,* Seria 23 (1967): 294–98; Hanna Nalepińska-Pieczarkowska, "Tylko Szczera Cnota Otworzy Te Wrota," *Stolica* 28, no. 14 (1973):16; a biographical sketch compiled by the Warsaw Uprising Museum; and correspondence from Alicja Mińska to Lucyna Kotarbińska, a writer involved in theater circles in Warsaw who was friends with Alicja and Hortensja. Biblioteka Narodowa, Korespondencja i papiery Lucyny Kotarbińskiej z lat 1887–1940, archival number 7043, microfilms 22311, 22312, and 22313.

22. Listek-Gorczyca, "Nad korespondencją Zygmunta Bartkiewicza," 296, 297. A biographical sketch in the Warsaw Uprising Museum asserts that Alicja limited her social life beginning in 1930, without giving any indication of why.

7

The "Road to Total Assimilation"

1. Shatzky, who gives 1904 as the year when Bersohn donated his art, cites an account from an archival director interested in Bersohn's collection who recounted a 1903 conversation with him. In that conversation, according to the account as told by Shatzky, Bersohn indicated that his children and grandchildren were not interested in Judaica because they had all converted (Shatzky, *Geshikhte fun Yidn in Varshe,* 3:331). On the history of the museum, see Marcin Urynowicz, "Adam Czerniakow a Muzeum im. Mathiasa Bersohna przy Gminie Żydowskiej Warszawie, 1908–1940," *Kwartalnik Historii Żydów* 4 (2008): 477–89, and Monika Kuhnke, "Muzeum im. Mathiasa Bersohna w Warszawie," *Cenne, Bezcenne, Utracone* 2, no. 14 (1999) (no page numbers). Two paintings from Bersohn's collection, by the painter Aleksander Gierymski,

240   Notes to Pages 177–180

made their way to Alicja, who later donated them to the National Museum. The donation is mentioned in a biographical sketch contained in the archives of the Warsaw Uprising Museum. Gierymski was a Realist painter who in the late 1870s and 1880s was associated with the circle of Positivist writers in Warsaw. One of his best-known paintings is titled *Jewish Woman with Oranges*, depicting a resident of Warsaw's Powiśle neighborhood. It is unclear which of his paintings were donated by Alicja.

2. Shatzky, "Alexander Kraushar and His Road to Total Assimilation," 173.

3. Joseph Lichten, "Notes on the Assimilation and Acculturation of Jews in Poland, 1863–1943," in Abramsky, Jachimczyk, and Polonsky, *The Jews in Poland*, 128. Of forty individuals from Jewish families whom Alicja mentions more than twice in her diary, at least thirty-three were baptized or had relatives who were (sometimes the diary includes only a last name). This number is based on biographical sources about the families referred to in Alicja's diary, as well as on two books that compiled lists and family trees of converts from Judaism to Christian denominations: Mieses, *Polacy-chrześcijanie pochodzenia żydowskiego*, and Teodor Jeske-Choiński, *Neofici Polscy: Materyały historyczne* (Warsaw: Piotr Laskauer i S-ka, 1904), a work motivated by an intention to "expose" Polish families of Jewish origin, as Todd Endelman notes in "Jewish Converts," 32. Kraushar was not listed in the Jeske-Choiński volume. Shatzky attributed this omission to the fact that Jeske-Choiński was on the staff of *Kurjer Warszawski*, which was co-owned by Hortensja Lewental, Kraushar's sister-in-law. (The Lewentals were also not on Jeske-Choiński's list.) "Many prominent Jewish converts were omitted from the book for similar reasons," Shatzky wrote. "These wealthy converts simply paid the author hush money" ("Alexander Kraushar and His Road to Total Assimilation," 170, footnote 38).

4. Porter, *When Nationalism Began to Hate*, 9; Brian Porter, *Faith and Fatherland: Catholicism, Modernity and Poland* (Oxford: Oxford University Press, 2011), 9. Jagodzińska wrote, "Integrationists wanted to become Poles—that is, fellow citizens; they wanted to become part of Polish society and to achieve cultural adaptation to it. The discourse that we call national consisted of different contents in the middle of the nineteenth century (for example, a community of land, history, common values) and was based on different categories (not yet ethno-racial) than what existed toward the end of the nineteenth century" (Jagodzińska, *Pomiędzy*, 41).

5. Jagodzińska, *Pomiędzy*, 69–75; Porter, *Faith and Fatherland*, 9. Jagodzińska's argument is based on an extensive analysis of newspaper polemics. Michlic (*Poland's Threatening Other*) argues that it was in the 1880s that ethnic nationalism developed fully in Poland as a way to consolidate Polish national identity, while Alina Cała emphasizes the end of the 1870s and early 1880s as the key time period for the development of political antisemitism,

Notes to Pages 181–183   241

which became a central part of Polish nationalism at the end of the nineteenth century (Cała, *Jew: The Eternal Enemy?*, 141).

6. Maciejko, *The Mixed Multitude*, 1, 259–60. On the descendants of Frankists in Warsaw, see also Endelman, "Jewish Converts in Nineteenth-Century Warsaw," 31–35. In the medieval and early modern period, according to Maciejko, at times "Christians themselves, while officially praising the apostates . . . privately voiced doubts concerning the sincerity of the converts and the very ability of the Jews to truly accept Christ." Maciejko, *The Mixed Multitude*, 1. On the historiography of Jewish conversion in medieval Europe, see Paola Tartakoff, *Conversion, Circumcision, and Ritual Murder in Medieval Europe* (Philadelphia: University of Pennsylvania Press, 2020). Magda Teter traces the exclusion of Jews and other non-Catholics from modern conceptions of the Polish nation to the early modern period, when the vulnerability of the Polish Catholic Church after the Reformation, even into the eighteenth century, led to the Church's "use of Jews, real or symbolic, as instruments for its wider struggles." This anti-Jewish rhetoric, Teter argues, while using Jews as symbols of broader threats to the Church's control, "propagated anti-Jewish sentiments in Poland and ultimately disseminated a virulent animosity against those real Jews with whom Polish Christians had daily contacts. Vilified and dehumanized from premodern times, Jews eventually found themselves permanently excluded from a Polish nation that increasingly saw itself as Catholic. . . . The creation of a Polish Catholic national identity had begun with the nobles in the early modern period and extended to other Polish Catholics in modern times. . . . The premodern anti-Jewish stereotypes that challenged the Jews' very humanity and extended beyond religion to permeate their very nature translated into racist anti-Semitism that denied even most assimilated Jews their identity as Poles. . . . The permanent exclusions of Jews, especially of converted Jews, was a contradiction of the Church's theology and of its ideals" (Teter, *Jews and Heretics in Catholic Poland: A Beleaguered Church in the Post-Reformation Era* [Cambridge: Cambridge University Press, 2005], 6).

7. Krzywiec, *Chauvinism, Polish Style*, 138. According to Porter, Catholic authors "tried to avoid the implication that the Jews were a radically alien community, impermeable to conversion," and Catholic theology viewed conversion as "both desirable and possible" (*Faith and Fatherland*, 276, 287–88).

8. Weeks, *From Assimilation to Antisemitism*, 10, 178. According to Krzywiec, "The practical basis on which racial ideas began to be adopted by nationalism, which was not necessarily associated with an acceptance of a highly-developed racist theory of history, was fighting political enemies and attempting to polarize the political scene" (Krzywiec, *Chauvinism, Polish Style*, 138; see also pp. 93–140, 266–310); Jedlicki, "Resisting the Wave," 67.

9. Krzysztof Teodor Toeplitz, *Rodzina Toeplitzów: Książka mojego ojca* (Warsaw: Iskry, 2004). About Maksymilian Horwitz, see Olczak-Ronikier, *W*

242   Notes to Pages 183–185

ogrodzie pamięci. On Polonized Jews who became active in Zionist politics, see, for example, the memoir of the Zionist activist and interwar Polish politician Apolinary Hartglas, born four years after Alicja, who became active in Zionist politics at the turn of the twentieth century and was a member of parliament and a Jewish political leader in interwar Poland: Apolinary Hartglas, *Na pograniczu dwóch światów*, ed. Jolanta Żyndul (Warsaw: Oficyna Wydawnicza, 1996). On Jews in the socialist movement, see Cała, *Asymilacja Żydów w Królestwie Polskim*, 303–14; Alina Cała, "Jewish Socialists in the Kingdom of Poland," in Antony Polonsky, Tomaszewski, and Mendelsohn, eds., *Polin: Studies in Polish Jewry* 9 ("Jews, Poles, Socialists: The Failure of an Ideal") (2008): 3–13; Alexander Guterman, "Assimilated Jews as Leaders of the Polish Labour Movement between the Two World Wars," *Gal-Ed* 14 (1995): 49–65; Joshua Zimmerman, "Feliks Perl on the Jewish Question," in Glenn Dynner, Antony Polonsky, and Marcin Wodziński, eds., *Polin: Studies in Polish Jewry* 27 ("Jews in the Kingdom of Poland, 1815–1918") (2015): 321–34. See also the biography of Zygmunt Heryng, an early socialist activist from a middle-class Polonized Jewish family: Marta Sikorska, *Zygmunt Heryng (1854–1931): Biografia lewicowego intelektualisty* (Łódź: Wydawnictwo Uniwersytetu Łódzkiego, 2011). On Jews in leftist and avant-garde cultural circles in the interwar period, see Marci Shore, *Caviar and Ashes: A Warsaw Generation's Life and Death in Marxism, 1918–1968* (New Haven: Yale University Press, 2009).

10. Steven Zipperstein, "Heresy, Apostasy and the Transformation of Joseph Rabinovich," in *Jewish Apostasy in the Modern World*, ed. Todd Endelman (New York, Holmes & Meier, 1987), 209; Endelman, "Jewish Converts in Nineteenth-Century Warsaw," 41–42, 52; Michael Stanislawski, "Jewish Apostasy in Russia: A Tentative Typology," in Endelman, *Jewish Apostasy in the Modern World*, 190–91; Shatzky, *Geshikhte fun Yidn in Varshe*, 99–109; Cała, *Asymilacja Żydów w Królestwie Polskim*; Cała notes, however, that it is difficult to determine definitively the pogrom's effect on Polonization.

11. Zipperstein, "Heresy Apostasy and the Transformation of Joseph Rabinovich," 208; Shulamit Magnus, *A Woman's Life: Pauline Wengeroff and Memoirs of a Grandmother* (Oxford: Littman Library of Jewish Civilization, 2016), 112–19, 124–26.

12. Referring to the Lutheran conversions of two Jewish men earlier in the nineteenth century who had attended the Rabbinical School in Warsaw, Jagodzińska noted, "Every Jewish conversion to Christianity created a stir in the Jewish community of the capital" (*Pomiędzy*, 74). See also Agnieszka Jagodzińska, "Reformers, Missionaries and Converts: Interactions between the London Society and Jews in Warsaw in the First Half of the Nineteenth Century," in Ruderman, *Converts of Conviction*, 9.

13. Endelman found that financial elites and professionals made up 71 percent of converts to all Christian denominations in Warsaw in the 1880s

Notes to Pages 185–188

243

but decreased in the 1890s to 59 percent ("Jewish Converts in Nineteenth-Century Warsaw," 38). Maciejko, in his study of the Frankist movement, found that most Frankists who converted in L'viv in 1759–60 were "poor and marginal" (*The Mixed Multitude*, 161).

14. Endelman estimates that more than nine hundred conversions to Protestantism in nineteenth-century Warsaw were connected to a London missionary group. According to Endelman, "No form of Christianity was attractive in its own right. Rather, Protestantism was the lesser of two evils, the least offensive alternative to being Jewish. In this respect, the behavior of Warsaw Jewish converts was similar to that of converts in Vienna, St. Petersburg, and Moscow, who often preferred (but not to the same extent) to become Christians under Protestant rather than Catholic or Orthodox auspices" ("Jewish Converts in Nineteenth-Century Warsaw," 48). See also Cała, *Asymilacja Żydów w Królestwie Polskim*, 346; Jagodzińska, "Warszawska Szkoła Rabinów w świetle źródeł misyjnych," 142–61.

15. Endelman, "Jewish Converts in Nineteenth-Century Warsaw," 42.

16. Ellie Schainker, *Converts from Judaism in Imperial Russia, 1817–1906* (Palo Alto: Stanford University Press, 1917), 4, 7.

17. Marion Kaplan, *The Making of the Jewish Middle Class: Women, Family and Identity in Imperial Germany* (Oxford: Oxford University Press, 1991), 64–84; Paula Hyman, *Gender and Assimilation in Modern Jewish History: The Roles and Representation of Women* (Seattle: University of Washington Press, 1995), 5–49. On recent research on Jewish women in Eastern Europe, see Elissa Bemporad and Glenn Dynner, "Jewish Women in Modern Eastern and East Central Europe," *Jewish History* 33, nos. 1–2 (2020): 1–6; this is an introduction to a special issue on the topic edited by Bemporad and Dynner. See especially Elena Keidošiūtė, "Marginality without Benefits: Converting Jewish Women in Lithuania Guberniyas," *Jewish History* 33, nos. 1–2 (2020): 7–27.

18. For Galician Jews in the Austro-Hungarian Empire, Rachel Manekin has found that education in Polish primary schools for girls instilled Polish patriotism in students through an emphasis on Polish language, culture, and history, establishing an important context for higher rates of conversion among Jewish women who grew up in traditional Jewish homes in villages and small towns. Such women were daughters of merchants, tavern keepers, and other professionals of the middle and lower-middle classeses (Manekin: *The Rebellion of the Daughters*, esp. 1–10, and, "The Lost Generation: Education and Female Conversion in Fin-de-Siecle Krakow," in Antony Polonsky, Chae-Ran Freeze and Paula Hyman, eds., *Polin: Studies in Polish Jewry* 18 ("Jewish Women in Eastern Europe") [2005]: 195–97, 201–3); Freeze, "When Chava Left Home," 162. In Galicia in the last decades of the nineteenth century, the Austro-Hungarian Empire was significantly less repressive of Polish culture and national identity than was the Russian Empire, and Poles had gained a

244 Notes to Pages 188–189

high degree of political autonomy beginning in the 1860s. For a discussion of assimilation in Galicia, see Rachel Manekin, "The Debate over Assimilation in Late Nineteenth-Century Lwow," in *Insiders and Outsiders: Dilemmas of East European Jewry,* eds. Richard I. Cohen, Jonathan Frankel, and Stefani Hoffman (Oxford: Littman Library of Jewish Civilization, 2010), 20–30. On Jewish women's education in Eastern Europe, see Eliyana Adler, *In Her Hands: The Education of Jewish Girls in Tsarist Russia* (Detroit: Wayne State University Press, 2011).

19. Iris Parush, *Reading Jewish Women: Marginality and Modernization in Nineteenth-Century Eastern European Jewish Society* (Waltham, Mass.: Brandeis University Press, 2004); Hyman, *Gender and Assimilation,* 50–92 (chapter 2: "Seductive Secularization"). See also Shaul Stampfer, "Gender Differentiation and the Education of Jewish Women," in *Families, Rabbis and Education: Traditional Jewish Society in Nineteenth-Century Eastern Europe* (Oxford: Littman Library of Jewish Civilization, 2010), 184. As Shulamit Magnus noted, in reality one of Wengeroff's sons converted to Russian Orthodoxy as much for cultural reasons as for opportunistic ones—a "cultural conversion," as Magnus termed it—and a third child, a daughter whom Wengeroff omitted entirely from her memoir, seemed to have undergone baptism as a result of religious affinity for Christianity (*A Woman's Life,* 87–93, 123–25); Pauline Wengeroff, *Memoirs of a Grandmother: Scenes from the Cultural History of the Jews of Russia in the Nineteenth Century,* ed. Shulamit Magnus (Palo Alto: Stanford University Press, 2010),

20. Parush, *Reading Jewish Women,* 191. In a later period, Mickute has shown in her study of interwar Poland that young women from traditional families often underwent a process of acculturation before turning to Zionism in the process of political maturity, influenced by their experiences of "double marginality" as both women and Jews. Mickute found a "handful of older-generation Zionist women who came from thoroughly assimilated, Polonized Jewish homes, and knew little about Judaism," a background approaching the radically assimilated environment of Alicja Lewental's home. But in her study of autobiographies of young Jewish women written in interwar Poland, Mickute found that moderate integration, rather than radical assimilation, was more typical of homes in which many young Zionist women were raised ("Modern, Jewish and Female," xiii, 241–42).

21. Endelman, *Leaving the Jewish Fold,* 10.

22. Stanislawski, "Jewish Apostasy in Russia," 202. Such incomplete social integration despite frequent interactions with Christian society, and Alicja's resulting disillusionment, echo the experiences of Jewish women that Deborah Hertz traced in her study of Berlin's salons a century earlier. About Berlin's salons, Hertz wrote, "The volatile social mix of the salon society led to hurt feelings, anger, humiliation, and self-deception on the Jewish side,

Notes to Pages 190–191

and arrogance, condescension, and sometimes explicit antisemitism on the Christian side. For there were definite limits on how many and which Jews could succeed in the salons. And, after all, enjoying a visit to the fascinating and déclassé territory of the Jewish salons was one thing, but marrying a Jewish salon hostess was something else entirely" (Hertz, *How Jews Became Germans: The History of Conversion and Assimilation in Berlin* [New Haven: Yale University Press, 2007], 53).

23. Endelman notes, "The fact that some Jews saw Judaism in a negative light and Christianity in a positive light was the outcome of historical circumstances, not spiritual yearning and speculation alone. Moreover, even if it were true that these conversions were spiritual transformations pure and simple, exceptional events removed from the common run of human experience, the language the converts used to describe their journey toward Christianity was rooted in the time-bound attitudes of the period. The invidious way in which they contrasted Judaism and Christianity, and the terms they used to disparage the one and exalt the other, emerged from the same negation of Jews and Judaism that motivated strategic conversions. Thus, conversions of 'convenience' and conversions of 'conviction' were not altogether dissimilar" (*Leaving the Jewish Fold*, 11). Alicja Lewental's ruminations on her conversion both support and complicate Endelman's argument that "for the younger generation, conversion was not a dramatic transformative experience. It did not mark a wholesale or decisive break with past practices and beliefs but was, rather, the final step in a lengthy and gradual process of disengagement from Judaism" ("Jewish Converts in Nineteenth-Century Warsaw," 45). Elisheva Carlebach notes that in early modern Europe, "language became part of the complex of Jewish identity, to be set against Christian identity" (Carlebach, *Divided Souls: Converts from Judaism in Germany, 1500–1750* [New Haven: Yale University Press, 2001], 157–61).

24. Ezra Mendelsohn, "Should We Take Notice of Berthe Weill? Reflections on the Domain of Jewish History," *Jewish Social Studies* 1, no. 1 (1994): 26.

25. Pamiętniki, vol. 3, February 14, 1899.

26. Cała and Silber, "Natanson Family," in Hundert, *YIVO Encyclopedia of Jews in Eastern Europe*; Mieses, *Polacy-chrześcijanie pochodzenia żydowskiego*, 142–43. There are few traces of Franciszka Perlmutter's life in the historical record. Her and her son's baptisms are listed in Jeske-Choiński, *Neofici Polscy*, 149, 159. Three years after her baptism, Franciszka married Henryk Loewenfeld, a Galician landowner of Jewish background whose mother had been baptized as a Catholic. Perlmutter was her first husband's name; she was from the Kempner family. There is no indication from extant documents whether her first husband was related to Abraham Perlmutter, chief rabbi of Warsaw in the early twentieth century, or to Dawid Perlmutter, a graduate of the Warsaw Rabbinic School.

246   Notes to Pages 192–197

27. Shatzky, "Alexander Kraushar and His Road to Total Assimilation," 146, 168-172.

28. Shatzky, "Alexander Kraushar and His Road to Total Assimilation," 173. Just before Kraushar died in 1931, however, he told an interviewer that "at the present time Zionism is the only positive manifestation of Judaism." The interview with Kraushar, by a Jewish journalist, is cited in François Guesnet, Howard Lupovitch, and Antony Polonsky, "Introduction," *Polin: Studies in Polish Jewry* 31 ("Poland and Hungary: Jewish Realities Compared") (2019): 4.

EPILOGUE

1. On converts to Christianity in the Warsaw ghetto, see Katarzyna Person, *Assimilated Jews in the Warsaw Ghetto, 1940–1943* (Syracuse, N.Y.: Syracuse University Press, 2014), and Peter F. Dembowski, *Christians in the Warsaw Ghetto: An Epitaph for the Unremembered* (Notre Dame, Ind.: University of Notre Dame Press, 2005).

2. A handwritten note in the personal papers of Korotyński, the journalist who was editor of *Kurjer Warszawski*, refers to Stefan Lewental's death in Sachsenhausen in 1941 or 1942. State Archive of the Capital City of Warsaw, *Zbiór Korotyńskich*, 72/201/0, archival number XI 1314, p. 3. The list of prisoners transported from Pawiak to Sachsenhausen is in Regina Domańska, *Więzienie Gestapo: Kronika 1939–1944* (Warsaw: Książka i Wiedza, 1978), 54.

3. Two sisters in hiding with a Polish family in Tarczyn survived after bribing a local Polish resident who threatened to denounce them to German authorities. Testimony of Jochwed Kantorowicz, archival number 301/2493, Jewish Historical Institute in Warsaw; *U.S. Holocaust Memorial Museum Encyclopedia of Camps and Ghettos*, vol. 2, 452. About the Jews of Brwinów during the war, see Lech Dzikiewicz, *Walka podziemna: Brwinów—Podkowa Leśna—Nadarzyn, 1939–1945* (Warsaw: Gminny Ośrodek Kultury, 2010), 86–87. Postcards that Bartkiewicz sent to Alicja during the war confirm that she was living in Jeżewice in 1940. Some details of Alicja's wartime circumstances are recounted in a biographical sketch in the archives of the Warsaw Uprising Museum.

4. Aleksander and Jadwiga Kraushar's daughter, Zuzanna Rabska, recounted the murder of Alicja's younger sister, Helena Gubrynowicz, Rabska's cousin, in her unpublished account of her wartime experiences and the fate of Polish intellectuals under German occupation. Rabska to Alicja. She wrote the following: "In the establishment of SS Felicjanek on Leszno [Street] during the uprising, the wife of professor Bronisław Gubrynowicz—Helena Gubrynowiczowa—was murdered by Ukrainians, together with an entire group of older women who hid there during the war. The Germans ordered

Notes to Pages 197–203

first of all the nuns, and then the patients who were able to walk, to leave the establishment. The bedridden patients, which included Gubrynowiczowa, were to remain in the building, which was to be set on fire. The nuns begged the Germans to allow Gubrynowiczowa, who, as a nurse of very sick patients and a librarian, had done a lot of service for the establishment, to leave with them. They did not agree. Gubrynowiczowa was killed in the burning building. The manuscript of [Juliusz] Słowacki's Król Ducha ['The Spirit King'], from which she was not separated during the war, burned with her." Archiwum Akt Nowych, collection 1349: "Dzienniki, kroniki, pamiętniki, 1939–1945," sygn. 231/III, t. 1: Zuzanna Rabska, "Kartki z pamiętnika, 1939–1945," p. 4; Listek-Gorczyca, "Nad korespondencja Zygmunta Bartkiewicza," 294–98; "Lista ofiar cywilnych," https://www.1944.pl/ofiary-cywilne.html; accessed October 5, 2017.

5. According to the sketch from the Warsaw Uprising Museum, based partly on accounts by nuns from the hospital, "Alicja Mińska died a tragic death together with all of the residents of the institution, whom she did not want to leave despite the possibility of saving herself disguised as a nun, on August 13, 1944, during the Warsaw Uprising." Alicja's death during the uprising is also referred to in *Monitor Polski,* July 1, 1947, no. 91, p. 13. A history of Jews in Brwinów gives a different account of Alicja Mińska's death. According to this account, she lived in hiding in Brwinów and was shot in nearby Milanówek days before war's end. Grzegorz Przybysz, "Kronika przerwanego życia," http://www.sztetl.org.pl/ru/article/brwinow/16,-/42708,grzegorz-przybysz-kronika-przerwanego-zycia-monografia-/?action=viewtable&page=8; accessed July 6, 2015. The link is no longer active.

6. On Jewish children at TPD schools, see Joanna Wiszniewicz, "Jewish Children and Youth in Downtown Warsaw Schools of the 1960s," in Leszek W. Gluchowski and Antony Polonsky, eds., *Polin: Studies in Polish Jewry* 21 ("1968: Forty Years After") (2008): 204–29.

7. The family narrative left by Jadwiga Hoesick-Podolska, based on her father's diary, refers to Zbigniew's working on his great-grandfather's history. It could not be found in archives.

Acknowledgments

The research and writing for this book were funded by the Institute for Arts and Humanities at the University of North Carolina, the Carolina Center for Jewish Studies, the Simon Dubnow Institute for Jewish History and Culture at Leipzig University, the Department of History at UNC, and grants from Monash University in Melbourne, Australia. I began the research as a postdoctoral fellow at the Frankel Institute at the University of Michigan, where I was fortunate to participate in a seminar led by Anita Norich and Joshua Miller. While at the institute, I also benefited from feedback and support from Deborah Dash Moore as well as Monique Balbuena, Marc Caplan, Benjamin Hary, Na'ama Rokem, and Kalman Weiser. Lucy Cleland of the literary agency Calligraph worked with me for a year to develop this book. Her invaluable feedback has helped to shape and improve it, and she has provided encouragement throughout the process. At Yale University Press, Adina Popescu Berk has been a supportive, extraordinarily patient editor, and Margaret Otzel and Eva Skewes have shepherded me through the publication process. I am also grateful to Bojana Ristich for copyediting the manuscript with such care and expertise and to the manuscript reviewers for their feedback.

I am indebted to archivists and others in Poland who provided access to materials: Maria Ejchman, Marta Kuźmińska, and Barbara Rogalska at the Museum of Printing, a branch of the Museum of Warsaw, and especially the late Michał Horoszewicz, who first made Alicja Lewental's diary accessible; Joanna Dziewulska, previously at the Polska Akademia Umiejętności in Krakow; and Marcin Majcz of the Warsaw Uprising Museum. In Brwinów, Andrzej Mączkowski was a warm host who generously provided access to archival materials. Todd Endelman's scholarship has had a significant influence on my work, and he provided insightful feedback on my research and a draft that became chapters of this book. Arndt Engelhardt, Moshe Rosman, and Marcin Wodziński gave helpful feedback during a seminar at the Simon Dubnow Institute for Jewish History and Culture. The most rewarding part of this project has been meeting descendants of Salomon and Hortensja Lewental, first of all Aneta Lewandowska, who generously shared a trove of family papers and welcomed me into her home, and to Joanna Plucinska as well as Hania Kielczewska, Teresa Lines, Małgosia Plucinska, and Janek Szymanowski for sharing information about their family and discussing their own lives. I am indebted to the residents of an apartment building in Jeżewice who generously gave food and drinks to my daughter when we were stranded there for hours in stifling heat.

The Department of History and the Carolina Center for Jewish Studies at the University of North Carolina have been my academic homes for the past decade, and I am lucky to have colleagues of such scholarly integrity and warmth. Flora Cassen has been part of this project in so many ways: helping to shape it by encouraging me to focus on Alicja Lewental's diary, reading parts of the manuscript, and maintaining a continuous dialogue about Jewish history, now from afar. Chad Bryant has been a constant source of insight and was exceptionally gener-

Acknowledgments 251

ous in providing feedback on the entire manuscript. Michelle King read chapter drafts, and her encouragement has helped to sustain me. Kathleen DuVal has been a wonderfully supportive mentor and connected me with my agent. I am grateful for all of my departmental colleagues, including Jennifer Grayson, Konrad Jarausch, Lauren Jarvis, Louise McReynolds, Susan Pennybacker, Cynthia Radding, Terence McIntosh, Louise McReynolds, Donald Raleigh, Ana Maria Silva Campo, and Katherine Turk. Miguel La Serna's leadership as department chair has guided me through recent times with integrity and unwavering support. He and previous department chairs, Fitz Brundage, Lloyd Kramer, and Lisa Lindsay, are models for the collegiality that makes the department such a supportive environment. I benefited from feedback at a departmental colloquium and a seminar of UNC's Center for Slavic, Eurasian, and East European Studies. I am also grateful to my colleagues in the Carolina Center for Jewish Studies, including Yaakov Ariel, Ruth von Bernuth, Andrea Cooper, Karen Gajewski, Michele Rivkin-Fish, Emily Katz, the late Jonathan Hess, and Patricia Rosenmeyer.

Conversations with other colleagues at UNC and other universities have been invaluable, especially Andrea Bohlman, who commented on a draft that became part of manuscript chapters and who has encouraged me throughout the process. I have been grateful to be part of a Polish studies community in Chapel Hill and Durham with Beth Holmgren, Eliza Rose, and Ewa Wampuszyc as well. Doctoral students Robin Buller, Alison Curry, Alma Huselja, Max Lazar, Morgan Morales, Elena Mueller, and Daniela Weiner have enriched my academic community, as has Oskar Czendze, who expertly and carefully checked my translations of Alicja Lewental's diary. The cohort of faculty fellows at the Institute for Arts and Humanities, led by Oswaldo Estrada, provided feedback on sections of the manuscript and a respite: Samuel Gates, Alicia Monroe, Antonia Randolph, Vincas Steponaitis, Brendan Thornton, Benjamin Waterhouse, and Waleed Ziad. At Monash University Leah Garrett, David Garrioch, Julie Kalman, Paula Michaels, and David Slucki provided feedback and support. I am grateful to Kata Gellen and Saskia Ziolkowski, who have made this project so much more enjoyable as friends and colleagues in Jewish studies. Antony Polonsky planted the seeds for this book by sparking my interest in this circle of Jewish families in nineteenth-century Poland and by his guidance in the study of Jewish history more broadly. Ellie Kellman and Eugene Sheppard have shaped all of my work in Jewish studies.

Colleagues and friends in Warsaw have provided me with an academic home in Poland throughout this project, especially Eleonora Bergman, Monika Krawczyk, Joanna Nalewajko-Kulikov, Monika Natkowska-Tarasowa, Agnieszka Reszka, and Martyna Rusiniak. Works by Alina Cała and Helena Datner have been a foundation for this book. Glenn Auerbach, Jeff Bauman, Joanna Bauman, Jeff Cioletti, Donna Davis, Teri Del-Giudice, Tony Gallotto, Jennifer Golson, Rebecca Hartman, Craige Moore, the late Jenny Park, Monika Rice, Stephanie Simon, and Emily Wax made it possible for me to make it through my peripatetic existence while I worked on this book.

No part of this project would have happened without the support of my late mother, Marsha Auerbach, who sustained me no matter how far away I was. Guy Ottewell, Tilly Lavenás, Miranda Ottewell-Swartz, and Krister Swartz have warmly embraced me as part of their family. Above all, Roland and Madeline have put up with my absences and numerous "almost finished" stages. They have made it all worthwhile.

This book is dedicated to the memory of my father, Robert Auerbach, who inspired my love of bookstores, and my grandmother, whose childhood in Warsaw began it all.

Index

Antisemitism, 85, 117, 127–28, 176, 201–02, 224–25n27, 225n31; in Central Europe, 8, 88–89, 138; Jewish responses to, 87–88; and Polish nationalism, 165, 181–82, 206nn7–8, 235n8, 236n9, 241n6, 241n8
Arct family, 222n16

Baliński, Stanisław, 41–43
Bałucki, Michał, 94, 99
Bartal, Israel, 97
Bartkiewicz, Eugenia, 175, 239n21
Bartkiewicz, Zygmunt, 175–76, 195–96, 239n21, 246n3
Bashkirtseff, Marie, 26
Bauer, Ela, 116
Benni family, 60
Benzizoune, Romaissaa, 13
Bersohn family, 48, 123, 124, 157, 190, 195, 200, 210n6
Bersohn, Hortensja. See Lewental, Hortensja
Bersohn, Jadwiga (Kraushar), 47, 59, 60, 156, 170; childhood and education, 63–64; friendships with writers, 65

Bersohn, Jan, 46, 56, 232n15
Bersohn, Maria, 157, 162, 234n42
Bersohn, Mathias, 45–46, 53, 72, 120, 203; and Judaica museum, 177, 193, 239–40n1; death of, 158–59
Bersohn, Me'ir, 45–46
Bersohn, Michał, 190
Bersohn and Bauman Children's Hospital, 57–58, 123
Blobaum, Robert, 165, 235n8, 236n9
Bobrowska, Barbara, 199
Boglewice, 191
Bookstores: and book rows in Warsaw, 50–51, 58; and bookselling cooperative, 169–70; as literary salons, 48, 50, 58–59, 67; and politics, 59; secondhand, 50, 54, 66–67, 71–73, 81–82, 168
Boycotts: of Jewish businesses, 167–69, 182, 236n9; of Jewish-owned bookstores, 73
Brandel, Konrad, 23
Breslauer, Jan, 214n22

254   Index

Brühl, Dawid Ludwik, 28, 48
Brwinów, 174–75, 194–96, 199, 239n21
Bund, 115, 118, 161, 173, 229n21

Cała, Alina, 183, 217n41, 226n36, 240n5
Cemeteries: Warsaw Jewish (Okopowa Street), 57, 120, 121, 122, 192, 204; Powązki, 156, 163, 174, 202, 204
Censorship, 44, 59, 80, 82, 95, 100, 170, 226–27n39
Centnerszwer, Gabriel, 214n22, 219–20n7
Chęciński, Jan, 63
Chopin monument (Warsaw), 198
Communism: before World War II, 161, 183; after World War II, 201
Communist Party of Poland, 173, 183
Conversion from Judaism, 38–39, 125, 134, 183–84, 186, 189–90, 195; and antisemitism, 8, 166, 180–81; to Catholicism, 185–86, 190–91; and economic class, 184–85; and gender, 16, 186–88; and language, 190; and Polish nationalism, 178–79, 186; to Protestantism, 65, 185, 191; of publishing families, 7, 191–92; to Russian Orthodoxy, 183
Czarniecka Góra, pogrom in, 196

Dabrowski, Patrice, 231n10, 232n16
Daniłowiczowska Street synagogue, 55, 212n11
Daszyński, Ignacy, 142, 232n17
Datner, Helena, 206n6, 223n23, 225nn34–35

Deotyma. See Łuszczewska, Jadwiga
Deutscher, Isaac, 34
Diaries: and gender, 17, 25–27; history of, 24–27
Dickstein family, 60, 227n44
Dmowski, Roman, 167. See also Endecja
Dreyfus affair, 128, 230n36
Dynner, Glenn, 214n21, 228n3, 238n18

Eisenbach, Artur, 211n7
Emancipation of Jews, 51, 62, 68, 83–85, 115–16, 148, 171, 231n13
Emancipation Proclamation, U.S., 92
Emancipation of serfs, 62, 106–7
Encyclopedias: Jews as publishers of, 78, 219n6; Polish, 78–80, 203
Endecja, 150, 165
Endelman, Todd, 185, 209n24, 211–12n8, 243n14, 245n23
Enlightenment, Jewish. See Haskalah

Fajans, Edward, 125, 143–44, 150
Folkspartey, 116, 229n17
Frank, Jacob, 64
Frankists, 64, 69, 181, 197–98, 241n6, 242–43n13
Freeze, ChaeRan, 39
Friedlein, Daniel, 219–20n7
Friedrich, Agnieszka, 93, 226n36

Galicia: Baron Maurice de Hirsch Foundation for Jewish Education schools in, 93; conversion of Jews in, 190; Jewish landownership in, 138–39; Polish nationalism in, 117; pogroms in, 136
Gay, Peter, 24

Index

255

Gebethner and Wolff publishers, 41, 60, 77, 90, 101, 227n45

Gebethner family, 60

Gieysztor, Jakób (Jakub), 83

Głos, 85, 91–92

Glucksberg family: conversion of descendants of, 191–92; and leadership in Jewish life, 83; publishing activity of, 77, 78, 80, 170, 218n5, 219–20n7, 221n13, 222n14; gravestones of, 192, 203

Glucksberg, Ernestyna (Lewental), 57, 76, 77, 192, 214n23

Glucksberg, Jan, 56–57, 76, 83

Glucksberg, Lewin, 76

Glucksberg, Michał, 222n15

Glucksberg, Natan, 76, 81, 192

Gomulicki, Wiktor, 96

Gorecki, Ludwik, 144

Great Synagogue (Warsaw), 46, 48, 55, 56, 57, 63, 155, 191

Grimké, Charlotte Forten, 27, 208–9n11

Grodzisk Mazowiecki, 196

Grossman family, 60

Gubrynowicz, Bronisław, 157, 158, 170

Gubrynowicz, Helena. *See* Lewental, Helena

Haskalah (Jewish Enlightenment), 51, 53, 54, 55, 183, 220–21n9

Ha-Tsefirah, 116

Hirsch, Baron Maurice de, 93

Hoesick, Ferdynand, 40, 158–59; and biography of Chopin, 163; as co-editor of *Kurier Warszawski*, 163, 203; and family bookstore, 168–69, 236–37n12; and Lewental salon, 40–41; marriage of, 41, 133, 155–56; and Salomon Lewental, 101–02, 213n16

Hoesick, Zosia. *See* Lewental, Zosia

Hoesick-Podolska, Jadwiga, 159

Holocaust, 196–197

Horwitz, Maksymilian, 183

Huizinga, Johan, 39

Interwar Poland, 160–61, 171–74

Izraelita, 48, 55, 87, 116, 214n19, 220n9

Jagodzińska, Agnieszka, 184, 240n4, 242n12

Jedlicki, Jerzy, 225n31

Jeleński, Jan, 69, 217n41

Jeż, Teodor Tomasz, 94

Jeżewice, 153, 161–62, 174, 194, 196

Journalism: antisemitism in, 85–86, 89–90, 93, 96, 167–68, 223n23, 225n31; development of in the Polish lands, 89; Jewish journalists in, 225n34; and Jewish owners of newspapers, 89–90

Judaica museum, Warsaw. *See* Bersohn, Mathias

Jutrzenka, 47, 61, 87

Kalwarya Zebrzydowska, 136

Kaplan, Marion, 187

Karłowicz, Jan, 227n44

Kempner, Jan, 107–8, 109, 128–29, 134

Kieniewicz, Stefan, 205n5

Kleinsinger, Arje, 67

Kłosy, 23, 74–75, 94, 95–96, 101, 225n35; criticism of, 91–93, 98–100, 102–3, 154, 227n45

Konopnicka, Maria, 42, 96, 142, 197; and attitudes toward Jews, 96–97; literary works of, 97, 227n45

Index

Korotyński, Władysław, 210n2
Korzeniowski, Józef, 84, 124
Kossak, Wojciech, 75, 127
Kotarbińska, Lucyna, 174, 239n21
Krasicki, Ignacy, 53
Kraszewski, Józef Ignacy, 30, 31, 69, 78–80, 217n4, 219n7, 220n8
Kraushar family, 66, 122; and salon, 64–65
Kraushar, Alexander, 48–49, 59, 67, 155–56, 170, 177; and conversion to Catholicism, 177, 192; education of, 36, 61; and response to Warsaw pogrom, 68–69, 141, 183; and views on Polish-Jewish relations, 62–63, 192–93
Kraushar, Jadwiga. *See* Bersohn, Jadwiga
Kraushar, Ludwik, 61
Kraushar, Zuzanna (Rabska), 36, 59, 64
Kronenberg family, 49–50, 190, 212–13n11, 217n41
Krzywicki, Ludwik, 100
Krzywiec, Grzegorz, 181, 206n8, 224n25, 235n8, 241n8
Kulikowska, Kasylda, 63–64
Kurjer (Kurier) *Warszawski*, 14, 57, 97, 155, 156, 162, 163, 175, 200, 203, 232n23, 235n4, 240n3; and anti–Jewish boycott, 167–68; and Hortensja Lewental, 168, 170, 174; political stance of, 150, 152, 161, 233n33; and Salomon Lewental, 74, 85, 86, 90–91, 93, 101

Lelewel, Joachim, 215n26
Leo, Anna, 60, 64, 108–9
Lessing, Gotthold Ephraim, 84
Lewental, Alicja (Mińska): and antisemitism, 111–14, 124–25, 126–29, 189; and attitudes toward Jewish background, 10–11, 16, 37–38, 74–76, 104–5, 107–8, 109, 111, 115, 119–20, 130–35, 138–39, 179; baptism of, 1–2, 145–48, 189–90; death of, 197, 203; during WWII, 196–97; and diary writing, 16–22, 28; marriage of, 149–50, 153–54; and reading, 16, 30–35, 161–62; photographs of, 18, 19, 23, 157, 158; and salons, 6, 16, 36–37, 112–14, 125, 189
Lewental, Dawid, 53
Lewental, Ernestyna. *See* Glucksberg, Ernestyna
Lewental, Fabjan, 122, 203
Lewental, Helena (Gubrynowicz), 157, 158, 163, 170; death of, 197, 246–47n4
Lewental, Hortensja (Bersohn): and attitude toward Jews, 70, 73, 108, 128–29, 132–33, 144–45, 149, 188; and Catholic women's group, 174, 182; charitable activity of, 32, 58, 188; death of, 174; education of, 63–64; friendships of, 48, 126, 151; marriage of, 57; religious practices and conversion of, 2, 7, 154, 182; salon of, 30, 41–43, 60
Lewental, Marta (Mrozowska), 15, 19, 123, 138, 144, 158, 163; descendants of, 197–98; and diary writing, 17, 28; marriage of, 152–53, 156; and survival of World War II, 195, 198
Lewental, Salomon (Franciszek Salezy): and anti-Jewish polemics, 71, 74, 83, 90–91, 96–103; arrest of, 150–51; and book publishing, 76, 84–85, 101;

Index

bookstore of, 51, 57, 101; childhood and education of, 52–55; conversion of, 154–55; death of, 154–56, 162–63; and entry into publishing, 56–57; and exile to Odessa, 152–53, 233–234n37; and Jewish communal leadership, 155; Jewish religious observance of, 121; and *Kurjer Warszawski*, 74, 86, 90–93, 150–51; and *Kłosy*, 74, 91–93, 98–100, 102–3; marriages of, 57; and Mickiewicz monument (Warsaw), 136, 231n9; as overseer of Bersohn and Bauman Children's Hospital, 57–58, 155; tombstone of, 157–58

Lewental, Stefan, 36, 134, 157, 158, 163, 196, 235n4, 246n2

Lewental, Zosia (Hoesick), 41, 155, 158, 160, 163, 200–201; and correspondence with family, 164, 169; marriage of, 41, 133, 156

Limanowski, Bolesław, 101

Lueger, Karl, 138

Łuszczewska, Jadwiga (Deotyma), 60, 66, 106, 215n28

Maciejko, Paweł, 181, 241n6

Manekin, Rachel, 243n18, 243–44n19

Markusfeld, Stanisław, 169, 236–37n12

Mendelsohn, Ezra, 190

Merzbach family, 77, 214n22

Merzbach, Henryk, 59

Merzbach, Ludwik, 215n26

Merzbach, Samuel Henryk, 59

Merzbach, Zygmunt, 59

Meyet, Leopold, 96, 97

Michlic, Joanna, 206n7, 240n5

Mickiewicz, Adam, 31, 145,

212n10; anniversary of birth of, 135, 136–37, 143; statue of (Krakow), 136–37, 156, 231n10; statue of (Warsaw), 136, 141–42, 156, 212n10, 231n9

Milanówek, 195, 198, 247n5

Miłkowski, Zygmunt. *See* Jeż, Teodor Tomasz

Minorities Treaties, 171–72

Mińska, Alicja. *See* Lewental, Alicja

Miński family, 194, 198, 200, 203, 233n32

Miński, Wacław, 174, 203

Miński, Zbigniew, 199, 200, 203, 237n15, 247n7

Miński, Zygmunt, 149–54, 156–58, 160

Mortkowicz, Jakub, 81, 221n13

Mortkowicz, Janina, 81

Mrozowska, Feliks, 156, 158, 203

Mrozowska, Marta. *See* Lewental, Marta

Myśl Niepodległa, 168

Natanson family, 28, 48, 120, 121, 203, 212n9; and antisemitism, 85, 223n21; conversion of, 191

Natanson, Antoni, 48, 121, 191

Natanson, Henryk, 48, 212n11, 214n22, 219–20n7, 223n23

Natanson, Kazimierz, 48, 121, 191

Natanson, Ludwik, 48, 69

Natanson, Volf Zelig, 48, 191

Natanson, Władysław, 191

National Democracy. *See* Endecja

National League, 181

Nationalism, Polish, 8–10, 45, 47, 67, 129, 165–66, 178–80, 240–41nn4–6; and Catholicism, 2, 9, 80, 178, 180, 186, 189, 241n6; in interwar period, 172; and publishing, 77–81

Index

Newspapers. *See* journalism
Nin, Anaïs, 24
Niwa, 86, 90, 223n23
Nowiny, 96
Nowodworski, Franciszek, 150, 151, 152, 167, 233–34n37

Odessa, 110, 152–53, 233–34n37
Olchowicz, Konrad, 174
Opalski, Magdalena, 97
Orgelbrand family, 77, 78, 80, 83, 90, 170
Orgelbrand, Maurycy, 77, 81, 83, 191
Orgelbrand, Samuel, 77, 78, 83, 192, 203; and publication of Babylonian Talmud, 78, 219–20n7; and publication of Polish encyclopedia, 78–80
Orzeszkowa, Eliza, 64–65, 124, 212n10; and attitudes toward Jews, 33, 93–96, 99; and Jadwiga Kraushar, 65; and Hortensja Lewental, 151; literary works of, 32–33, 95–98, 124; and Polish Positivism, 32; and Salomon Lewental, 33, 84, 94–96, 99, 151

Paderewski, Ignacy Jan, 29, 50
Parush, Iris, 188
Pawiak prison, 196, 246n2
Penslar, Derek, 117, 118
Pepys, Samuel, 25
Peretz, I. L., 43, 44, 203, 210n4
Perlmutter family, 48, 126, 131, 133–35, 152, 191, 245n26
Pietkiewicz, Antoni (Adam Plug), 93, 100, 226n37
Piłsudski, Józef, 172
Piltz, Erazm, 96
Plucinska, Joanna, 197, 202

Plucinska, Małgosia, 202
Plug, Adam. *See* Pietkiewicz, Antoni
Pogroms (1881–1882), 68, 95, 117, 183–84; in Warsaw, 45, 68, 69, 93, 141, 183; and Jewish politics, 115
Pogroms (1903–1906), 164, 165
Pogroms (1918–1921), 171, 237n15
Poliakova, Zinaida, 26, 208n9
Polish-Lithuanian Commonwealth, 30, 31, 64, 106, 228n3
Polish Socialist Party, 167, 173
Porter, Brian, 85, 241n7
Positivism, Polish, 84, 92, 96–97, 117, 124, 162, 197, 216n39
Prawda, 92
Prus, Bolesław, 60, 67, 84, 93, 96, 98, 226n36
Przeworski, Jakub, 82

Rabbinic School (Warsaw), 51, 52, 54, 55, 56, 61, 83, 213n17; Protestant conversions of graduates of, 185
Rabska, Zuzanna. *See* Kraushar, Zuzanna
Rabski, Władysław, 170
Raoul, Valerie, 28
Rola, 85, 90, 93, 217n41, 223n21
Rotwand family, 49, 190
Rozen, Mathias, 53
Rundo, Hershl, 192
Russian Revolution (1905–1907), 164, 165–66, 181–82
Russian Revolution (1917), 171

Sachsenhausen, 196, 246n2
Salcstein, Gecel. *See* Zalcstein, Gecel

Index

259

Salons, Berlin, 244–45n22
Salons, Warsaw, 2, 3, 36, 44, 59–61, 67, 105, 112–14; and Jews, 65–66, 125; in the Lewental home, 15, 30, 40–42, 44
Sanacja, 172
Schainker, Ellie, 186
Sei Shōnagon, 24
Shatzky, Jacob, 59, 61, 63, 64, 65, 183, 192
Sienkiewicz, Henryk, 31, 42, 142, 143
Słowacki, Juliusz, 31, 246–47n4
Słowo, 86
Sokolow, Nahum, 116
Spinoza, Baruch, 34
Stanislawski, Michael, 189
Świat, 91
Świętochowski, Aleksander, 65, 84, 92, 93, 97, 227n44
Szabsio (tailor), 40
Szkoła Główna, 64
Szymanowski family, 198

Tarczyn, 196, 246n3
Teter, Magda, 241n6
Tetmajer, 42
Treaty of Versailles, 171
Treblinka, 196
Treitschke, Heinrich von, 88–89, 224n27

Ulanicki, 105–11, 126–27, 131, 135
Unger, Józef, 214n22
Uprisings, Polish, 47; in 1830–1831: 59, 83, 179; in 1863–1864: 31–32, 44, 45, 49, 59, 61–63, 83, 159, 179. *See also* Warsaw Uprising
Ury, Scott, 228–29n16

Wagner, Richard, 87
Warsaw Uprising, 197, 198, 203, 247n5
Wawelberg family, 190, 203
Wawelberg, Hipolit, 49, 212n10
Wawelberg, Jadwiga, 190
Weeks, Theodore, 85, 166, 182, 217n41, 223n23, 235n8
Wengeroff, Pauline, 184, 188, 244n19
Wertheim family, 60
Włocławek, 52, 53, 56
Wolff, Gustaw, 170
Wolff home, 60, 70
Woolf, Virginia, 24, 26
World War I, 160, 170–71, 174
World War II, 5, 41, 160, 194, 195–97

Yiddish, 16, 56, 73, 118–19, 123, 149, 173, 188; and bookstores, 50–51; development of modern literature in, 43–44; haskalah views of, 53, 54; Polish Positivist views of, 32, 68; publishing in, 213n13, 218n5

Zalcstein, Gecel, 66
Zaleski, Antoni, 86, 91, 232n23
Zaleski (fiancé of Alicja Lewental), 145–48, 152, 232n23
Zapolska, Gabriela, 42, 162
Zawadzki publishers/family, 83
Zawadzki, Jan, 170
Zawadzki, Józef, 222n14
Zionism, 115–18, 165–66, 173, 174, 228–29n16, 236n9, 241–42n9, 244n20; and First Zionist Congress, 117
Zipperstein, Steven, 183, 184
Żmichowska, Gabriela, 66